This History
of
Stagecoach Robbery
in
Arizona

is

dedicated

to

Ursula L. Wilson,

my wife

other
Arizona history
books by

R. Michael Wilson

Drenched in Blood,
Rigid in Death

the true story of the Wickenburg massacre

Tragic Jack

the true story of Arizona pioneer John William Swilling

Encyclopedia

of

Stagecoach

Robbery

in

Arizona

by

R. Michael Wilson

RaMA Press; Las Vegas, Nevada

Encyclopedia of Stagecoach Robbery in Arizona

is published by:

RaMA Press

1566 E. Juniper Twig Avenue
Las Vegas, NV 89123-7116

Library of Congress Cataloging-in-Pulbication Data

Wilson, R. Michael, 1944-
  Encyclopedia of stagecoach robbery in Arizona/by R.
Michael Wilson. -- 1st ed
  p. cm.
  LCCN: 2003092274
  ISBN: 0-9665925-3-0

  1.Stageoach robberies--Arizona--Encyclopedias.
2.Brigands and robbers--Arizona--Biography. 3.Outlaws--
Arizona--Biography. 4.Coaching (Transportation)--
Arizona--History. I.Title

HV6661.A6W55 2003   364.15'52'09791'03
                                QB133-1344

Table of Contents

Introduction

INTRODUCTION

Stagecoach robbery was among the most sensational and well-documented events of the Territorial period. Only a few themes seemed to dominate the news of Arizona and the search for mineral wealth seemed relatively routine, but was the basis for most exciting events. Where ore was found a boom resulted, accompanied by the sudden intense influx of every sort of pioneer. A town would suddenly spring up and the pages of the local newspapers would be filled with the details of cutting and shooting affrays and murders which resulted, the lynching or execution of the murderers, and Indian depredations. Road agents rushed to every boom and the command to "Halt! Throw down that box!" was soon heard. The reports of stagecoach robbery fascinated the population.

After sixteen years the railroads finally crossed the Territory but, rather than end travel by stagecoach, the lines prospered and proliferated. Train robberies soon commenced but did not replace stagecoach robberies, which continued for two decades.

Hollywood has never done justice to the era of stagecoach robbery, nor could it have done so until the events were documented. The record reveals that the truth was far more exciting and incredible than fiction, and exposed the many myths and misrepresentations which persisted. A carefully designed methodology was designed to dispell the misconceptions about the business of stagecoach robbery.

Only events involving a stagecoach were included, thus it became necessary to determine what constituted a stagecoach in the days of the Old West. This was an easy task as it was not the vehicle but its use at the time which made it a stagecoach. Nearly every type of horse-drawn four wheeled vehicle was, at some time or other, used as a public conveyance to carry express, mails, and passengers. Mule trains carrying treasure or mail and individual riders were excluded, as were buggies and wagons on private or military excursions, even when they carried treasure.

Robbery meant a "stagecoach robbery," or that the target for theft was a stagecoach and its contents – the U. S. mail, treasure express, or passengers. In some events only the treasure box was taken, in others only the mails, or the robbers might take only valuables carried by passengers, but many times the plunder was determined by the simple expedience of what was available. A robbery included failed attempts to stop a coach and events where the coach was successfully stopped even though nothing was stolen. One event involved the theft of treasure – silver bullion – which had just arrived by stagecoach and was being unloaded at the depot, but was still in the care of the stagecoach driver. Events involving highway robbery of persons traveling by private conveyance, on horseback or afoot were excluded.

The designation "Arizona" excluded those thrilling events which occurred in New Mexico, in California and in Nevada, even when stagecoaches began their journey in Arizona or ended there.

"Road agents" excluded Indians making raids on stagecoaches, such as the Wickenburg massacre. There were no recorded events where Indians attacked a stagecoach for plunder. Road agents included male robbers who were Mexican or American bandits and, in one single instance, a woman named Pearl Hart and her paramour.

The best, first source for information on these thrilling events was the newspapers of the Territorial period. Newspapers provided Arizona's population with news from around the Territory, the country and the world. The mails brought newspapers and magazines published outside the Territory from which articles were selected for reprint, often weeks after original publication. Local newspapers usually subscribed to or exchanged news items with other newspapers in Arizona, and often reprinted those stories which were of Territorial interest, especially those sensational in detail.

There were two newspapers printed before the Territory was established – the *Weekly Arizonian* at Tubac and later at Tucson, and the *Mesilla Times*. During the Territorial period there were over two hundred newspapers published in sixty settlements. Several of the earliest newspapers survived into the twentieth century. During the heyday of the road agents newspapers appeared at Globe, Tombstone, Pinal City, Florence, Mineral Park, St. Johns, Benson, Casa Grande, Bisbee and many other towns whose names appear within the thrilling stories of stagecoach robbery or in the masthead of the chronicle reporting it.

The first newspaper published in the Arizona Territory was the *Arizona Weekly Miner*, which put out its first edition on March 9, 1864 from the Army Post at Fort Whipple. The capital of the Territory was moved to Prescott as soon as the Territory was established and the *Weekly Miner* moved its presses into the town, only a short trip from the fort. Other newspapers, such as the *Arizona Gazette* which appeared at La Paz in 1866 and was moved to Prescott the following year, would also appear and disappear at Prescott over the next five decades, but the *Daily Miner* and *Weekly Miner* survived to announce statehood. The *Miner* was published within the Third Judicial District.

In 1866 the *Southern Arizonian* appeared at Tucson, a continuation of the *Weekly Southern Arizonian* which had been silent since 1859. The following year the paper dropped *Southern* from its name and two years later again changed its masthead, this time to read *Arizona Citizen*. Numerous other newspapers would appear in Tucson over the years, but the *Arizona Citizen* continued to be published throughout the Territorial period and covered all the news of significance. The *Citizen* was published in the First Judicial District

Nothing occurred in the newspaper industry for another two years until, in 1872, the *Sentinel* was established at Arizona City, later to be renamed Yuma. The *Sentinel* was still being published when the Territory became a state. The *Sentinel* was published in the Second Judicial District.

The records of the Territorial Prison provided a cross reference of persons sentenced on territorial charges of highway robbery. Those sentenced on U.S. charges were transferred to a federal facility – the Detroit House of Corrections through the late 1880s and California's San Quentin Prison in the 1890s and beyond, and their records provide a cross reference for cases of federal jurisdiction. The minute books of the various justice courts provide another cross reference for criminal cases since the preliminary examinations were held in these lower courts, though often these records are deplorably abbreviated. The Territory's archive of proclamations and pardons provides yet another source of pertinent information.

Many people were instrumental in making this work possible. I am pleased to give those most helpful the recognition they deserve:

Special recognition is due Nancy Sawyer of the Arizona State Library, Archives in Phoenix and Linda Ollney, Park Ranger II at the Arizona Territorial Prison Historic State Park near Yuma.

Others who have contributed significantly include John Gibson of the Detroit Public Library; Bill James of the Arizona State Library, Archives; and, Betsy Towle, of the Postal History Foundation.

ARIZONA

The founding fathers recognized that the nation would grow and they wanted it to develop in logical phases. They designed, two years before the Constitution was written, an orderly process that would create a Territory which could then evolve into a state. In its infancy a future territory was a vast wilderness with little population. Its boundaries were surveyed and it was named. Federal law prevailed, with little provision for local law or structure.

Once the population within the boundary reached five thousand settlers a Territory was organized. The President would appoint a governor, judges, and those other officials who rely upon the federal government for their authority. The Governor would immediately call for an election and the two houses of legislature would be elected, whose members then enacted the Territorial laws. There was a shift to local authority and the governor could charter counties and issue a proclamation establishing a sheriff in each, or he could ask the U. S. Marshal and his deputies to serve as officers of the territorial courts, using the judicial districts as boundaries of jurisdiction.

As early as 1854 the Territory of Pimeria, which would later become Arizona, was proposed in a memorial to Congress. Congress never acted on that memorial but instead, in 1855, attached the area to the New Mexico Territory as Doña Anna county. Tubac was then the population center and the county seat remained there until 1861, when it was moved to Tucson. In August of that same year a secession convention was held there and a delegate was sent to the Confederate Congress at Richmond, a move which would prove disastrous for Tucson when the Arizona Territory was established by President Lincoln several years later.

Territories initially encompassed immense parcels of land, so that as the population grew it was natural to divide the original territories into several smaller, more manageable tracts. This was the situation on February 24, 1863 when President Lincoln divided the New Mexico Territory roughly in half and named the western portion the Arizona Territory. The place for establishment of the government was controversial but finally it was decided to avoid Tucson, the major population center for Americans, because of its unsavory Confederate record and its strong Mexican influence.

The Early Days

Newly appointed Governor John N. Goodwin initially assembled a small party of men to establish the territorial government. They gathered forty miles west of Zuni at Navajo Springs on December 29, 1863. During the festivities Secretary of the Territory Richard C. McCormick gave a speech and hoisted the Stars and Stripes. Reverend H. W. Read then delivered a prayer, which was followed by a salute of fifteen guns fired from two anvils. The small crowd of Arizonians attending this momentous event sang "Battle Cry of Freedom" and the Territory was established.

Governor Goodwin immediately issued the first Territorial Proclamation and declared that the capital would be located near Fort Whipple:

TO THE PEOPLE OF ARIZONA

I, John N. Goodwin, having been appointed by the President of the United States, and duly qualified as Governor of the Territory of Arizona, do hereby announce that by virtue of powers with which I am invested by an Act of the Congress of the United States, providing a temporary government for the Territory, I shall this day proceed to organize said government. The provisions of the Act and all laws and enactments established thereby, will be enforced by the proper Territorial officers from and after this date.

A preliminary census will forthwith be taken and thereafter the Judicial Districts will be formed and an election of members of the Legislative Assembly, and the other officers provided by this Act, be ordered.

I invoke the aid and co-operation of all citizens of the Territory in my efforts to establish a government whereby the security of life and property will be maintained throughout its limits, and its varied resources be rapidly and successfully developed.

The seat of government will, for the present, be at or near Fort Whipple.   By the Governor:

JOHN N. GOODWIN

Richard C. McCormick
Secretary of the Territory
Navajo Springs, Arizona
Dec. 29, 1863

The *Arizona Miner*, the first newspaper published in the new Territory, issued its inaugural edition from Fort Whipple on March 9, 1864. It gave the contents of the Governor's address to the people of Arizona. The section titled "Stages and Mails" summarized the condition of the Territory at that early time: "Immediate and extensive provision should be made for furnishing the Territory with proper traveling and mail facilities. At present it is not only impossible to get here and to move about except by private conveyance and at heavy expense, but we are entirely dependent upon military expresses, infrequent and necessarily irregular, for our mail matter.

"Several stage lines might at once be established, with profit to the owners. A line from Los Angeles to Fort Yuma and thence to Tucson is much needed, and one from there to Mesilla. From Los Angeles or San Bernardino to La Paz and from La Paz to the Weaver diggings over the Ehrenberg Road. If not to this point, another line is demanded, and still another line San Bernardino to Fort Mohave and from that Fort here would be likely to pay. A stage should be run from

Tucson through the Pima Villages, the Weaver, Hassayampa and Walker diggings to this post, and we should have stage communications from here to the Rio Grande via Zuni and Fort Wingate by the Whipple Road or a more direct one. All of these routes are feasible and would, in our judgement, be well patronized from the start. They should all be declared mail routes. It is due to the Territory and its rapidly increasing population that there should not be a moment of unnecessary delay on the part of the Government in giving us ample mail facilities.

"With such lines of stage road opened, passengers might reach Tucson or this post from Los Angeles or San Bernardino in from five to six days while from the Rio Grande with the establishment of posts they could come in seven or eight days, and we should at once be put in communication with the outer world. Sufficient military force is already in the Territory to protect such of these routes as run through an hostile Indian country."

On March 23, 1864 the editor of Prescott's *Miner* wrote of the circumstances at the time the new Territory was formed. He said, "No Territory has been organized under more favorable auspices than has Arizona. The population contained within her boundaries at the time of passage of the organic act was small – so small indeed as to create wonder that Congress should pass a law to create for them a separate government. Hence it is not because of the numerous population that we say the organization was propitious. The scarcity of inhabitants is one of the favorable circumstances attending the organization.

"The rich mines of gold which exist there were no doubt the moving cause of the Territorial organization, and they will prove sufficiently attractive to draw in a population large enough to make up, in a short time, for the lack that formerly existed. And that population will be of the right character for the new government. It will be composed mainly of miners and those engaged in pursuits connected with the mining interests. Hence all being new, the government and the governed to the country there will be no old prejudices to overcome, no inimical laws to contend with and no conflicting interests of long standing to be reconciled. All will start anew in the midst of an old country. Upon the arrival of the civil functionaries, now on their way to the Territory, the military authority which has been temporarily established there by General Carleton will give place to regularly appointed officers of the Federal Government and we presume the machinery of the Territorial government will, of course, be men familiar with the mining business and cognizant of the wants of a mining population. ..."

The land was rugged and desolate, and this required a true pioneer spirit to open the country by locating traces and trails where water, grass, timber and game was plentiful. Roads would later be developed along these routes, and only then could the stagecoach lines be established. Distances in these primitive lands seemed immense. The wagon road to Tucson via Weaver and the Pima Villages, seemed to be practicable. The military express, at the time, covered it in seven days and wagon trains made the entire distance of two hundred forty miles in from twelve to fifteen days with no serious delays or difficulties occuring in crossing either the Salinas or Gila Rivers.

The people of La Paz were anxious to have a good road to the new mines. The route to Weaver was promising as it was a comparatively level country, with an abundance of good grass, but a lack of timber and water. To supply the latter the citizens of La Paz dug wells at several points and Mr. Tyson, superintendent of the Apache Chief Mine, had completed a good well fifteen miles from La Paz. It was less than one hundred forty miles from La Paz to Weaver. Mr. Ehrenberg wrote the Governor the particulars of the condition of Arizona's roads:

> To make the road valuable and serviceable for extensive travel some money must be expended in opening more watering places than are now found on the route. We have now a few men out to improve those found by us, which will open the road for transportation, but it should be made a first class road.
> The route to Walker's and Fort Whipple will not go to Weaver, but at a point of mountains called Cañon Water by us, and 75 miles from La Paz, it will turn in a more northerly direction either by Rhode's Ranch, Date Creek, or at a point between the two, thence I am told an excellent road exists.

At Cañon Water the road will also turn off for Tucson, striking
the Weaver wagon route about 25 or 30 miles south of that place.
I estimate the distances from La Paz as follows, viz: To Los
Angeles 260 miles; to Cañon Water 75; to Weaver 110; to Walker
130; to Tucson 250; to Albuquerque 560 (not by the foot of the
San Francisco mountain but by a more direct line crossing the 34th
parallel, and striking over the little Colorado); to Fort Yuma 110
miles; to Williams Fork 60; to Fort Mohave 140 ...

Finding trails that could be made into roads was not an easy
task, or even as feasible as was initially predicted. Mr. S. H. Herring,
a California Volunteer, accompanied Major Willis from the Rio Grande
to Fort Whipple. They were directed to find a direct and practical
wagon road from Fort Whipple to the Colorado River. They were not
successful in discovering any, except to Fort Mohave, and reported
that between Fort Whipple and Fort Mohave were three ranges of
mountains of granite, quartz, and sandstone, and volcanic formations
which ran North and South with intersecting hills and plains. Along
the route there was little land that could be cultivated because of a
lack of water; but, there was sufficient water along the road for trains,
and the longest stretch without water was only a span of twenty-five
miles between one of the tributaries of Williams Fork and Hualpais
Spring. Grass was abundant and the hills were wooded with cedar
and pine to within forty miles of Mohave, but from there it was a
desert. Game was plentiful along the route.

After striking the Beale route, the party found a few miles of
graded road, though it was quite steep. The only really bad places
between Whipple and Mohave, with the exception of some heavy
sand near the Colorado, were the ranges of mountains. They found a
succession of spurs and ravines which they were able to cross easily,
but these would make the route difficult for heavy wagons.

Roads had to be established and they were, eventually, in sufficient number and quality to allow for the transport of four wheeled
conveyances, including stagecoaches. In the meantime, however, the
population of the Arizona Territory demanded that their mail be delivered by whatever means were available.

Mail Matters

Early in the development of the frontier there were trails and paths to the west, but the first road along the southern route was not blazed until 1846. The army marked the road through the southwest but did nothing more to improve it for travel or transport.

For the next four years there was a continuous plea from the west for mail service. Mail came by way of ship, either around Cape Horn, to Panama and across the isthmus, or through Nicaragua by mule and boat. The mail arrived months after it had been sent, if it arrived at all. Finally, in 1850, Congress granted the first contract for mail delivery to Salt Lake City. By 1851 Congress extended that contract to Hangtown, later renamed Placerville, California.

Many stagecoach lines sprang up along this central route to take advantage of the lucrative contracts and many, as quickly, failed. This route suffered from heavy snows in the several mountain ranges that had to be crossed and from Indian attacks at many points along the route. But, chiefly, the mail routes suffered from regionalism and politics as southerners and northerners fought for the routes to be established through their part of the new country. These political battles delayed, for several years, successful stagecoach operations into the west.

James Birch was finally granted, on June 6, 1857, the first mail contract along the southern route. His route from San Antonio to San Diego, about one thousand four hundred seventy-five miles, skirted the Mexican border the entire way. He was required to make two trips per month and allowed thirty days for travel in each direction, a schedule he never met.

San Diego was six hundred miles from the gold fields, where the demand for mail service was loudest, and Californians protested. Congress responded and established a mail route from the Mississippi River to San Francisco. John Butterfield won that contract and began setting up his stagecoach line. The agreement, which was signed on September 16, 1857, required Butterfield to establish a southern route within one year covering twice the distance of Birch's route – more than two thousand eight hundred miles – and allowed him five days less for the trip, only twenty-five days in all.

Butterfield was an experienced stagecoach man. He realized that his coaches had to cover one hundred twelve miles a day in any weather and despite any obstacles or problems that might arise. This meant running men and coaches twenty-four hours each day, and would require many changes of horses. In one stretch of the new route no white man lived for nine hundred miles; in another of seventy-five miles and yet another of forty miles there was no water. Through the desert there was no feed for the stock. Between Fort Smith and Los Angeles there were only two towns, El Paso and Tucson, so Birch had established a station at Maricopa Wells, which Butterfield used. All these problems had to be overcome before the first coach left Fort Smith, Arkansas.

Butterfield's plan was to establish one hundred stations along the route, to be expanded later to two hundred fifty stations. He began by ordering two hundred fifty coaches, two thousand horses, hundreds of sets of harness and scores of freight wagons, thousands of picks and shovels, stagecoach horns, halters, horseshoes and nails, and equipment for dozens of blacksmith shops. The wagon train started out for California, dropping off men and supplies along the way at the point where each station was to be built.

From the beginning it became clear that Indians would cause problems as they raided the stations to steal horses. The horses on the stagecoach line were of much better quality than prairie mustangs, and most Indians wanted one. Butterfield countered by having all the horses in Indian country replaced with mules. This, however, did not solve the problem as Indians preferred mule meat to any other, and the raiding continued.

The distance between stations in Indian country was so great that herds of mules had to be driven ahead of the coach to provide team changes along the way. It was always necessary to carry full canteens when the coaches entered the arid zones, and at many points water storage tanks were built and water hauled in by wagon.

The mail started west on September 16, 1858, one year to the day after Butterfield signed the agreement with the Postal Department. It took the first coach twenty-three days and twenty-three hours to reach San Francisco, completing the trip a day ahead of schedule.

Butterfield was able to overcome all the obstacles set before him and planned to bring the travel time east or west downward to twenty days. Neither the weather nor the Indians could stop the stagecoaches or the mail, but politics finally did.

With the beginning of the Civil War the Overland Mail route was removed from the southern route and once again established along the mid-continental route from St. Joseph, Missouri to Placerville, California. This shorter route continued to suffer from severe weather, especially in winter, and from frequent Indian attacks. It never achieved the same efficiency as the Butterfield Line on the southern route, but the mail continued to be delivered to the west.

Before the end of the civil war the Arizona Territory had been established. As soon as it was formed the Governor observed the need for mail service and addressed that need in his address to the first Assembly. In July 1864 the problem persisted, and Prescott's *Weekly Miner* reported, "There is naturally much inquiry regarding the improvement of our mail facilities, or, we should say, the establishment of mails for as yet we have none whatever, and are only permitted to communicate with the outer world by courtesy of the military authorities."

By October the postmaster at Prescott, Rev. H. W. Read, was asked to learn the particulars of several roads, anticipating that these would then be designated postal routes. The presumption was correct and by early November a post road was designated from San Buena Ventura, California to Fort Mohave, then on to Fort Whipple and finally to Santa Fe, New Mexico. Another was designated from Los Angeles to La Paz and thence to Prescott and Santa Fe. A third post road which would benefit the Territory was between Denver, Colorado and Santa Fe, New Mexico. The Post Office Department published their request for proposals to carry the mails:

> Proposals will be received at the Contract Office of this Department until 3 p.m. of Tuesday, the 15th of November next (to be decided by the 17th) for conveying the United States mails in the Territory of Arizona from the 1st of January, 1865, or as soon thereafter as practicable to the 30th of June 1866 on the route and by the schedule of departures and arrivals following:

14466 From Albuquerque (New Mexico) ... Jacob's Well (Arizona), Leroux Springs, and Woolsey's Ranch to Prescott, 450 miles and back once a week.

Leave Albuquerque Sunday at 12m;
Arrive Prescott in 6 days by 12m;
Leave Prescott Thursday at 12m;
Arrive Albuquerque in 6 days by 12m.

After the routes had been in operation for sixteen months the service was still poor, when the *Miner* reported, "there is much complaint regarding mail service in the Territory ... it is now some weeks since a mail arrived or departed on time, or since one was brought or taken away by the regularly employed carrier... there is a screw loose here somewhere and we wish the contractor would hasten to put it right." The newspaper said that the service was notorious and that, "it is equally notorious that no part of the contract has to this time been faithfully, or even tolerably, fulfilled." In July mail contractor J. S. Poston was reportedly on his way to Prescott, and the newspaper's editor said of him, "no white man has done them [the people] and the Territory so great an injury."

Mr. James Grant had offered to buy the contract at a profit, offering Poston fifteen hundred dollars a quarter, but Poston refused and the *Miner* warned, "In almost any other Territory a man who had done so much to annoy and injure the public interests would be hung to the nearest tree, without benefit of judge or jury." The population of Arizona took mail matters seriously.

By early 1867 a resolution was introduced at Congress to re-establish Butterfield's southern route, and by mid-May G. F. Stanley had arrived to begin stocking the road. The *Miner* reported, "After nearly six years in experimenting other routes, the Post Office Department became satisfied that the Butterfield line was the safe and practical one in all seasons, and acted accordingly. We therefore expect for the future, a permanent overland line that will only be discontinued when the Southern Pacific Railroad will render it no longer necessary." Service began weekly, but within six months had already expanded to a tri-weekly service. In May 1867 the mail began to arrive under contract to Sanderson, Barlow & Co. The next month the Governor made a fresh application to establish a continuation of a route along the 35th parallel from Albuquerque to Prescott.

In 1868 James Grant was awarded the mail contract for three stagecoach lines north of the Gila River. Stagecoaches ran from Wickenburg to Maricopa Wells to connect with Capron's stagecoaches, which ran from Los Angeles, California to Tucson, A. T. By 1869 there was even greater interest in the mails as the Postmaster-General proposed to deal quite liberally with the Territory in the matter of mail service.

In April 1870 James Grant, owner of the California and Arizona Stage Company, received the mail contracts for the next four years, commencing from July 1st, and the mail came and went with great efficiency during those years. However by 1878, with James Grant dead three years, the new manager announced that the mails and passengers would be carried in buckboards rather than in celerity or concord coaches, and the *Daily Miner* complained that, "Cheap and nasty mail contractors are now the scourge that afflicts Arizona. Total failure to place service occurred this month on several routes; and even where no actual failure took place, some mails are being carried in a shabby and scandalous manner... ."

In only fifteen years the Territory had progressed from a situation where there was no mail to one where the residents could complain about the quality of conveyance and efficiency, confident that the mails would be delivered even if a bit tardy.

Wells, Fargo and Company Express

Before 1849 express companies were active throughout the east and mid-west but there was only one small operation on the Pacific coast – C.L. Cady's Express was first announced in the *Californian* on April 24, 1847. The need for express operations changed dramatically when gold was discovered at Sutter's Mill on January 24, 1848. There was an immediate need for expanded express operations to bring mail to the miners in isolated gold camps and to bring out the gold to a place from which it could be shipped. Several express companies sprang up almost overnight but the Adams Express

Company, by 1852, had established itself as the major express company in California and by 1854 dominated the entire Pacific coast.

The men behind Wells, Fargo & Company watched the situation in California and finally opened their Pacific express business in 1852. Their first public notice appeared in the *New York Times* on May 20, 1852:

> WELLS FARGO & CO. CALIFORNIA EXPRESS
> Capital $300,000
> A joint stock company.
> Office 16 Wall Street
> ... This company having completed its organization as above is now ready to undertake the general forwarding agency and commission business; the purchase and sale of gold dust, bullion and specie, also packages, parcels and freight of all description in and between the City of New York and the City of San Francisco, and the principal cities and towns in California ...

A similar notice appeared in the *Alta California* in early June 1852, before the company had opened an office and even before its representatives arrived on the Pacific coast. Once established the company quickly grew and soon adopted a policy of acquiring its smaller competitors. As early as November 1852 they had bought Gregory and Company's Express; in September 1853 they acquired Reynold's, Todd and Company Express; and in July 1854 they added Hunter and Company's Express. That left them with only one major competitor in the west – Adams Express Company.

Many factors led to the state of economic conditions in the mid-1850s, but in California it was lack of water that most affected mining operations during 1854. Water was necessary for placer mining so, with a drought at hand, many miners sat about idly during much of that year. There was far less gold to be shipped by express, while merchants and financial concerns over-extended credit to the miners.

Adams and Company concentrated upon their waning express business in association with Page, Bacon and Company, a banking firm which was situated in the same building. The parent bank, in St. Louis, had invested heavily in the Ohio and Mississippi Railroad.

When that venture failed the parent bank was forced to close its doors. The San Francisco branch had just sent one million dollars in assets to the parent bank so, when word of the St. Louis closure reached San Francisco on February 23, 1855, the local branch was unable to meet the demand and also had to close its doors. Adams and Company at San Francisco followed suit, never to reopen there.

When gold and silver were discovered in Nevada, Wells, Fargo & Company, now the dominant express company in the west, added stagecoach lines to their operations. They purchased the Pioneer Stage Line in 1864. On November 1, 1866 they added the entire Holladay Overland Mail & Express Company and within a few weeks all interests, including the stagecoach lines, the Overland Mail, and Wells, Fargo & Company, adopted the name Wells, Fargo and Company. In 1869 Wells, Fargo and Company sold their stagecoach lines and thereafter contracted the handling of express in their "green treasure boxes" on whichever stage lines operated regionally.

The little green treasure box became the standard for carrying express, and other companies included making up boxes as part of the process of stocking the road. The treasure boxes used by Wells, Fargo and Company were manufactured by J. Y. Ayer of San Francisco.  He used Ponderosa pine for the body which he reinforced with oak rims and iron strapping. A box measured twenty inches long by twelve inches high by ten inches deep and weighed nearly twenty-five pounds 'lean.' At first the boxes were loaded in the office and deposited into the driver's boot or inside the passenger compartment, but the familiar command of "throw down that box" led to its being bolted into the boot by the early 1870s.

During the early years of express operations in California road agents did not steal gold shipped with express men. Alexander Todd gave a personal account of the early days of excitement and profit. He said, "An express man on the road was almost exempt from interference because everybody was interested, and if an express man had been attacked, and his assailant discovered, punishment would have been very speedy. ... An express man though carrying large sums of money, bore almost a charmed life in those days."

In 1860 Wells, Fargo & Company had established an office at Tucson, in what was then the New Mexico Territory. This agency, however, was short lived. As the war between the states loomed, the southern stagecoach route was abandoned and all the rolling stock and animals were moved north to support the central route. Without the stagecoaching business the Tucson office soon closed.

Before the end of the war it became clear that the area which was becoming known as Arizona was filled with mineral treasure. President Lincoln was convinced of the need to declare it a separate Territory, even though the population was still quite sparse and, with the free reign of hostile Indians in the absence of troops, the populace was barricaded in their towns. In early 1863 President Lincoln split the New Mexico Territory roughly in two on a perpendicular line and proclaimed the western portion the Arizona Territory.

By the end of the Civil War, Wells, Fargo & Company had expanded its transportation of treasure and express operations in the west to include stagecoach lines, pony express, wagons and buckboards, as well as sleighs and dog sleds in colder climes. They also contracted for shipments on stagecoaches, railroads and ships owned by other companies.

Wells, Fargo & Company never operated a stagecoach line in the Arizona Territory, and for many years they had no offices within the Territory. In 1863 the first agency was established at La Paz, where gold had been discovered a year earlier. Two years later an agency was established at Fort Yuma on the California side of the Colorado River across from Arizona City – later renamed Yuma. It was another six years before an agency was established at Ehrenberg, successor in significance to the town of La Paz. All these agencies, however, were on the boundary with California. This made it necessary for express and treasure to be delivered to these few agency offices.

This need was met by entrepreneurs, with large and small express companies starting and failing regularly over the first decade. Two of the first express companies in the Territory advertised in the

Miner as early as July 1864. Express was transported to the Colorado River towns by any means available including horseback, buggy, wagon, buckboard and, in later years, by stagecoach. Mr. James Grant established an express from San Bernardino to La Paz, and thence to Prescott. On December 14, 1864 the *Miner* newspaper announced, "Grant's express reached here on Saturday last with San Francisco dated to Nov. 22d."

There is no record of any early shipments being intercepted by highwaymen. Perhaps it was easier to allow the treasure to accumulate at the Colorado River agencies and then "jump" the stagecoach in California, where the familiar green treasure box would be delivered on command.

Not all of Wells, Fargo and Company's competition were shoestring operations. In 1875 the Arizona and New Mexico Express Company tried to capitalize on Wells, Fargo's absence in the Territory. A meeting was held at the Horton House in San Diego on a Thursday evening with Henry Wells of Wells, Fargo presiding. The meeting was to decide upon the formation of a company to carry on an express business between San Diego and Tucson with a view to later extend the line through New Mexico. At the end of the meeting stock in the amount of two hundred thousand dollars was subscribed by the participants. It was decided that the new express company routes would extend from San Bernardino to Hardyville, Cerbat, Mineral Park,

---

EXPRESS LINES.

PRESCOTT TO LA PAZ.

The Pioneer Express.

The undersigned will run a Pony Express semi-monthly, from Prescott and the various mining districts of northern Arizona to La Paz, connecting with Grant's and Wells, Fargo & Co.'s expresses to California and the Atlantic States. Offices: Lynx Creek, Wertheimer's store; Prescott, Juniper House; Weaverville; Howell's store; La Paz, Chris. Murr's saloon:
ROBERTSON & PARISH.
Prescott, July 28, 1864.   n10

L. Dukes & Co.'s Express
————FROM————
MOHAVE TO PRESCOTT, ARIZONA.

We will run a regular semi-monthly Express from Mohave, near Fort Mohave, to Prescott and Fort Whipple, Arizona, connecting with the Government Express from Fort Mohave.

Leaving Prescott and Fort Whipple on about the 1st and 16th of every month, and Mohave on or about the 10th and 25th of every month.
Rev. H. W. Read. P. M., Agent at Prescott.
L. DUKES & Co., Proprietors.
July 30th, 1864.   n10 v1

ARIZONA AND NEW MEXICO Express Company.

CAPITAL, - - - $500,000.00.

HENRY WELLS, Pres't.   HENRY WICK, Treas.
   Aurora, N.Y.   Cleveland, Ohio
C. H. WELLS, Gen'l Supt., Tucson, Arizona.

This Company is now prepared to transact a
GENERAL EXPRESS BUSINESS

Between Prescott and the Terminus of the Southern Pacific Railroad, now at Whitewater, Cal., running via Wickenburg and Ehrenberg, making close connections with their stages for Phoenix, Florence, Tucson and Southern Arizona, and selling tickets at their offices good over the Central and Southern Pacific Railroads to San Jose, San Francisco, Sacramento and intermediate places, and thence to all principal cities and town of the United States. Quickest and easiest route to San Francisco. Large and comfortable Kimball four and six-horse coaches.
Shortest desert crossing, good water, and good stations

Five and a half days to San Francisco. Two days to Tucson.

The Arizona and New Mexico Express Company, having completed its organization of lines, offices and employes, has entered upon a

GENERAL CARRYING BUSINESS
....BETWEEN....
PRESCOTT, TUCSON
AND THE
**Terminus of Southern Pacific
RAILROAD,**

Where they will make connection with WELLS, FARGO & CO., for express matter destined to all parts of the United States and Europe, are now ready to carry passengers and do a general Express business.

LETTER POUCHES

Will be carried on all our stages, three times each week, each way. Government stamped envelopes will be sold by us at all our offices, with our frank, carrying letters to any part of the United States and Europe.

BULLION AND CURRENCY

Will be received and forwarded with dispatch and safety. McNeale & Urban's Cincinatti Bank Fire and Burglar Proof Safes at our Prescott and Tucson offices.
Orders for the purchase of goods at San Francisco and elsewhere, will have prompt attention. The collection of Notes, Drafts, Accounts and Acceptances will have special dispatch.
Through Rates given to New York, Boston, Philadelphia, Baltimore and New Orleans.

Stages Leave Prescott Mondays, Thursdays and Saturdays at 4 P. M.
CHAS. H. WELLS, General Sup't.,
                    Prescott.
F. W. BLAKE, Agent.   Tucson, A. T.
February 18, 1876.

and Prescott, thence via Wickenburg to Phoenix, Florence, and then Tucson; and, from San Diego the line would extend to Tucson, where express from the other route would connect, and from there to Silver City, New Mexico with such other extensions and branches as business warranted, including a branch from some point in Mohave County to the Sandy River and an extension from Silver City to Albuquerque, New Mexico via Camp Wingate.

Henry Wells and other capitalists were planning their express utilizing the California and Arizona Stage Line as their carrier, while the Texas Pacific Express Company was planning on using the stagecoach line of Kerens & Mitchell. In October 1875 the Texas Pacific Company already had perfected "all steps over the line, made boxes, etc." while their competitor, the Arizona and New Mexico Express Company, was planning to open business with four horse coaches connecting their Prescott office with the Southern Pacific Railway.

In December the Arizona & New Mexico Express Company had decided to build and stock four stations before initiating operations, which delayed their beginning service date to mid-January 1876. Their first stagecoach finally arrived in Prescott on January 31st. By July the company had suspended operations and never resumed; and, the Texas Pacific Express Company was not yet operating to fill the void. Once again the Territory was without express service. It was about this time that Wells, Fargo and Company began to seriously consider expanding into the Territory's interior.

Finally, in 1877, Wells, Fargo established agency offices at Florence, Hardyville, Phoenix, Prescott, and Tucson. The following year agencies were added at Aubrey and Signal. With the arrival of the familiar green treasure box stagecoach robberies commenced, as the *Miner* observed, "with a frequency that, a few years ago, we saw Apache murders."

Stagecoaching in Arizona

When the term "stagecoach" is uttered one is reminded of a beautifully decorated Concord coach rocking along behind six powerful, perfectly matched horses. Passengers are envisioned reclining in the roomy interior while the roof and rear boot is laden with their luggage, goods and express booked for the next destination. This was the dream of early stagecoaching in the Arizona Territory, a dream which came true much later in its evolution.

As roads began to replace trails and traces, and these were further improved, stagecoach lines were established. Coaches used on these early lines were often no more than a buckboard, spring wagon, surplus Army ambulance, or celerity wagon. These conveyances lumbered along behind teams of horses or mules, often mismatched in size and appearance. The teams consisted of two, four or six animals, but when a buggy or cart could be substituted it was pulled by a single horse, mule, or donkey. Some animals were so poor that they were referred to as "skeletons covered with horse hide, which the company fondly hoped would make this trip before dying ... ."

Passengers were allowed twenty-five pounds of luggage, two blankets, one canteen, a dust coat, hat and clothing. They were given a cramped space in which to sit, sometimes sharing the interior with mail sacks or express packages. The rocking and rolling of the coach could cause a passenger to become queasy, and they would be subjected to sand gnats, a lack of bathing facilities, and little sleep.

There were worse times for some passengers, however. A stagecoach might be delayed for days due to swollen rivers or because the current of the river was too swift. A coach might be mired in mud, requiring the passengers to disembark and pull it and the horses out. Temperatures could be unbearably hot or, as stage line entrepreneur James O. Grant noted while crossing the desert in 1870, "it was so cold that it almost froze the driver and passengers." A stagecoach might also career out of control and roll over or drop off a steep edge, or some mishap might lead to the loss of the team and perhaps even the driver, but matters could be worse still:

ANOTHER INDIAN OUTRAGE – A week ago today, as the stage containing the U. S. Mail, the driver Mr Tingley, Joseph Todd of this place, and George Jackson of Petaluma, California (brother of our fellow townsmen Cal and Sol Jackson) was passing through Granite Wash, about mid-way between Wickenburg and La Paz on its way to the former place, it was attacked by about 30 Indians, who lay concealed in the brush on each side of the road. The

Indians were armed with guns, and tried their best to kill and capture the party in the stage, all of whom were wounded. The driver, Mr. Tingley, received three wounds, Mr. Jackson was wounded slightly, Joe Todd was wounded in the spine and as he was just recovering from sickness and medical treatment it is feared he may die from the effects of his wound ... .

"Stage" in stagecoach referred to the division of a route into segments or "stages" of travel, no more than fifteen to twenty miles under ideal circumstances, with a way station at each terminus. At each station passengers experienced a delay of up to fifteen minutes while a fresh team of horses was harnessed. After several stops, the period would be extended to twenty minutes to allow the passengers to consume a quick meal; and, the driver and the coach might be exchanged after a day's travel on a through-coach.

In desert circumstances the distances between stations could be considerably longer, as these stations were at first situated where water was available. If the distance was too great a dry station would be established and water hauled to a tank built by the company. Later, as these routes became better established, wells were dug at regular intervals and stations built at those sites.

Stagecoach companies would spring up and then fail, as no stage line could survive on passenger transportation alone. The basis of survival was the mail subsidy, while success lay in the additional revenues which came from contracts for carrying express. Two years had passed since the first Governor had called for stage and mails service and, in his address to the 3rd Assembly in October 1866, the Governor noted that there had been little progress, "I am ashamed to say that to this day there is not a stagecoach running in Arizona, although the Territory has been organized nearly three years. Lines from Wilmington and San Diego to Fort Yuma and from San Bernardino to Hardyville have lately been established. Connecting lines to Tucson, La Paz, Prescott and the Rio Grande should be provided by some of our enterprising citizens without delay. ... Until well conducted lines of coaches are established we cannot look for a great increase of population, however tempting our mineral wealth ... ."

By mid-1867 the line of Tomlinson & Co., which operated from San Diego to Fort Yuma, had been extended to Tucson. The *San Bernardino Guardian* reported on May 25th, "On Monday evening last, Tomlinson & Co.'s great through line of United States mail stage-coaches from Los Angeles to Tucson was put in full and complete operation. The stage arrived here from the former place and immediately thereafter the passengers were transferred to another stagecoach, and sent on their way rejoicing. ... Tomlinson & Co. deserve great credit for the energy and efficiency displayed by them in so promptly organizing a line of stages, nearly a thousand miles in extent."

On August 14, 1869 Prescott's *Miner* reported that James Grant, the mail contractor from La Paz to Prescott, was making the necessary arrangements to run a weekly line of stagecoaches on the same route. The coaches used for this service were being built at the carriage and wagon factory of Todd & Kelly in San Bernardino. These stagecoaches would connect La Paz with the San Bernardino stages, and passengers would be able to procure through passage to Prescott."

By October 2, 1869 Prescott's newspaper announced Grant's arrival in a brand new Concord coach drawn by six mules. The new stagecoach line had an advertisement elsewhere in that edition of the newspaper which proposed a weekly trip to La Paz and from there to Prescott to connect with the stagecoaches of Noble A. Waters. The editor of the *Miner* seemed concerned that the stage line might fail if it did not receive the support of its citizens, and admonished, "Now that a line of stages runs between Prescott and La Paz, we hope the citizens along the route and at both ends of it will do all they can to keep it going. This can be done only by taking passage upon the stages and giving them packages, etc., to carry. We, ourself, have felt the want of stage communication with California; have 'blown' for it, and now that we have it, we mean to do everything in our power to support it."

By the end of 1870 stagecoach lines had been extended and improved to a point that quality of service was becoming a primary issue. The *Miner* on December 17, 1870 published under the headline OUR STAGE LINES: "It is gratifying to be able to state that travel by stage to this Territory is increasing. ... Central Arizona needs people and they should not be deterred from coming here by poor stages, sickly teams, and bad fare. The other line from San Diego to Tucson and the East does not appear to be run in the interest of the Territory … ."

Another stagecoach company established within the Arizona Territory was the Kerens & Mitchell line. It had taken over the route between Fort Yuma and Tucson and, in August 1875, announced that they were going to put new coaches on the route. In early October the *Sentinel*, established at Yuma in 1872 by C. L. Minor, reported that James A. Wilson had arrived from San Diego with a fine Concord coach drawn by six horses with three more horses in reserve, leading behind, and seven passengers for Tucson. The newspaper said, "It is the finest stagecoach that we have ever seen in Arizona," but was disappointed when Wilson informed the editor that the coach was intended for the run between Florence and the Pinal mines. Kerens & Mitchell extended their service to include the Black Canyon route about September 19, 1878. In 1880 they sold all their stock and wagons to H. C. Walker, who continued to run the line.

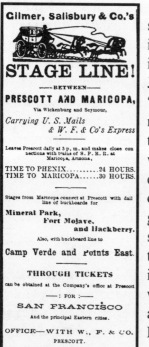

Gilmer, Salisbury & Co.'s

STAGE LINE!

— BETWEEN —

PRESCOTT AND MARICOPA,

Via Wickenburg and Seymour,

*Carrying U. S. Mails
& W. F. & Co's Express*

Leaves Prescott daily at 5 p. m. and makes close connections with trains of S. P. R. R. at Maricopa, Arizona,

TIME TO PHENIX..........24 HOURS.
TIME TO MARICOPA......30 HOURS.

Stages from Maricopa connect at Prescott with dail line of buckboards for

Mineral Park,
Fort Mojave,
and Hackberry.

Also, with buckboard line to

Camp Verde and Points East.

THROUGH TICKETS

can be obtained at the Company's office at Prescott

— : FOR : —

SAN FRANCISCO

And the principal Eastern cities.

OFFICE— WITH W., F. & CO.
PRESCOTT.

Gilmer, Salisbury & Company began stagecoach service in the Arizona Territory in 1879 as a result of mail contracts awarded in the fall of 1878. M. Salisbury wrote to John J. Gosper, Secretary of the Territory, "… we will do our utmost in the way of furnishing good, comfortable and speedy facilities for stage traveling to and from all points when our stages run. We have been at great expense and trouble getting the mails started on new routes awarded our firm at the last general mail letting and generally buying the stock and vehicles from the former contractors … We intend putting the Arizona service in a little better shape than any we have, as we think Arizona will justify us in so doing, and have already ordered from Abbott, Downing & Co., Concord, N.H. coaches specially adapted for your country. ... If the people of Arizona will have a little patience with us, they will be amply repaid."

There were independent stagecoach lines in operation as well, but these often did not do well. The firm of Caldwell and Levalley, as but one example, ran a line between Phoenix and Prescott in anticipation of winning the mail contract when it came up for bid, but were disappointed when Kerens & Mitchell underbid them. They reduced their semi-weekly to a weekly service and then, on one trip, refused to take a shipment of gold bullion saying that their coach was disabled and would be repaired at Prescott. However, when they got to their station on the Agua Fria they put Levalley's family into the coach, had a Mexican employee drive their stock alongside, and they "skipped the country" toward New Mexico via the Little Colorado. A constable went in pursuit with an attachment for their property, but not a warrant for their arrest. He overtook them and, when they made good on the debts listed, he allowed them to continue.

During the late 1870s stagecoach companies had great concern over the advancing railroads. Many thought that the completion of a transcontinental railroad would spell an end to stagecoaching operations. The Southern Pacific Railroad reached the California side of the Colorado River in the early summer of 1877. At that point they fell into a dispute with other railroad companies so that the bridge across the river could not be completed until September 30, 1877. The laying of track would not commence again until November 18, 1878 and by February 1879 only sixty-four miles of track had penetrated the Territory eastward. By early summer the tracks ended at Maricopa Wells and in mid-May the crews reached Casa Grande, but again work stopped until January 24, 1880. Now the track layers worked in earnest, reaching Pantano on May 1st, Benson on June 22nd, the tracks crossed Dragoon Summit on July 30th, reached San Simon on September 15th, and finally entered New Mexico a week later.

The railroad brought in new populations and new commerce, and the stagecoach lines found that their businesses flourished. Many new routes and lines were added to bring passengers, express and mail to the railroads, and to take the same away to every town and settlement in the Arizona Territory. As late as July 1, 1894 another major stage line started operating in the Territory – The Black Canyon Stage Company which operated over the Black Canyon Road from Prescott to Phoenix; and, as a new century dawned new stage lines were still being established. Railroads did finally spell an end to stages, as more lines operated over shorter distances, often point to point and back without any stops, or "stages," between. But, it was the automobile that wrought the end of "coaches" as the means of public transportation. In December 1909 Florence's *Blade-Tribune* announced the "New Automobile Stage Line."

> The Arizona Automobile Stage Company, whose name fully describes its purpose, has recently been organized with a capitalization of twenty thousand dollars. The officers and principal stockholders of this company are: Robert A. Lewis, of Tucson, President; W. P. Grigsby, of Florence, Vice-president; J. H. McCann, of Phoenix, Secretary. Nearly two-thirds of the capital stock is already subscribed and the promoters anticipate no difficulty in placing the balance, and indeed there should be no difficulty in this as the proposition will be a money-maker from the very start; this company is the first in the field and is officered by capable business men who are well acquainted with all the conditions necessary to be anticipated in overland travel on the desert. Then this is an age when time is worth money and no business man wants to poke along in the dust behind a team of horses when he can get over the ground with less discomfort in one-tenth the time. The Arizona Automobile Stage Company has ordered four cars and the first, a seven-passenger 35 horse-power Elmore, will be on the ground in a few weeks. The first schedule, as planned now, will be between Casa Grande, Florence, and Superior, with headquarters at this city. Eventually they expect to extend their territory to include regular trips from here to Mesa and Tempe, and on to Phoenix. Then from Florence to Tucson and to Globe would also fill a long felt want, since at the present one has to almost circumnavigate the Territory to reach either of these two points from this place by railroad. This is a first-class enterprise any way you look at it and will have our hearty sympathy and support.

Stagecoach lines continued to operate in remote areas into the late 1920s, when the highway to Young, Arizona was finally paved and the mail coach was replaced by a Ford.

Stagecoach Robbery in the Arizona Territory

The situation in the Arizona Territory was not favorable for road agents during the eighteen-sixties and early seventies. The construction of roads was in progress and coaches were often no more than a spring wagon or buckboard, and usually carried little of value. When valuables of any consequence were carried the military might provide an escort. Mails were irregular and came by way of military express during the early days, and treasure express had not yet come to the Territory in regular fashion.

Indians were so active throughout the Territory that it was not safe to be out in small groups, not even for "hard-game" road agents, and travelers went well armed and alert at all times.

Although a stagecoach was stopped in 1875 and an attempted robbery occurred at the end of 1876, stagecoach robberies did not reach epidemic levels until 1877.

After only one year of frequent highway robberies the editor of Tucson's *Citizen*, in their January 11, 1878 edition, remarked:

"Road Agents" are successfully pursuing the business of robbing stages of mails and express matter and passengers ... perhaps before this is given to our readers, the mails and express will again be plundered and the letters and other like matter be scattered over the country. Thus far we hear of a few arrests of innocent persons – at least testimony in each case was to that effect. All seem to agree that the same "agents" committed the several robberies referred to. They therefore must have been along the public highway and perhaps at some way stations during the period of those depredations. Can it be possible that they have escaped notice of every honest man along the road? Or can they be such honest looking fellows that when seen they attract no special notice? Have the sheriff's and other peace officers exerted themselves to the full extent of their duty to ferret out and arrest these land pirates? It would seem as if, stimulated by large rewards offered by the Territory, the United States and Wells, Fargo & Co., that extraordinary and successful efforts should have been put forth to capture these men who are more infamous than the Apaches ever have been and who, if their career be not arrested, will inflict incalculable injury upon the prosperity of the Territory. Individually Messrs. Kerens & Mitchell have much interest in the matter and they should have all station keepers instructed to carefully note passers by or callers at their stations, and report the same, when their suspicions are aroused as to their legitimate pursuit of such people. Sheriffs in California and other States have made themselves so valuable to the public in hunting down, arresting or destroying this class of public enemies, that no matter what change occurs in political sentiment in their counties, they are re-elected as often as they will consent to serve the people. As officers, sheriffs and constables should use every possible effort to capture highwaymen, and as men they have a large interest in doing so. With a united and determined effort on the part of such officers, station keepers and stage men, at least a measure of success would surely soon be achieved. ... with reference to the present American road agents. Their operations are stopping travel; deterring men of means from coming to the territory; preventing remittances and generally having a disastrous effect on the public at large. They should be arrested dead or alive – better dead, but arrested in some condition.

The editor of Prescott's *Enterprise* voiced frustration over the frequency with which stagecoaches were being robbed during 1877, and wrote "Confound our road agents. They are growing bolder and bolder, and no wonder, as none of their tribe have, as yet, met with just punishment in the Territory. Those of them that have been caught should have been shot, hanged, or sent to Congress. The scoundrels are almost as great nuisances as savings bank men or 'literary' thieves. We're down on them, horse, foot, and dragoons. They deter people from carrying money into the Territory, which is wrong. They prevent people from taking any out of it, which is right; but this is all the good they do. If the civil authorities cannot corral and intimidate these roadsters, we are in favor of declaring martial law against them and letting the military commander hunt them out of the Territory or into their holes."

The *modus operandi* of stagecoach robbers in the Arizona Territory was fairly consistent throughout three decades of operation. They did not ply their trade from the back of a horse, except for three robberies – May 1881 in Yavapai County, October 1888 in Pinal County, and May 1890 in Graham County; nor did road agents alert the driver of their presence and then try to ride down the coach in a harrowing chase, except for the robbery in Cochise County on January 6, 1882. Typically, road agents carefully selected a site along the route where the stagecoach must necessarily slow down, such as the incline of a hill or while traversing soft sand, or might create the circumstance by stretching a rope across the road or building a barricade. Once the coach had slowed or stopped the highwaymen would appear on foot, gun in hand, and order the driver to yield; or, they would fire a volley simultaneously with their demand; though on a very few occasions stagecoach robbers did "shoot first and ask questions later."

Officers of the law were not motivated to chase stagecoach robbers unless there was a strong likelihood that at least one of the criminals could be captured. It was a policy of the times to withhold reimbursement for unsuccessful pursuits. Often, reimbursement was only guaranteed if the crime was so heinous – such as a murder in the course of the robbery – that the community would demand or even subscribe reimbursement for the effort, or that the treasure was so great that potential rewards were a worthy gamble, or that sufficient information was provided to ensure an arrest. In the December 1888 edition of the *Flagstaff Democrat* the editor complained, "the law should be amended so as to allow the sheriff, undersheriff and constables fees for pursuing criminals, whether captured or not." The editor emphasized that the law did not contemplate that an officer should do something for nothing, and to expect so was unjust.

However, this policy persisted into the twentieth century. The *Citizen* reprinted an article in May 1900 which said, "Experience has shown that under our present laws it is almost impossible to wipe small gangs of criminals out of existence. When a crime has been committed a sheriff will go after the criminals. If he catches them it is only after a long and expensive trip he is allowed mileage, and it is seldom that the mileage pays the expenses of the trip. If he does not get them he gets nothing. Now, sheriffs are but human and while many of them put up a good bluff as to the work they have done to catch outlaws, yet but few of them feel able to hunt outlaws for weeks at a time and over hundreds of square miles of territory ... ." More than half the stagecoach robberies remained unsolved because the road agents were not pursued, or if pursued were not captured.

In 1875 the first stagecoach to be halted by road agents was stopped soon after leaving Tucson, and one passenger was robbed. The record does not indicate if other passengers were aboard and the contents of the coach were not molested.

In 1876 an attempt was made to stop a coach, but the robbers failed. Stagecoach robbery commenced in 1877 with six stagecoaches being robbed by eleven men. Three robberies remained unsolved. Four robbers were captured, convicted and sent to prison while another robber, a year later, would resist arrest and be killed.

During 1878 there were ten stagecoach robberies committed by twenty-four men. Four stagecoach robbers were captured, tried and convicted and one was killed. Three robberies remained unsolved. On one occasion two stagecoaches were "jumped" a few miles apart by the same robbers on the same night and in another incident, for the first time, robbers carried away silver bullion. One driver was wounded.

There were ten stagecoach robberies in 1879 committed by thirteen men. Eight of the robberies remained unsolved. Four men were captured but two were released when the Grand Jury declined to indict them. Two robbers were convicted, one receiving a prison sentence while the other was executed for a murder which occurred during the robbery; and one robber was killed while resisting arrest. One messenger was wounded.

There were two stagecoach robberies in 1880 committed by five men. One robbery remained unsolved. Two men were arrested but never tried for their crimes. A messenger was killed and a driver wounded.

There were eleven stagecoach robberies in 1881 committed by at least twenty-three men. Six robberies remained unsolved. None of the guilty parties identified were convicted of their crimes but, with two exceptions, were killed under unrelated circumstances. One driver and one passenger was killed.

There were eight stagecoach robberies in 1882 committed by nineteen men. Four robberies remained unsolved. None of the men arrested or identified were convicted of stagecoach robbery. Several robbers were killed in unrelated events and one escaped jail while awaiting trial. Two passengers were killed.

There were fourteen stagecoach robberies in 1883 committed by thirty-one men. Seven robberies remained unsolved. Nine men were captured, tried and convicted of stagecoach robbery and sentenced to prison terms, but one robber escaped while en route to the territorial prison near Yuma. Two robbers were killed following a pursuit and one robber and an accessory were lynched for a murder committed during a robbery. One driver was killed.

There were nine stagecoach robberies in 1884 committed by nine men. Two robberies remained unsolved. Six men were captured and tried. Four robbers were convicted of stagecoach robbery while two were acquitted.

There were nine stagecoach robberies in 1885 committed by at least sixteen men. Five of the robberies remained unsolved. Five men were captured, tried, convicted, and sentenced to prison terms. Four men were delivered to prison while the fifth man died trying to escape while en route to the penitentiary. Two robbers were released for retrial and one escaped to Mexico, the other was convicted and returned to prison. The robber who escaped was extradited from Mexico in 1891 and tried on the 1885 stagecoach robbery charge, but the case was dismissed.

There were two stagecoach robberies in 1886. At least four men were involved. Both crimes remained unsolved.

There were two stagecoach robberies in 1887 committed by one man. In one instance two stagecoaches were robbed. The robber was killed in an unrelated event.

There were eleven stagecoach robberies in 1888 committed by four men. Six robberies remained unsolved. One robber was captured, tried, convicted and sentenced to prison terms twice for a single robbery. Four robberies were committed by the same two men, but shortly after their tenth robbery on June 2, 1891 one road agent was killed while another was convicted and sent to prison.

There were four stagecoach robberies in 1889 committed by five men. One robbery remained unsolved. Three men were captured, tried, convicted and sentenced to prison while a fourth robber was killed while resisting arrest shortly after he and an accomplice committed their tenth robbery on June 2, 1891.

There were five stagecoach robberies in 1890 committed by two men. One robbery remained unsolved. Four robberies were committed by the same two men – on June 2, 1891 one robber was killed while the other was convicted and sent to prison.

There were four stagecoach robberies in 1891 committed by four men. There were no unsolved robberies. Two men were captured, tried, convicted and sentenced to prison. One man was captured the following year after another stagecoach robbery, and the fourth robber was shot to death while resisting arrest.

There were two stagecoach robberies in 1892 committed by two men. One robbery remained unsolved. One man was captured, tried, convicted and sentenced to prison.

There was one stagecoach robbery in 1893 perpetrated by the stagecoach driver. He was tried, convicted, and sentenced to prison.

There were seven stagecoach robberies in 1894 committed by at least eleven men. Four robberies remained unsolved. Five men were captured, tried, convicted and sentenced to prison. One driver was badly beaten during a robbery.

There were two stagecoach robberies in 1895 committed by two men. One robbery remained unsolved. One man was captured, tried, convicted, and sentenced to prison.

There were no stagecoach robberies in 1896.

There were two stagecoach robberies in 1897 committed by four men. One robbery remained unsolved. In the other robbery two men were arrested, examined, held for the Grand Jury, and released on bail; but they were never tried as they eluded capture.

There were two stagecoach robberies in 1898 committed by three men. Both robberies remained unsolved.

There was one stagecoach robbery in 1899 committed by one man and one woman. Both were captured, tried, convicted, and sentenced to prison.

There were no stagecoach robberies in 1900.

There was only one stagecoach robbery in 1901. The robber escaped to Mexico but was extradited the following year. He was never indicted.

There were two stagecoach robberies in 1902 committed by three men. One robbery remained unsolved. One man was captured, tried, convicted and sentenced to prison.

There was only one stagecoach robbery in 1903 committed by two men, and it remained unsolved. The era of stagecoach robbery ended as it had begun, with a controversial crime in which a particular victim in posession of specific plunder seemed the target, rather than the stagecoach on which she rode.

Three Decades of Stagecoach Robbery

Between 1875 and 1903 there were one hundred twenty-nine stagecoach robberies in the Arizona Territory. Five robberies involved two coaches each, bringing the total number of stagecoaches robbed to one hundred thirty-four. More than half the robberies remained unsolved.

Passengers William Thomas, Peter Roerig and two unnamed Chinese passengers were killed during robberies. Drivers Budd Philpott and F. M. Peterson and messengers Chavis and Johnny Collins were killed, while drivers Nathan Powell and John Henry and messenger William Blankenship were wounded.

More than two hundred men and one woman engaged in the business of robbing stagecoaches. Most road agents remained unknown but seventy-nine men and the only female stagecoach bandit in the Arizona Territory were identified. Most were tried, convicted and sentenced to prison. One sentenced prisoner escaped and one prisoner died during an escape attempt while en route to their new home at the Territorial prison. One stagecoach robber, the accomplice of the female bandit, escaped from the Territorial prison and, as with the one who escaped en route, was never recaptured.

Five road agents were killed while resisting arrest. One man was executed and another was lynched for murders committed during a stagecoach robbery. No man was ever lynched or legally hanged in the Arizona Territory for robbing a stagecoach. Convicted stagecoach robbers received prison sentences, but never served an entire term as they received credit for good time as required by law, or they were granted an early pardon. Most of the stagecoach robbers who served their sentence were granted pardons to restore citizenship, particularly their right to vote.

Typical of the myths found in the record is the story of George Johnson. George was among the earliest arrivals at Tombstone, with wife Nancy Independence and a large brood of small children. He was a heavy drinker who only occasionally held a job. In October 1882 he inexplicably came into possession of a fine brace of pistols, and the belts to hold them, which motivated him to embark upon a criminal career.

George proceeded to hold up the stagecoach from Bisbee with Mr. and Mrs. M. E. Kellogg aboard. He halted the coach at gun point but his horse bolted and threw him, his six-shooter misfired, and Mr. Kellogg fell dead. George fled afoot.

The stage driver unhitched two horses from his team and sent Mrs. Kellogg for the sheriff while the driver went after George, whose tracks circled back to Tombstone.

Mrs. Kellogg alerted the sheriff, who led a posse to the scene. Meanwhile the stagecoach driver captured George and brought him to town. They arrived shortly after the sheriff departed so, with no lawmen present to protect the prisoner, the citizens promptly hanged George.

The sheriff brought in the coach and body and announced that Mr. Kellogg had died of a heart attack so, in those times, George was not responsible for his death.

The town's people took up a collection to compensate George's widow and children while George and Mr. Kellogg were buried side-by-side on boot hill. Visitors can see the gravemarkers there to this day.

But, the first record of this event appears after 1930.

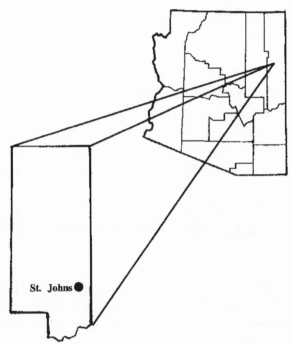

Stagecoach Robberies in Apache County

In 1879 Apache County was formed from the eastern part of Yavapai County. The new county established its county seat at Snowflake, which moved to St. Johns that year, then to Springerville in 1880, and back to St. Johns the following year. Navajo County would not be formed from the western half of Apache County until 1895, after both stagecoach robberies were committed in that region

September 19, 1882

The stagecoach which left Fort Thomas bound for Willcox on Tuesday morning was robbed of all mail matter by two masked men about five miles north of Cedar Springs. Thirty-eight registered packages were taken, containing an aggregate of over three thousand dollars, which belonged principally to soldiers.

The robbers were never identified.

September 1, 1885

The buckboard carrying the mail left St. Johns for Navajo Tuesday morning and was stopped by two highwaymen at Zuni bridge, about twelve miles north on the St. Johns and Navajo road. The pouch containing the Springerville mail and the entire southern and St. Johns' matter was rifled. Dr. Yarrow of the Smithsonian scientific exploration party was the only passenger, and he contributed a very valuable watch in addition to whatever funds he may have had for traveling expenses.

The report of the robbery was brought in by F. C. Lewis' express man, who saw the robbers fleeing in the direction of the Zuni villages. Sheriff Hubbell sent out a strong force of men well acquainted with every watering place and trail, who were determined to capture the robbers.

J. O. Culver, Post Office Inspector, issued a notice of a two hundred dollar reward "for the arrest and conviction of each of the robbers who were implicated in robbing the United States mails ... on September 1st, 1885."

The robbers were never identified.

October 30, 1887

The Tonto Basin is located east of the Verde River and north of the Salt River. Within the basin is Pleasant Valley, a relatively isolated basin beginning at the head of Cherry Creek under the rim of the Mogollons and entirely surrounded by mountains. Earle R. Forrest, in *Arizona's Dark and Bloody Ground*, wrote, "with its tranquility, its wild, rugged beauty, and its vast, untrammeled distances, covered with that mystic purple haze peculiar to the Southwest, this land fascinates the wilderness traveler." By 1886 the valley was well settled with cattle ranches. In August 1887, however, a blood feud had erupted from disputes between the Graham family and the Tewksburys, and residents were forced to choose sides or leave.

An Indian was killed first, but on August 10th the first white blood was drawn at the Middleton ranch, and law enforcement was quick to respond. Sheriff Mulvenon of Yavapai County invaded the valley with a large force, determined to see an end to blood shed before the feud worsened. His efforts failed and after more men died he brought another large force of men into the valley on September 21st. He made nine arrests, but missed William Bonner and Louis Parker, who were Graham partisans. As Sheriff Mulvenon was leaving the valley he met Sheriff Commodore Perry Owens with a force of thirty men entering the valley. Owens searched for the men Mulvenon had missed, but could not find them.

With law enforcement's attention focused to the west and south it must have seemed a great opportunity for adventure and fame to the young cowboy William Bonner. He traveled eastward in search of a fortune, perhaps to share with the Grahams or to finance his own exit from the valley. On Sunday, October 30th Bonner hid along the road between St. Johns and Navajo. When the stagecoach was about eight miles out of Navajo, and just as the coach was driven amongst some scrubby cedars, Bonner jumped out from the side of the road with pistol in hand and ordered the driver to "throw up," which he did. The highwayman then searched to see if the driver had any arms and, finding none, proceeded to cut open the mail bags and examine the registered matter. After he had satisfied himself with the contents of the mail pouch he searched the driver and took eighty dollars belonging to Wells, Fargo and Company's express.

The robber ordered the driver to put the mail matter back into the sacks and onto the buckboard and then boarded next to the driver. He made him drive towards St. John's for about five miles when Bonner stopped him again, ordered the driver off the stagecoach and joined him on the side of the road, where they waited for the buckboard from St. Johns. After waiting about four hours Bonner was rewarded by the appearance of the stagecoach, which he stopped and ransacked in the same manner as he had the one from Navajo.

The northbound stagecoach had one passenger, who was unmolested, while the southbound stagecoach had no passengers. The driver of the southbound stagecoach could only describe the robber as tall and slender and wearing a light colored hat, even though he was with him for over four hours on a night when there was hardly a cloud in the sky and the moon was nearly full. Sheriff Commodore Perry Owens went in pursuit but came up empty-handed.

Bonner fled southwest and on November 7th robbed a stagecoach in Maricopa County before returning to Pleasant Valley. On November 9th Prescott's *Miner* reported that the body of William Bonner had been found in Pleasant Valley fifteen feet from a road frequently traveled by cowboys. Bonner's remains had been covered with sagebrush and it was supposed from the circumstances that Bonner had been ambushed by the Tewksburys, rivals of the Graham family. Bonner was counted as the twentieth death in two months growing out of that feud, and many of the deceased were murdered from ambush.

THE NAVAJO, ST. JOHNS
— AND —
Springerville Stage Line.
TIME TABLE.

GOING SOUTH.	STATIONS.	GOING NORTH.
*6.00 A. M.	lve. Navajo ar.	6.00 P. M.
6.00 P. M. } arr.	St. Johns.	6.00 A. M. } lve.
7.30 A. M. } lve		5.45 P. M. } arr.
5.45 P. M.	Springerville.	†6.00 A. M.

*Except Saturdays.
†Except Sundays.

EXPRESS RATES.

Over 50 pounds ....3 cents per pound.
Under 50 pounds ....5 cents per pound.
No package carried for less than 50 cents.

Carrying Passengers, Express, and the United States Mail, between Springerville and the Atlantic and Pacific Railroad.

Principal office St. Johns, Arizona. Branch offices and local agents at Springerville and Navajo.

W. W. WALL, Proprietor.

From the St. Johns Herald, October 1885

It was reported, "... on good authority that Bonner was the party who recently held up the stage between Fort Apache and St. John's, securing quite a sum of money. ... He has participated in all manner of crimes that have stained the annals of Arizona, and there is no question but his death is a welcome one."

Bonner, it was believed, was wanted in Colorado for murder and was also suspected of rustling twenty horses from the San Juan country a little over a year previously.

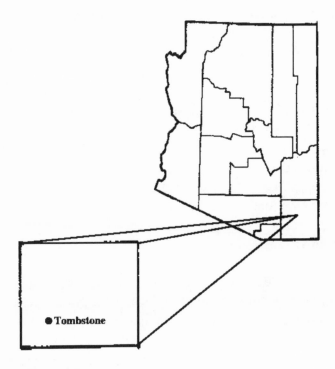

Stagecoach Robbery in Cochise County

In 1881 Cochise County was formed from southeastern Pima County, and established its county seat at Tombstone. This was the era of conflict between the Earps and the "cowboys," often misrepresented as a feud only with the Clantons. The pro-cowboy factions implied that the Earps, or at least "Doc" Holliday, were involved in stagecoach robberies. However, the Earps, in searching for business opportunities, followed the "booms," as did the road agents seeking outgoing bullion and incoming payrolls. This gave the impression that stagecoach robberies started when the Earps arrived.

Wyatt Earp was the first member of that family to arrive at Tombstone in December 1879 and all the Earps were gone by March 1882, a period of only twenty-seven months. It was often said that Tombstone "had a man for breakfast and a stage robbed by sunset," but during the time the Earps were in Tombstone there were only eight stagecoaches robbed in the County.

February 25, 1881

The first stagecoach robbery in the newly created Cochise County occurred on February 25th when the stagecoach between Tombstone and Contention was robbed. The coach was three and a half miles from Contention when it was stopped. Only one hundred thirty-five dollars was found in the box, this being an off-night for express. Neither the passengers nor the mails were molested. The robbers were not pursued.

On March 15th the robbers would "jump" another stagecoach near Contention.

March 15, 1881

On Tuesday night, eight miles from Contention and about two hundred yards from Drew's Station, the Tombstone to Benson stagecoach was attacked by two road agents. The coach was going up a small incline when a man stepped out on each side of the road and called "hold!" Mr. Paul replied, "I don't hold for anybody," and at the same time brought his gun to his shoulder and fired both barrels at the robbers, and said later he thought he might have hit one or both. Shots by Paul and the robbers were nearly simultaneous and it was difficult to tell who shot first. At the same instant the driver fell forward and down between the wheels.

The horses jumped into a dead run at the first sound of gunfire, the reins falling from the driver's hands. The team ran nearly a mile before they could be stopped, which saved the stagecoach from being robbed. Once they were under control Paul found that driver Budd Philpott was killed and a passenger named Peter Roerig was wounded. There were eight other passengers on the coach, but none of them was injured. Paul brought the coach into Benson with the body of Philpott and the wounded passenger, who died a short time later.

Wyatt Earp formed a posse and arrested Luther King four days after the robbery on suspicion of being one of the perpetrators. King submitted to arrest peaceably even though he had a Winchester, two six-shooters and twenty boxes of cartridges with him. He confessed but insisted that he had only held the horses, and then revealed that his accomplices in robbing the stagecoach were the notorious cowboys Billy Leonard, Jim Crane, and Harry "the Kid" Head. Sheriff Behan insisted on taking King to Tombstone's jail and the Earps, anxious to get on the trail of the three named robbers, agreed. They failed to find the trio.

Leonard, Head and Crane laid low in the vicinity of Eureka, New Mexico Territory, but by June their funds had dwindled and they needed a new stake. The three stagecoach robbers, with other members of the Clanton gang, decided to rob the store of Bill and Ike Haslett. However, instead of surrendering their cash the Hasletts went for their pistols, which they kept strategically placed under the counter. During the gunfight Head was killed and Leonard mortally wounded. As he lay dying, Leonard named Crane as the stagecoach robber who had killed Budd Philpott.

Unaware that Leonard had identified him as the murderer, Crane felt obligated to exact revenge on the Hasletts for killing his friends. He approached Curly Bill Brocius, who gathered a small army of gang members which may have included Frank Stillwell, Pony Deal, Pete Spence, Jim Crane and at least five other men, to assist in killing the storekeeper-brothers. In the running gun battle that erupted in Eureka in July, two obscure members of Curly Bill's party were killed and three wounded before the Hasletts fell, murdered. Crane fled into Mexico.

In August, Newman H. "old man" Clanton went to Mexico on a cattle rustling venture with five men, including Charlie Snow, Dick Gray, Bill Byers, Harry Earnshaw, and Bill Lang. The rustlers, with their stolen cattle, crossed the international border onto U. S. soil and camped in Guadalupe Canyon, where Jim Crane joined them.

Mexican Commandant Filipe Neri, knowing of the old Apache trail used by northbound American rustlers and southbound Mexican smugglers, sent troops onto American soil where they ambushed the gang and recovered the cattle. Crane along with Clanton, Snow and Gray were killed. Bill Byers, Harry Earnshaw and Bill Lang survived the attack but Lang was mortally wounded and died a short time later.

Luther "Sandy" King managed to escape from Sheriff Behan almost as soon as he reached the Tombstone jail. A reward for "arrest and conviction" was posted and the search continued, but Luther King was never heard of again in the Arizona Territory. However, a desperado working under the sobriquet "Sandy" King appeared in the southwest section of the New Mexico Territory about this time. In the fall of 1881 Sandy King tried to "take the town" of Shakespeare and was soon in jail, shortly to be joined by "Russian Bill" Tattenbaum who was captured riding a stolen horse. A group which called itself the Law and Order Committee was determined to be rid of the bad element in their town, so they took the two men from jail and suspended them from a ceiling beam in the banquet hall of the Grant House.

August 17, 1881

Not every stagecoach robbery occurred on the road. Occasionally road agents might allow the treasure to be brought into town and unloaded for them. On Wednesday, August 17th the coach arrived in Benson and drove up to the depot platform to unloaded bars of silver bullion sent by way of Wells, Fargo and Company's express. While the messenger was taking the heavy bars into the building one at a time, necessitating his absence from the platform only for a few seconds each trip, some person stole one of the bars valued in the neighborhood of two thousand dollars. Diligent search was immediately made but no clue was found to identify the robber.

Wells, Fargo and Company offered a reward of one hundred fifty dollars for the recovery of the bullion and three hundred dollars for the arrest and conviction of each party implicated in the theft. Neither the robber nor the bullion was found, and the fact that the silver ingot or a part of it never turned up was baffling.

A stagecoach was robbed in Maricopa County on May 10, 1882 by William Miller, and he was arrested. He admitted that he alone was the man who had stolen the bar of bullion on August 17, 1881, but that he had hurriedly buried it nearby because of its great weight. He said that, fearing discovery, he moved it several days later and buried it again, but had hidden it so well that he was never able to find it again.

Miller managed to escape from the Maricopa County Jail and was never seen nor heard of in the Territory again.

September 8, 1881

The stagecoach for Bisbee left Tombstone on Thursday afternoon at the usual hour, having as passengers E. T. Hardy, S. W. Rae, Owen Gibney, and Mat Delahan. The coach was stopped by three masked men at a point about five miles from Hereford and twelve miles from Bisbee. The robbery occurred about half-past ten and resulted in a loss to Wells, Fargo and Company of two thousand five hundred dollars in coin. Passengers E. T. Hardy contributed a gold watch and chain valued at one hundred fifty dollars and eight dollars in currency, and S. W. Rae contributed six hundred dollars in money. The mail pouch was cut open and its contents rifled. Two robbers were seen doing the business while the third remained hidden, but was always near at hand so that he could keep up communication with his partners. One of those seen was described as a tall man while the other was a heavy set man of medium stature.

Mr. Stillman, who was the agent for Wells, Fargo and Company at Bisbee, started across the country by trail for Tombstone, thinking that the robbers would come that way rather than by the road, but nothing in the way of fresh tracks was seen. Marshall Williams, Wells, Fargo and Company's agent at Tombstone, informed Undersheriff Woods of the crime and Woods was soon in the saddle en route to the scene of the robbery.

On Friday a posse consisting of Wyatt and Morgan Earp, Deputy Sheriffs Breakenridge and Nagle, Marshall Williams, and Frederick Dodge started to hunt for the trail of the highwaymen and arrived at the scene of the robbery at dusk. By that time all tracks had become obliterated except one from a barefoot horse, which had been ridden in the direction of Bisbee, and a narrow boot heel was visible in the mud near where the coach was stopped. From there the posse followed the trail.

At about 9 o'clock Sunday morning Frank C. Stillwell, the Deputy Sheriff at Bisbee, and Pete Spence, a resident of Tombstone who was engaged in business in Bisbee, were arrested upon a territorial warrant sworn out by Marshall Williams. They were brought to Tombstone and lodged in jail.

The two men appeared before Justice Spicer, but before any proceeding could commence they were rearrested by deputy U. S. Marshal Wyatt Earp upon a federal warrant sworn out by Marshall Williams, and both defendants were charged with robbing the United States mail. The examination on the federal charge was scheduled for Thursday and upon the Territorial charge the following Monday.

On Thursday morning, October 20th, the preliminary hearing for Pete Spence and Frank Stillwell commenced before U. S. Commissioner Stiles at Tucson. They were charged with robbing the U. S. mail. The first witness was the driver, Levi McDaniels, who testified, "... the first I knew the lead horses jumped out of the road to the right and somebody said 'hold on!' I saw a man standing near my near leader with a double barreled shotgun, looking to the right I saw another man with a six-shooter walking toward me. It was near 11 o'clock; the man with the six-shooter walked up to me and I said 'boys, don't shoot, there's no need of it.' He stepped two or three steps toward me and told me to throw out the mail sack, which I did. The same man then said, "throw out everything in the boot," so I threw out everything. He then told the passengers to get out on the opposite side of the coach from him and hold up their hands and he walked around and commenced robbing them. When he was done he ordered the passengers into the coach and told me to drive on.

"I started when the man with the shotgun said 'hold on there' and to the man with the six-shooter said, 'look on top.' The robber with the six-shooter stepped up on the boot of the coach and went through the man sitting by me, saying as he came up, 'maybe you have got some sugar.' The men were disguised with handkerchiefs tied just below the eyes, their hats were drawn down, and they were roughly dressed."

It was well known in that part of the country that Frank Stillwell always used the term "sugar" in referring to money; but the most damning testimony came from John Hiles of Bisbee, who overheard a conversation between the two defendants. Hiles testified: "Stillwell said, 'We are suspected for this stage robbery and we must put this money away for I expect we will be arrested.' Spence answered, 'Let's let John know about this and we can have him for a witness.' Stillwell said, 'It is not necessary to let him know anything about it.'" Hiles testified to the identity of the person who had made narrow boot-heel tracks in the mud near where the stagecoach was overhauled and D. W. Weldt gave expert testimony in identifying the tracks of men and horses at the scene of the robbery. Shoemaker Dever then testified that Stillwell had him replace the narrow heels of his boots with broader ones just after the robbery.

Frank Stillwell and Pete Spence were held to answer before the U. S. Grand Jury, but posted bail and gained their freedom following the hearing. The hearing in the District Court on the Territorial charge was postponed pending the outcome of the trial in the U. S Circuit Court. They were never convicted of this crime.

October 8, 1881

The stagecoach from Benson to Tombstone left the former place at 9 o'clock a.m. on Saturday, October 8th but was stopped by five masked men five miles after leaving Contention. The robbers spooked the horses and they ran away, upsetting the coach, but no one was seriously hurt. The robbers relieved the passengers, eight men and one lady, of all the money and valuables they had and, seeing that they had done well, gave each five dollars for expenses. They waited for half an hour for the down stagecoach which was supposed to have a heavy run of coin and bullion, but it was an hour late and the robbers decided not to wait longer, so they bade their victims 'Good bye, boys' and left.

Cochise County's Board of Supervisors offered five hundred dollars reward for the capture of the five robbers, or one hundred dollars for any one of them. There was also the standing reward of three hundred dollars from Wells, Fargo and Company for each robber, and the same amount offered by the Territory.

On October 14th two familiar suspects were arrested – Frank Stillwell and Pete Spence. Wyatt and Virgil Earp arrested them on a charge of robbing the Benson stagecoach. Stillwell had not been in town for some time but immediately upon his arrival, at about half-past four o'clock in the afternoon, he was jailed by Wyatt Earp.

Shortly after being arrested Stillwell asked that a man be sent out on the road to inform Spence. Upon hearing this Virgil and Wyatt started on horseback towards Charleston, from where Spence was expected, with the intention of arresting him. The two lawmen saw Spence riding toward Tombstone, but waited until he came into town and then jailed him. Both prisoners were taken to Tucson.

On November 9th Stillwell and Spence waived further examination and the case was closed pending a hearing before the territorial Grand Jury. Stillwell and Spence were once again released on bail.

December 14, 1881

On Wednesday, December 14th, an attempt was made to rob a stagecoach four miles from Tombstone. The circumstances suggested that the real target of the attempt might have been the assassination of John P. Clum, editor of the *Tombstone Epitaph*.

The six horse team was driven by Jimmy Harrington and the bullion wagon was driven by "Whistling Dick." They had just left Malcolm's Station, the last house on the road to Contention and only about four miles from Tombstone, and were moving along at a rapid gait when the order to "Halt!" was given. From the roadside, and almost simultaneously, a volley was fired at them. The off-leader of the coach's team was struck in the neck and all the horses became unmanageable. Dick was hit in the calf of the leg, receiving a painful flesh wound, but kept his seat and his wagon right-side up. The coach horses, followed closely by the wagon, ran about half a mile when the wounded horse weakened and fell from loss of blood.

Clum, with the assistance of other passengers, cut the leaders loose and continued on with four horses. It was generally the impression that all the passengers were aboard. Mr. Clum had been riding on the inside and he was missed, but it was supposed by his fellow passengers that he had taken a seat on the outside; while the driver supposed that Clum had joined his fellow passengers inside. Consequently, Clum's absence was not noticed until the arrival of the stagecoach at Contention.

Sheriff Behan and Mr. Reppy arrived at Contention between four and five o'clock where they learned from Mr. Danham of Philadelphia, who was on the stagecoach, the particulars of the affair. Upon learning the facts Behan and Reppy started for Tombstone and, upon arriving at the place where the attack was made, examined the locality carefully. However, no trace of Clum could be found.

The second party left Tombstone about four o'clock a.m. and, after arriving at Malcolm's Station, continued down the road about a half mile beyond the attacking point where, by the light of a match, two large pools of blood were found on the right where the off- leader had given out and been unharnessed from the team. The animal had wandered several hundred yards to the right of the road, marking his trail by his ebbing life, where it had already fallen prey to skulking coyotes. No rifle cartridge shells could be found on the ground, and all parties claim that there were from fifteen to twenty shots fired in quick succession.

The party, not being able to discover any trace of Clum, proceeded on to Contention where they learned that Clum had been heard of at the Grand Central mill. The party proceeded there and found that the mayor had taken the ore road to the mill from whence, after resting, he had gone by saddle to Benson, arriving about eight o'clock that evening.

Two teamsters, who were camped near the point of attack, had not only heard the noise of the shooting but could distinctly see the flashes, the attack having been made about the apex of the first rise beyond. The teamsters and Mr. Danham stated that the flashes seemed to come from both sides of the road, and the wound received by the bullion driver and the killing shot to the team's leader were made by revolvers, suggesting that the attack was not intended to rob the stagecoach.

Mr. O'Brien, one of the teamsters, said that the attackers had probably fled up the gulch to the northeast just above Malcolm's, as about one hundred yards from the road there was evidence of the repeated hitching of horses in the thick brush, and shortly after the shooting the sound of flying hoofs came from that direction.

The robbers were never identified.

January 6, 1882

W. W. Hubbard & Company's stagecoach left Tombstone for Bisbee at eight o'clock on Friday morning with passengers Mrs. J. D. Watson, Col. S. A. Moore, E. T. Hardy, and J. C. Stewart, Charles A. Bartholomew as messenger for Wells, Fargo and W. S. Waite driving.

The stagecoach had proceeded as far as Lewis' Spring, about six miles above Charleston, when five mounted men were observed on the opposite side of the river galloping rapidly, evidently with the intention of getting ahead of the coach. Proceeding on to Hereford, and fearing trouble, Mr. Bartholomew procured a Winchester rifle in addition to the shot-gun which the messenger always carries. In the meantime the horsemen had disappeared among the foothills. About three o'clock p.m. the stagecoach had reached a point eight miles from Bisbee when three men suddenly appeared in the road seventy-five yards ahead of the coach.

Without a word of warning the robbers opened fire with rifles, firing twelve to fifteen shots, some of which struck the coach and two shots hit one of the wheel horses. The driver turned the team and took the back track while Bartholomew and one passenger, who were on top, jumped off as the messenger returned fire at the robbers with the Winchester. The coach had gone some distance when it stopped and waited for the messenger and passenger to catch up.

The robbers mounted their horses and charged after the coach about five miles, where the wounded horse weakened and the coach was compelled to stop, so the driver rounded them up by the side of an arroyo. For the entire distance Bartholomew kept up his fire though, on account of the jolting of the coach, his aim was very uncertain.

When the coach stopped the rustlers made a circuit around out of rifle distance and came out on the road ahead. There they met a Mexican woodhauler whom they compelled to carry a message to the beleaguered passengers. The message was to the effect that if Wells, Fargo and Company's treasure box was not thrown off the "entire outfit would be killed."

The box contained six thousand five hundred dollars, principally in coin, which was being taken out to pay miners at the Copper Queen. For a long time the messenger refused to surrender but at last the passengers persuaded him to yield. All except the driver left the coach and went several hundred yards to one side of the road. The three robbers then came up, two of them having their faces concealed by dirty silk handkerchiefs while the third robber, who was the spokesman of the party, was not disguised.

They approached the coach and held a conversation with the driver, who thought they seemed familiar to him although he did not recognize any of them. They disclaimed all intention of hurting any of the passengers or robbing them, saying all they wanted was the treasure box. The unmasked man asked the driver if he would know him the next time he saw him, and Waite was compelled to admit that he would. The reply was in plain English, "Well, if you do know me, and ever give me away, you won't live a minute."

After breaking open the box and securing the coin the robbers ransacked the coach, but did not take anything. One of the robbers then remarked to the driver, pointing to a coach horse, "That horse jumps pretty well, I believe I'll take him along," and the animal was unharnessed and led off. The passengers and the messenger then returned to the coach and the remaining two horses were hitched-up.

The robbers watched them from a distance but, before they could get underway, the robbers drew their six-guns and ordered a halt. The driver dismounted, went to them, and asked why they had halted him again. The answer was an order for him to go to Bisbee. Waite argued that it would be impossible to get to Bisbee with only two horses, and at last they agreed that he should return to Hereford. At Hereford fresh horses were procured and the stagecoach proceeded on to the copper camp.

The first report of the robbery came to Tombstone Saturday morning about ten o'clock, being sent from Charleston by Bartholomew who had returned from Hereford. Wells, Fargo and

Company offered a reward of five hundred dollars for each of the robbers and one fourth of all the treasure recovered. The five robbers included Frank Stilwell, Pete Spence, Ike Clanton, Curly Bill Borcius and Pony Deal.

Stillwell and Spence were free on bail from several previous arrests for stagecoach robbery when they participated in the murder of Morgan Earp at Tombstone on the 18th of March 1882. Within three days Frank Stillwell was discovered in the railroad yard west of the depot near Porter's Hotel in Tucson with four rifle balls and two loads of buckshot imbedded in his body. The train carrying the body of Morgan Earp had passed through the previous evening with the Earps and "Doc" Holliday aboard, and it was assumed that Wyatt and Doc had dispatched Stillwell. Virgil Earp, in an interview at San Francisco on May 27th, confirmed that his party was responsible for Stillwell's death, but declined to provide specific details.

Ike Clanton, the man who backed down at the O.K. Corral, was never arrested for robbing the stagecoach. He was implicated in the attempted assassination of Virgil Earp and quickly thereafter fled south of the border where he remained for several years. Once the Earps had permanently vacated Tombstone, Ike returned to the territory and resumed his career as a cattle rustler. Commodore Perry Owens, the newly elected Sheriff in 1887, was determined to clean up his county. His posse trapped a gang of rustlers in their base camp that year and a gunfight ensued, during which Ike Clanton was killed.

Pete Spence or Peter Spencer, whose real name was Elliott Larkin Ferguson, was implicated in the murder of Morgan Earp by his wife. Spence was in jail when the Earp's visited his wood camp, which saved his life. After his release from jail he remained in Arizona until late 1882, where he was having some difficulties with Judge Burnett at Charleston. Spence avoided a confrontation with Burnett by moving to New Mexico. There he served as a lawman for a short term before returning to Arizona, where he soon pistol-whipped Rodney O'Hare to death and was sent to the Territorial Prison for a short stretch. He was pardoned by Governor Kibbey in late1894 and later settled on a farm at Webster Springs near Globe. Pete Spence died of pneumonia on January 30, 1914.

"Curly Bill" Brocius and Pony Deal robbed another stage-coach the following day.

January 7, 1882

Mr. Sheldon, a driver on Sandy Bob's stagecoach from Benson to Tombstone, reported that his stagecoach was stopped just north of the arroyo, about half way between Tombstone and Contention, at 4 o'clock Saturday morning. Sheldon was ordered to halt by two men and then compelled to get down and hold his leaders. Two more men appeared in the dim moon light, there being four robbers, and one of them held a shot gun at the window pointed at the inside passengers, and forbade any one of them to stir on pain of instant death.

There were nine passengers aboard, all males, eight of whom were inside and one outside with the driver. The outside passenger, on coming down with the driver, was relieved of a six-shooter which one of the robbers remarked was needed in his business. Most of the inside passengers were asleep when the driver pulled up and had no opportunity to resist.

Among the inside passengers was J. B. Hume, chief detective for Wells, Fargo and Company, who was on the back seat, but before he was sufficiently awakened and able to take in the situation the driver was at the front holding the leaders and the outside passenger was standing near the wheelers with hands raised. Hume had on his person two fine revolvers but, instead of making use of them on the robbers, he stepped out with the rest of the passengers and gracefully surrendered them. He later said that any attempt to use his revolvers under the circumstances would inevitably involve a sacrifice of the lives of several of the passengers, and as there was nothing of his employer's treasure on board he considered he would be acting in the best interest of all to refrain from violent measures.

The road agents first demanded that Wells Fargo's express box be handed out, and were evidently disappointed when the driver responded that there was no treasure on board. They proceeded to go through the passengers. The inside passengers were told to hold up their hands and come out, to which order they obeyed. After they had filed out one by one they were ranged in line on the roadway, still holding their hands up, and rapidly gone through by one of the thieves while the other kept them constantly under cover with his weapon. In most instances only one pocket was searched and watches and valuables other than money were not disturbed. There was from twelve to fifteen hundred dollars among the passengers but only seventy-five dollars and three revolvers were secured, as various ploys were resorted to by the passengers to secure their valuables. After this hasty search the passengers were allowed to re-enter the coach and the driver was ordered to resume his journey.

The two robbers who first halted the coach were well disguised with black cloth masks. One of them was a tall man who wore a tight fitting suit, such as are used by the "leg-maniacs" in the Christmas pantomimes. The other, a short man, wore a gunny sack over his head and clothes, with holes cut for his eyes and for his arms. Both of them had powerful firearms but made no apparent attempt to use them and no shot was fired during the transaction. The robbers, though firm in their commands, were polite in their language and evidently were not novices at the business.

Even though disguised, the two robbers who first appeared were identified as "Curly Bill" Brocius and Pony Deal. The other two men, though unmasked, were never identified. Marshall Williams, Wells, Fargo and Company's agent, authorized the standing reward of three hundred dollars for the arrest and conviction of each robber.

"Curly Bill" Brocius, whose real name was William B. Graham, was involved in the attempted assassination of Virgil Earp and, consequently, was one of the men sought by Wyatt. He was killed in a gunfight at Iron Springs. Wyatt and his party had just dismounted at Iron Springs to rest and water their mounts when their party of six men was ambushed by a party of nine men who were a part of the ruffians known as "the cowboys." Reports suggest that when fired upon, instead of seeking cover, the Earp faction charged the cowboys, who were entrenched behind good cover, and put them to rout. Other accounts say the Earp faction retreated, except for Wyatt who charged the group firing a shotgun and pistols. Curly Bill was the only man killed, taking the full load from Wyatt's shotgun in his chest.

Charles T. Ray went by the name Pony Deal, sometimes spelled Diahl or Diehl. Deal left Arizona in late 1881 or early 1882 but was arrested with two other men at Cisco, Texas on February 18th, charged with the Bisbee stagecoach robbery of January 6, 1882. It was said that he would be extradited to Tombstone, but that rumor proved false. Deal was reportedly killed in a gunfight at Clifton, New Mexico in late 1882, possibly to throw lawmen off his trail. He killed John O'Rourke to avenge the killing of John Ringo and for that offense was sentenced to serve five years in the New Mexico penitentiary. He was pardoned March 14, 1887 and not heard of again.

November 1, 1888

The stagecoach between Bowie and Solomonville was robbed Thursday when three miles from Bailey's Wells by two young Mexicans. Mr. S. W. Pomeroy, county treasurer of Graham county, was the only passenger and was relieved of thirty-five dollars in currency and a fine gold watch and chain. The robbers also took three mail pouches. The pair was well mounted, one riding a dun horse and the other a chestnut bay. The direction taken by the men after the robbery was not known.

A reward of three hundred dollars was offered by the post office department for the arrest and conviction of parties robbing the mails. Marshal Meade was in Tombstone at the time of the robbery and was "on the ground giving the matter his personal attention."

The two Mexicans were not captured following this robbery, but on June 2, 1891, after robbing their tenth stagecoach, the robbers were run to ground. One was killed resisting arrest and the other captured, convicted and sentenced to prison.

December 24, 1888

The stagecoach running between Bowie and Solomonville, the same that was robbed November 1st, was held up by two men on Monday near Bowie and the mail sack and everything of value taken. Miss Fitzgerald of Tucson was in the coach but was not molested.

The matter was reported to Marshal Meade in Tucson, who telegraphed to J. Windmiller, the deputy postmaster at Bowie, to start a posse after the highwaymen. Unknown to Windmiller two stockmen who lived near the scene of the robbery took the trail early the next morning and found that the robbers had left the road westward and went about two miles before they dismounted and opened the mail sacks. The robbers opened all of the letters and left a number of postal notes and checks on the ground, but took along the contents of the registered letters. Their tracks indicated that they afterwards left in the direction of Stockton Pass. The stockmen brought the mail matter to town and delivered it to the postmaster.

Three men Windmiller had formed for the official posse were ready to start the following day and left at about 10 a.m., an hour before the stockmen arrived in town. However, they were unable to overtake the highwaymen.

From the description it was clear that these were the same two Mexicans who had robbed four stagecoaches during the past two months. On June 2, 1891, after robbing their tenth stagecoach, the robbers were run to ground. One was killed resisting arrest and the other captured, convicted and sentenced to prison.

October 17, 1890

The Bowie and Solomonville stagecoach was held up Friday afternoon about seven miles from Ft. Bowie by two Mexicans wearing masks. The mail was rifled but the passengers were unmolested.

The two robbers were not captured following this, their eighth, stagecoach robbery. On June 2, 1891, after robbing their tenth stagecoach, the robbers were run to ground. One was killed resisting arrest and the other captured, convicted and sentenced to prison.

October 31, 1890

The Fort Thomas and Bowie stagecoach, en route to Bowie, was robbed on a Friday evening near the ranch of F. A. Kreigh on the San Simon. The robbers rode up to the stagecoach from the rear and one of them covered the driver with a six-shooter before he was aware of their intentions. The other robber went through the coach and took every mail sack and package, and even the driver's coat. It was not known whether they got any money in the robbery, but I. E. Solomon had one thousand seven hundred dollars in checks and drafts in the mail and Captain Thomas had about one thousand dollars in checks.

The driver described the robbers as Mexicans, one a tall man and the other short and heavy set. They both rode bay horses and fled west. It was reported on Sunday that two men answering the description of the robbers had traveled through the Stockton Pass on Friday evening.

The two Mexicans were not captured following this, their ninth, robbery but on June 2, 1891 after robbing their tenth stagecoach the robbers were run to ground. One was killed resisting arrest and the other captured, convicted and sentenced to prison.

May 16, 1891

On Saturday afternoon the Bowie and Thomas stagecoach, with three passengers aboard, was held up by a young Mexican who went through the passengers and safely escaped. He got away with considerable money, though the amount was not reported. The passengers proceeded through to Florence by train.

The driver of the Bowie stagecoach circulated a description of the robber to his many friends, asking that they be on the lookout for the road agent. When Jesus Arvisu was arrested at Willcox on a minor offense, J. F. Smith went to the jail to look over the prisoner, and immediately recognized him from the stagecoach driver's description. He contacted the driver, who then identified Arvisu and swore out a complaint against the robber. Arvisu remained in jail, this time being held for deputy U. S. Marshal Jack O'Neill, who brought Arvisu from Willcox and lodged him in the Pima county jail.

Arvisu's examination on the U. S. charge of robbing the mails was scheduled before Commissioner Aines on August 5th and continued through August 7th. The most important witness was the stagecoach driver, who positively identified Arvisu as the robber and reported that he had ridden a sorrel horse and was unmasked during the robbery of the Bowie stagecoach. The driver testified that Arvisu had demanded the mail sack in very good English and, upon being given a bundle of newspapers, fumbled with his gun as he demanded the leather sack. Witnesses from the Casa Grande stagecoach robbery of April 1st testified that Arvisu looked very much like the robber but could not positively identify him. He was held for the Grand Jury on five thousand dollars bond, and to wait for additional witnesses who could testify about the April 1st robbery.

Arvisu was indicted by the U. S. Grand Jury and on October 20th was taken to Florence by deputy U. S. Marshal Paul for trial in the circuit court. He was convicted on a charge of robbing the U. S. mail, but the more serious charge of using a gun and placing the driver's life in jeopardy was dismissed. Arvisu was sentenced on December 21, 1891 to a ten year term to be served at San Quentin.

Arvisu had also robbed the stagecoach in Pinal County on April 1, 1891 but, with the long sentence already received in the U. S. circuit court, there seemed no need to add the expense of prosecuting him for that Territorial charge.

June 2, 1891

The Tombstone and Bisbee stagecoach, driven by Engle, was held up on Tuesday morning at ten o'clock by two Mexicans when it was about nine miles west of Bisbee. They secured forty dollars for their trouble. The passengers, a man and a woman, were not molested. A posse started in pursuit two hours later.

The posse pursuing the robbers did not capture them. At first it appeared that they had failed though their pursuit had been relentless, allowing the robbers little opportunity to rest their horses. On June 11th three Mexicans rode up to Walter Vail's ranch, quickly dismounted and exchanged a worn-out saddle horse for a fresh mount. They then went to Jones' ranch nearby and made a similar exchange. Vail contacted Constable Gray of Benson, who assembled a posse consisting of W. T. Hughes, Chico Orosco, D. H. Logan and W. H. Gibson. They struck the trail and the chase was in hot progress, with the prey showing they appreciated the life and death nature of the posse's resolve. The posse went to Bohn's ranch and there Sam Bohn joined them. At Pool's ranch Sam Morgan joined the posse. At some point along the way George Wilson also joined in the pursuit. When they left Pool's ranch the Mexicans were only a short distance ahead of them so they ran their horses, the best going on ahead while Orosco and Gibson were left a short distance behind.

The posse finally overtook the three fugitives thirty miles down river from their starting point at the foot of the Rincon mountains. Mr. Hughes hallooed them in Spanish four or five times, which caused one to stop and turn his horse while the other two put spurs to their horses and started off in a lope. The fleeing men pulled their six-shooters and commenced firing. The posse outgunned the robbers with rapid firing Winchesters having eighteen inch barrels and a range far exceeding the .44 caliber six-shooters used by the Mexicans.

Logan rode to the crest of a small knoll and fired three shots at the fleeing men while other posse members returned the robber's gunfire from below. One of the fleeing Mexicans fell from his horse, dead of his wounds, after riding only two hundred-fifty yards. After the shooting the dead Mexican was identified as "Geronimo." His six-shooter was examined and found to have three spent cartridges.

The second fleeing Mexican continued another two hundred yards, jumped his horse into a water ditch, and there it bogged down. He fell from his horse and made a dash for the heavy brush, firing continuously until he hid himself, and then ceased fire so as not to give away his position. Most of the posse members stayed behind to search for the second man while a party started for Benson with the Mexican who had stopped upon being hallooed, Victoriano Sandoval, and took along the body of the dead man tied across his saddle.

The fugitive, upon being discovered, made a fight of it but finally his ammunition gave out and he surrendered, whence he pleaded with the posse, "cut my throat, hang me, take me to Hell, but don't take me to Tucson," and gave his name as Guadalupe Redondo. An hour later George Wilson overtook the party headed for Benson and told them that Redondo had been captured, and they turned back so that they could take in the three robbers together.

Sandoval, who had surrendered upon being hailed, identified the dead robber as the "Geronimo" who had been robbing stagecoaches on the American side of the border – not to be confused with the Mexican train robber of the same period also known as "Geronimo" nor the Apache Indian known by that name. Sandoval continued his confession and implicated Geronimo, whose real name was Santiago Moreno, in nearly every stagecoach robbery in Southern Arizona during the past two years. The list of robberies included stagecoaches in Cochise County on November 1 and December 24, 1888, October 17 and 31, 1890, and June 2, 1891; in Graham County on May 1, 1890; and in Pinal County on October 2 and November 22, 1888, October 2, 1889 and March 20, 1890.

The posse recovered three stolen horses, two belonging to Jones and the other to Wakefield. Several other stolen horses had been set free by the robbers as the pursuit progressed. The rewards earned by the posse included three hundred dollars from Wells, Fargo and Company and five hundred dollars from the Southern Pacific Company; and it was thought that a United States reward might also be collected, but territorial and county rewards had not been proffered.

Moreno's body was taken to Tombstone where it was kept on ice for four days so that a number of people could confirm his identity as "Geronimo" the stagecoach robber. The *Citizen* commented, "As desperate and daring a character as Southern Arizona has ever known was laid low last Friday, full of bullets and fighting and cursing to the last. Stagecoaches throughout Pima, Cochise, Graham, and Pinal counties have occasionally been called upon during two years past by a Mexican of 25, sometimes alone, oftener with one or two confederates, to hand over what treasure might be aboard ... "

Victoriano Sandoval, an informant who had infiltrated Geronimo's gang on the orders of Cochise County's Sheriff John Slaughter, had participated in the Bisbee and Tombstone stagecoach robbery because, he said, Moreno would have been suspicious if he had refused. To prove he had been there he described the man and woman on the stagecoach, told how much they got, and related the conversation they had with Engle, the driver. He assisted the officers in identifying Geronimo and was released.

Guadalupe Redondo was lodged in the county jail at Tombstone, examined, and held over for the Grand Jury. A charge of stagecoach robbery could not be proved, but he was indicted for grand larceny for stealing a horse, tried and convicted at Bisbee. Guadalupe Redondo was the 797th prisoner to arrive at the Territorial prison near Yuma. He was admitted on December 8, 1891 to serve a sentence of three years. Redondo was a heavy-set Mexican, five feet tall, with black hair and eyes, thirty-six years of age who could read and write. He served his entire sentence and was discharged on March 27, 1894.

December 23, 1902

The regular stagecoach reached a point one mile outside of Fairbanks, en route to Tombstone, when two men jumped out with rifles and called "hands up." Wells, Fargo and Company's express box was pulled off by the robbers and the stagecoach driver was then ordered to proceeded. On Christmas morning the box was found in the foothills broken open and rifled.

The loss was not reported but it was suspected that the men who held up the stagecoach acted on a tip, but missed calculations by one night. Had they intercepted the stagecoach the night before they would have made a haul of twenty-eight thousand dollars, which constituted the pay roll for the Consolidated mines.

Posses went out and tracked the men back into Fairbanks. The tracks of one man showed high heeled boots while the other had his feet muffled in sacks. Still, the robbers were never identified.

One of the most thrilling robberies involving W. F. and Co. treasure did not involve a stagecoach. It occurred on Sunday morning, August 20th when a mule-train carrying treasure into Globe was taken-in on the Pioneer trail. The express box was under the watchful eye of Andy Hall, stagecoach driver and messenger. The treasure, $5000 belonging to Fisk, Waldridge & Co., was loaded onto the mule from a stagecoach by Hall, mail carrier Frank Porter and Cicero Grimes.

Cicero had cut the telegraph wires earlier and then rode ahead of the train to alert his brother, LaFayette "Fate" Grimes, and Curtis B. Hawley that the box was heavy. Fate and Curtis attacked the train from behind breastworks, drove off Porter, wounded Hall in the leg, and killed the treasure-laden mule. They emptied the box, took their plunder and fled into the hills.

The road agents soon came to Bremen's road, where they met and murdered Dr. W. F. Vail. Hall followed their trail, which he believed had been made by Indians, and met Fate and Curtis. The three men continued on together until the two robbers got the drop on Hall and murdered him. They buried their booty and returned to Globe.

Suspicion soon turned to the Grimes boys. Fate had not responded to the alarm as he always did. A dimunitive bootprint at the scene of Hall's murder matched Fate's boot; and Cicero, while at the gunsmith's shop, acted suspicious while cartridges from a murder weapon were being examined. Fate was arrested and soon confessed. Curtis and Cicero, in quick order, joined him in jail .

On August 24th a citizen's committee was assembled. They took the prisoners out of jail and escorted them to Stalla's Hall, where they were tried. They were found guilty, but Cicero was returned to his cell to await a legal trial as he had not participated in the murders.

Fate and Curtis were taken to the large sycamore tree on Main Street near Pinal Creek. The saloons closed and church bells rang continuously as the men were slowly pulled up by their necks and left dangling until they had strangled to death.

Cicero was later sentenced to twenty-one years in prison but feigned insanity and was taken to the asylum in California, from which he soon escaped and was never heard from again.

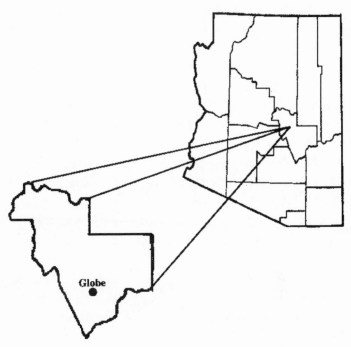

Stagecoach Robbery in Gila County

In 1881 Gila County was formed from the southwest portion of Apache and southeast portion of Yavapai, with its county seat at Globe. In 1889 Gila County annexed an additional portion of southeastern Yavapai County.

February 16, 1881

On Wednesday at 11 o'clock p.m. the westbound stagecoach was stopped and robbed by two highwaymen near Dripping Springs. The mail sack was gutted of its contents, letters opened and valuables taken. Wells, Fargo and Company's express box was rifled.

The robbers were closely masked and, consequently, were never identified.

June 11, 1881

On a Saturday night about half past nine, as the stagecoach was coming toward Globe, it was stopped by two men one and a half miles from Riverside. A request was made to hand over Wells, Fargo and Company's treasure box, which was complied with. There was only one passenger on board the stagecoach, a lady, who was badly frightened but not molested.

The robbers were apparently satisfied with the contents of the treasure box, as nothing else on the coach was disturbed and they ordered the driver to proceed.

If an investigation or search followed it was not reported and was without results, as the robbers were never identified.

November 29, 1881

The Globe stagecoach was coming down the canyon Tuesday night when a suspicious looking individual stepped out in front of the horses. The driver brought the horses to a halt and Andy Hall, the messenger, covered the nocturnal traveler with a Wells, Fargo shotgun. Taking in the situation the individual asked a few foolish questions and passed on. It was supposed that he intended to rob the stagecoach, but lost his courage when he discovered a messenger on board training a double barreled "mountain howitzer" on him.

The robber was never identified.

Andy Hall was killed by highwaymen on August 20, 1882 while driving a treasure-laden mule train into Globe.

March 2, 1883

The Globe to Florence stagecoach was robbed Friday night just after it passed Dripping Springs. There were five passengers aboard at the time but they were not disturbed by the highwaymen. Only the treasure box was taken and it contained little of value.

Two robbers were seen but, with nothing of significance taken, they were not pursued and were never identified.

April 16, 1883

The Globe stagecoach was taken in on a Monday night a short distance beyond Dripping Springs. The same two men who robbed the stagecoach on March 2nd took the express box, but again it contained nothing of value.

Although the highwaymen had made "water hauls" both times they seem to have retired from the business as no further robberies occurred at or near Dripping Springs. The robbers were not pursued and were never identified.

September 1, 1894

The stagecoach between Verde and Globe, via Tonto Basin, was robbed and the driver beaten into insensibility. It was determined that the robbers obtained less than two hundred dollars.

The driver was not in a condition to give information about the robbers and, with the small amount stolen and no description, there was no pursuit, so the robbers were never identified.

Stagecoach stations were often characterized as rudimentary structures with few accomodations; often pictured by Hollywood as a hut or mud shack with one room, a table and a fireplace. However, many stations were substantial and modern, by contemporary standards, and provided travelers everything they needed to continue their journey. Maricopa Wells was one of the first, and best, but many new stations were established along the many routes in Arizona and advertising became common to encourage every sort of traveler to stop.

Stagecoach Robbery in Graham County

In 1881 Graham County was formed from the northeastern portion of Pima and south eastern portion of Apache with its county seat first established at Safford, but moved to Solomonville in 1883.

December 3, 1882

On Sunday at nine o'clock p.m. the southbound Clifton stagecoach reached a point two miles south of York's ranch when two Mexicans stepped out from behind the rocks and ordered the driver to halt. They took the mail sacks from the coach, found them light and returned them unmolested. They disarmed the driver and ordered two Chinese passengers to get out of the coach, stood them up for what valuables they had and then shot them dead for no apparent reason, as they had not resisted and had already been robbed of all valuables. The robbers took nothing from the stagecoach and did not even ask about an express box.

The only explanation offered for the murders was that there was a secret organization at Clifton and in the surrounding country committed to cleaning out the Chinese employed by the Arizona Copper Mining Company. It was theorized that the robbers were either part of that organization or sympathetic to its cause. On December 4th the remains of the murdered men were still lying where they were killed. The robbers were never identified.

February 4, 1883

Three men held up a stagecoach on the Clifton and Lordsburg road on Sunday night and took the mail pouch. They were recognized and were soon captured by William McCormick, William Cestney, J. F. Corkle and G. W. Bryan and jailed at Solomonville.

One of the robbers, Alfred Briggs, was considered an honest, industrious and trustworthy man, so that his connection with the robbery was a surprise to those who knew him. About a month before he quit working for the Detroit Copper Company and went to Lordsburg, where he met his two accomplices. They gave their names as Arthur Craymond and Billy Coleman. Coleman was supposed to be a deserter from the army.

On June 12th the robbers were turned over to deputy U. S. Marshal J. W. Evans for transfer to Safford. Evans said that when he took custody of Coleman the robber said, with much bravado, "Oh, I'm a bad man," and laughed as if he enjoyed the fun. Evans said of Coleman, "[he] is anxious for notoriety and will do anything to be known abroad as a bad, bold man. In Graham county just after his capture he was shackled with two big log chains, and fastened to a bull ring in the floor, and had his hands cuffed behind him." They were removed from Clifton to Safford, the county seat, where they were each held on eight thousand dollar bonds to await the action of the U. S. Grand Jury.

On July 2nd the case came before the U. S. Circuit Court and a request was made for continuance to the next term because the subpoena's for the defendant's witnesses had not been returned, nor had the subpoena for George De Jarnett, the stagecoach driver who was the principal witness for the prosecution. Hugh Farley, attorney for the defendants, stipulated to De Jarnett's testimony.

On July 7th Crawford and Craymond, suspecting that Briggs had turned state's evidence, withdrew their plea of not guilty and entered a plea of guilty. They were ordered to return to court at five thirty p.m. for sentencing, at which time each man was sentenced to a term of five years to be served at Detroit's House of Corrections.

Briggs at first refused to change his plea from not guilty, even though he had provided the information which had incriminated all three men. He later reconsidered, pled guilty, and was ordered to return the following Wednesday for sentencing. Briggs, who had co-operated and had been willing to testify against Craymond and Crawford, was given two years at the same institution.

On the morning of July 27th U. S. Marshal Tidball, accompanied by A. H. Jackson and J. H. Simpson as guards, departed for Detroit with the prisoners. All three were admitted on July 31, 1883, said they were Protestants, had children, and drank alcohol.

William Coleman, a Georgian, was thirty-five years of age and in good health when he arrived at the Prison. He had been a clerk before becoming a stagecoach robber. He could read and write. He was released on August 1, 1887 after serving his five year sentence.

Arthur Craymond, a Texan, was twenty-five years of age and in good health. He had no particular skill, listing his occupation as laborer, but could read and write. He was released on August 1, 1887 after serving his entire five year sentence.

Alfred Briggs was born in Vermont. He was forty-two years of age; in good health; and was literate. He had been a blacksmith before becoming a stagecoach robber. He was released on March 31, 1885 after serving his entire two year sentence.

November 5, 1883

Three masked men held up the stagecoach due in Clifton on Monday night getting one hundred twenty-five dollars from the passengers. With little stolen, and the mails and express unmolested, a posse was not mobilized. The robbers were not identified.

November 6, 1883

The three robbers, who had taken such a light haul the previous evening, returned on Tuesday night to rob the stagecoach from New Mexico to Clifton. Ben Crawford, who was returning from Silver City, contributed sixty-five dollars. Again the mails and express were not molested. Apparently the small sum of money obtained in the two robberies was satisfactory as the three Clifton stagecoach robbers retired. They were never identified.

May 1, 1890

The stagecoach which left Bowie Thursday morning for Solomonville, Fort Thomas and intermediate points, was robbed by two Mexicans four miles south of Bailey's Wells and about fifteen miles north of Bowie. W. T. Clemens of Central was the only passenger, occupying the front seat with the driver. The robbers rode up to the stagecoach, one on each side, and the first the driver saw of them he and Clemens were covered with six-shooters. The leader was a tall man, not very dark, with short whiskers all over his face; he wore a large straw hat with a chin strap, and had on a blue jumper and overalls. The second robber was short with little chin whiskers and a short mustache; he wore what was originally a white shirt and brown vest. The short man rode a buckskin horse and the other a bay, both looking to be excellent animals.

The driver was ordered to throw out the mail and packages, which he did immediately, and was then ordered to drive on. The mail sacks for all points in the valley, including the San Carlos pouch, were taken. There was not money of any consequence in the mail as rarely any comes that way, the money invariably going the other direction. Two express packages, thought to be of small value, were also taken.

On arriving at Bailey's Wells the driver secured a horse and returned to Bowie while Clemens drove the empty stagecoach on to Solomonville. Clemens reported the particulars to Sheriff Whelan who immediately dispatched Deputy Pink Robinson, with a posse, to take the trail.

These robbers had taken-in the stagecoach previously and on those occasions they took refuge in the Graham mountains, so Robinson and his posse left towards the Graham mountains via Thorpe's ranch.

The driver later reported that on Wednesday these same robbers had followed the stagecoach for some distance when going to Bowie, beginning at about the same place. They evidently intended to rob the stagecoach then but evidently thought the undertaking too much for them, as it was loaded heavily with U. S. Marshal Paul, M. E. Cunnington, and Constable McCarty on board.

Deputy Pink Robinson and his posse were unable to overtake the fleeing robbers, so they were not captured following this robbery; but, on June 2, 1891, after robbing their tenth stagecoach, the robbers were run to ground. One was killed resisting arrest and the other captured, convicted and sentenced to prison.

March 20, 1894

The southbound stagecoach between Thomas and Bowie, driven by Ira Kempton, was held up by two masked men, six miles below Solomonville, and the passengers and mail robbed. The stagecoach was rolling along and the passengers were talking and laughing when, suddenly, two men appeared from behind a little knoll at the side of the road. The horses were so frightened that they almost threw the passengers out into a wash.

The highwaymen ran up to the side of the stagecoach and aimed a Winchester and six-shooter at the driver and passengers and ordered them to throw up their hands. The driver obeyed the order to throw out the mail sacks. One of the robbers told the passengers to get out of the stagecoach, but his companion interrupted, "except the ladies," meaning Mrs. Wickersham who was the female passenger. The men were stood up with their backs to the robber who was cutting open the sacks while the other robber guarded them, with instructions that "the first man who moves, blow his head off."

The mail sacks were cut open and the registered mail taken, including three hundred and fifty letters known to have been in the mail from Safford. After rifling the sacks of registered mail a demand was made on Wickersham, Will Brookner, and the driver for valuables. Wickersham gave up his gold watch and chain and a purse containing sixty dollars but the robber, still dissatisfied, said, "I want that roll of bills," and it was handed to him. Brookner took out a handful of change, about seven dollars, from which the robber took a five dollar gold piece and gave back the change. Wickersham handed over five hundred dollars in checks, but these were of no use to the robber so he gave them back. Brookner had a roll of bills in his vest pocket and Wickersham had over fifty dollars in his purse, which they did not find.

A team was heard coming down the road, so the robbers ordered the men back into the coach and ordered the driver to proceed. When the stagecoach had gone half a mile, Mr. Wickersham got out of the stagecoach and ran over to the freighting road, about two hundred yards distant, and at his request a freighter took a horse from his team and rode back to Solomonville.

Both robbers were Americans of medium build. The leader was about five feet ten and wore a long yellow slicker and light broad brimmed hat; he had very red and inflamed eyes; on the right side of his nose between the eyes he had a mole or sore; he had a light sandy mustache; he was armed with a short Winchester. The shorter man was about five feet seven or eight inches in height and wore a short, dark coat and white hat with red gilt Mexican band; and, his feet were muffled in gunny sacks but his high necked boots were exposed above the sacks; he was armed with a six-shooter. Both men wore blue overalls and were riding small dark bay horses, with something like a new yellow slicker tied behind on the saddle.

The sheriff and posse started in pursuit within two hours of the robbery. They came upon the robbers nine miles west of Solomonville and had a running fight with them, during which one of the robbers' horses and a six-shooter was captured. The posse failed to capture the robbers. However, much of the registered mail was recovered a short distance from the scene of the robbery, including several checks and money orders which were left behind because of the risk of detection involved in any effort to convert them to money.

Six days later deputy sheriff George Olney telegraphed that he had captured one of the stagecoach robbers near Curtiss. Frank P. Martin was taken without a struggle and soon provided a full confession. He had been living on the ranch of Webb, the man in jail for the stagecoach robbery of January 6th, which gave the impression that there was an organized gang of stagecoach robbers in the vicinity. On the same day the Sheriff's office from Bowie telegraphed that the second robber, John Jackson, had been caught on the 22nd near Cave Creek in the Chiricahua mountains ten miles south of Galeyville. When arrested he had one hundred ninety-five dollars in greenbacks on his person. Jackson had been at Wickersham's ranch the night previous to his capture and was bound for Sonora.

Ira Kempton, the stagecoach driver who had been the principal witness against Felshaw and Webb for the January 6th robbery, testified against Jackson and Martin. Jackson was identified as the man in control at the scene of the robbery while Martin was identified as the man who guarded the passengers as Jackson rifled the mails.

Jackson had been a criminal for some time, had served a term in the New Mexico penitentiary, and had recently broke jail at Silver City on another criminal charge. John Jackson received a life sentence to be served at San Quentin Prison. Martin was a newcomer to the business and cooperated in the investigation and trial. His assistance earned him a lighter sentence of five years, also to be served at San Quentin.

July 9, 1897

Charles Colbath, the driver, and his nine year old brother came into town at 12:45 p.m. riding two coach horses. Colbath delivered one leather pouch at the post office and reported that the king pin on the stagecoach had broken, so he left the stagecoach on the other side of Holmes' Well where the road crosses the wash from Coyote Holes to Gibson's. There was registered mail and a box containing one thousand dollars on the stagecoach, of which the driver was aware.

Postmaster Temple and George W. Hunt, the stagecoach agent, urged the driver to procure a light rig and return to the coach. Colbath left town within fifteen minutes for the scene of the alleged break-down, taking with him his mother and a companion named Joe Chrain. About 3:30 p.m. Colbath returned with the stagecoach, registered mail, and the empty box which contained the one thousand dollars in bright new silver coin. The money had been shipped by Rice Jones from El Paso through Wells, Fargo and Company, and was addressed to himself in care of Thomas Stevens, Globe, Arizona. Wells, Fargo and Company's responsibility ended at Bowie and D. B. Lacey, one of the proprietors of the stage line upon receiving the sack of money at Geronimo, placed it in the box and forwarded it to Globe.

Colbath stated that he had left the box, a small canned goods case marked "hardware" and addressed to Mr. Hunt, hidden under the mail sacks but upon his return from town found it lying empty on the ground in front of the stagecoach. He claimed that someone must have broken it open and taken the money during his absence, but left a note. With the coin was a package of photographic plates for A. Miller, and on this package was written in pencil, "Go to Hell, you S*** of B******," later believed to have been written by Chrain, as the writing strongly resembled his chirography.

Upon hearing of the robbery, Sheriff D. H. Williamson and Undersheriff Joe T. McKinney went out to where the stagecoach had been abandoned, which Mr. McKinney estimated was about ten miles from town. They made a rather cursory examination of the ground, which did not reveal anything, and Sheriff Williamson returned to town while McKinney went on to Gibson's and remained overnight.

While in Gibson, McKinney met Chief of Police Tuttle and a party of Indian trailers from San Carlos. On Saturday morning the posse went to the scene of the robbery and made a careful examination of the ground, the Indian trailers circling the spot for some distance, but not a sign of a track was found nor anything to indicate where the money had been cached.

Suspicion began to focus upon the stagecoach driver and, when McKinney and Tuttle returned to Globe, Colbath and Chrain were placed under arrest. The stagecoach had recently been overhauled at Middleton & Pascoe's blacksmith shop and at the time the king bolt was examined and found to be in good condition.

Mr. Jones arrived from El Paso and, with Mr. Lacey, waited for the preliminary examination of the defendants. The examination before Justice of the Peace Harry Temple had been postponed several times and as often adjourned. A question of jurisdiction was raised, proposing that since the crime had been committed on the Indian reservation the federal court alone had jurisdiction, in which event the hearing would have to be before Court Commissioner A. Kinney.

Finally it was determined that the preliminary examination would be held before Justice of the Peace Temple on the Territorial charge. The trial was postponed when the defense attorney, dissatisfied with the decision that this was not a U. S. case, withdrew and a new attorney had to familiarize himself with the facts. The hearing was finally held on July 16th and 17th, and both men were held to answer before the grand jury on one thousand dollars bond. The local newspaper observed that there was strong evidence against Colbath, "but little to connect Chrain with the crime, unless it was as an accessory after-the-fact, and if he was guilty then the woman [Mrs. Colbath] would be guilty also."

The driver's father, H. M. Colbath of Gold Hill, New Mexico and Mr. Neel, a relative from Solomonville, went to Globe on August 9th to investigate the charges. H. M. Colbath became convinced that Charles knew more about the matter than he had disclosed and persuaded him to reveal the location of the money. On Tuesday afternoon H. M. Colbath, P. T. Robertson, Sheriff D. H. Williamson and the prisoner, Charles Colbath, went out on the road to San Carlos to a place about seven and a half miles from Globe and one and a half miles west of where it was alleged the stagecoach broke down and there within a few feet of the road, under a mesquite bush, the money was found buried. It was in the original sack in which it was shipped from El Paso, and not one of the silver dollars was missing. The money was returned to its owner, Rice Jones.

The following day, in consideration of the evidence that Chrain had not been a party to the robbery, his bail was reduced to five hundred dollars and he was released on his own recognizance. Charles Colbath was also released on one thousand dollars bail, being furnished by Messrs. Taylor, Parks, and Tidwell of Solomonville.

In the ensuing months the case was determined to be a federal matter and the U. S. Grand Jury brought an indictment for grand larceny against Colbath and Chrain, who remained free on the posted bail. When the court convened in October the men failed to appear. They were never apprehended nor were they heard from again in the Territory.

April 20, 1898

The stagecoach on the Geronimo and Globe line, on a Wednesday, was held up about four miles from Geronimo by two men having the appearance of cowboys. They demanded the express box, but there was none aboard, so they requested that the five passengers pungle. Only five dollars was shown up which the cowboys refused to take and, after accepting two oranges to relieve their parched throats, they permitted the stagecoach to proceed.

Neither the passengers nor the driver could provide any clue to the identity of the bandits, but Sheriff Birchfield went in pursuit anyway. He followed the trail to Black River where it was lost on account of about one thousand head of cattle being driven across it.

The robbers were never identified.

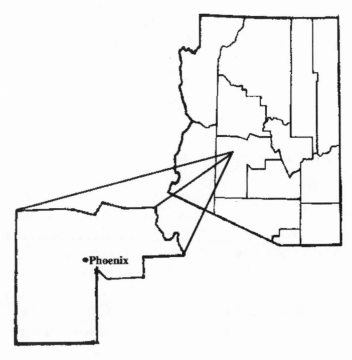

Stagecoach Robbery in Maricopa County

In 1871 Maricopa County was formed from the southwest corner of Yavapai County and established its county seat at Phoenix. In 1875 Maricopa County annexed a portion of the territory located in the northwest corner of Pima County.

May 12, 1877

Sheriff Bowers of Yavapai County had the opportunity to witness a stagecoach robbery first hand as he was transporting Mary E. Sawyer, a demented woman, to the California asylum for the insane. Three masked men stopped the westbound stagecoach one mile west of Wickenburg and took four hundred fifty-seven dollars and a pistol from the sheriff, but failed to find several other packages of money he was transporting. The Wells, Fargo and Company's treasure box was opened and examined. The mail bags were cut, rifled and their contents badly mutilated. The mail was later returned to

Prescott to be "fixed up for a new start." The Sheriff reported that from their physical characteristics, voices and gestures he would be able to identify the robbers.

Frank Luke was the only passenger on the stagecoach and surrendered his wallet containing sixty-five dollars in currency and an order on parties in San Francisco for two hundred fifty dollars more. The robbers returned the order, it being useless to them. Satisfied that they had all Luke's valuables, they failed to search him further and missed three hundred forty dollars in gold coin in his pockets.

During the early evening hours of May 16, 1877 two men slipped quietly into the tiny border town of Ehrenberg, Arizona Territory, too late to board the ferry which crossed the Colorado River to California. They put up their horses in the corral at the east end of town and stowed their tack and gear. It would be dawn before the ferry crossed again and their aim was to be as inconspicuous as possible while they passed the hours ahead. By daybreak they sensed they were being watched and had become suspicious. The men moved up the street toward their horses, but an apprehensive Thomas Brophy stopped in front of Mill's Saloon to watch the street while John Sutton went on to collect their gear and stock.

Joseph W. Evans, who was the line superintendent for the California & Arizona Stagecoach Company, recognized the men as soon as they appeared. Sheriff Bowers had given a good description of the men who robbed the stagecoach near Wickenburg on the 12th and Evans was sure these two were "the right birds." Evans and George "Crete" Bryan had figured throughout the night on the best way to take the two robbers without a fight, and had decided to make the arrest as they boarded the ferry, while their hands were filled with gear and reins. But that plan was afoul as the robbers had become cautious, so the two lawmen approached Brophy and demanded his surrender.

Bryan had armed himself with a shotgun while Evans sported a six-shooter on his right hip. Brophy had only his six-shooter, his rifle being among his gear at the corral. Evans and Bryan watched Brophy's hands to see if they went up or down. They went down, and just a bit too fast for Evans.

The first shot was fired by Brophy and glanced off Evans' forehead just above his left eye. Bryan immediately let loose both barrels, but had not checked the load of his borrowed shotgun. The small shot, which struck Brophy in the face and right arm, was not enough to knock him down.

Evans, hardly able to see because of the blood gushing into both eyes, got off his first shot. The bullet struck Brophy in his wounded arm and he went down from the force.

Three men "stood game," firing at each other until Brophy's pistol emptied. Brophy, unable to reload because of his wounds, then lay still as bullets whizzed over his prone body. John Sutton had returned as far as Salado's Saloon and was firing at the lawmen with a Henry rifle.

Stagecoach driver O. Mercer came to the aid of Evans but, before he could get off a shot, was hit in the shoulder with a rifle ball and went down in the middle of the street. He too hugged the ground as bullets whizzed over him.

Faced with rapid fire from a Winchester repeating rifle, Evans and Bryan retreated behind the Ehrenberg Hotel while Sutton backed into Salado's Saloon. The exchange continued for several more minutes until Evans called for Sutton's surrender and, seeing that there was no hope of escape, the robber stepped out and surrendered.

The entire battle had lasted fifteen minutes, more than sixty shots were exchanged and three men were wounded. Both robbers were then arrested and a search of their gear revealed several bars of gold bullion taken from the express box.

This was the wild west and men, good or bad, who faced death bravely were much admired. Yuma's *Sentinel* newspaper said of them, "Good pluck was shown by all parties and none showed any signs of flickering ... ."

In the fight Evans, who would later become one of the most controversial lawmen of Arizona's territorial period, favored a six-shooter because he could not manage another. Evans had lost his left arm in 1875. Perhaps Sutton and Brophy had dismissed, or at least underestimated, the danger posed by this one-armed man; but Evans was already much admired for enduring an amputation under the most primitive conditions; and, he had been the first man in the Territory to arrest stagecoach robbers – Vance and Berry in Yavapai County.

At first the two robbers identified themselves as the Johnson brothers but later John Sutton, who had come through the shoot-out unhurt, gave his true name. He was then mistakenly taken to Prescott but was immediately brought back to Ehrenberg where he boarded a steamboat for Yuma. While en route to Yuma Sutton threw over-board all the dishes within his reach and tried to throw a Chinaman after them and, but for his heavy irons, would have escaped.

The wounded robber, Thomas Brophy, remained at Ehrenberg. On July 4th his right arm was amputated above the elbow by Dr. Loring. The newspaper reported on July 7th that he was fast recovering his health and was "up, dressed and singing." The doctor had "staid with him five days and nights and is entitled to even more credit for his untiring fidelity to his patient than for the consummate skill displayed to treatment."

Sutton and Brophy were prosecuted by H. H. Pomeroy, H. N. Alexander, and Col. B. O. Whiting of Los Angeles, and defended by C. W. C. Rowell of San Bernardino and an attorney from Prescott. The trial and consideration lasted four days and the jury was dis-charged standing six for and six against conviction. The defendants, under the advice of Rowell and against the solemn protest of their Prescott attorney, pled guilty to the lowest crime known to the law under the indictment and were sentenced to five years to be served at the Territorial Prison near Yuma.

John Mantle, the third robber who claimed to be a detective for the Postal Service but had also been characterized by stage line owner J. A. Stewart as a detective for his line, was chastised by the United States Grand Jury of the 2d Judicial District of the Territory for his "detective experiment." The grand jury said:

> In examination of the robbery cases of the United States mail, a state of facts was brought to light which in the opinion of the Grand Jury is deplorable in the extreme. We find one John Mantle, while in the service and under the authority of the Postal Service Department of the United States, planning and executing a robbery of a stagecoach and of the U. S. mail.

We find that he was sent to this Territory and appointed Director to work up the facts concerning stagecoach robberies and bring to justice the perpetrators of any stagecoach robberies which might occur within the Territory. Mr. Mantle came here heralded by secret letters to two or three stage agents, but without notice to a single U. S. official within the Territory and no officer, either of the United States or the Territory, was ever informed of his intentions.

We find that in the town of Prescott he, with others, planned to rob the stagecoach passengers and mail traveling from Prescott to Ehrenberg. That his plan was put into execution whereby the passengers were robbed and placed in jeopardy of their lives, and the mail was broken into and robbed.

The different stage agents along the road of the contemplated robbery were notified, but neither the passengers nor the stagecoach driver knew what was coming.

Ed F. Bowers, sheriff of Yavapai County, was one of the passengers.

The robbing was committed a few miles from Wickenburg, and the stage agent – Pierson – of that place knew at the time the stagecoach reached his office what was to happen, yet neither Mr. Bowers nor the others were told a word so that they might have provided for what was coming, and to save their effects and perhaps secure the robbers.

The robbery was committed under cover of guns and pistols, and the least motion of resistance by any of the passengers might have lead to loss of life of one or more of the passengers. As it was, all the money had by the passengers was taken from them – some four hundred and fifty dollars from sheriff Bowers, and valuable letters mutilated and destroyed. The money taken has never been returned by the Postal authorities or anyone else.

The Grand Jury cannot too severely condemn this light-handed experiment of the Detective branch of the Postal Service and its execution, showed in the opinion of the Grand Jury, an almost criminal lack of common sense...

The Grand Jury went on to find that John Mantle had instigated the robbery "through his peculiar intellect," and the jurors said of Sutton and Brophy, "there are many unfortunate people in the world who, through poverty and destitution, might be led by a stronger will to the commission of crime and who, untampered with, would honestly struggle on."

Sutton and Brophy were delivered to the Territorial Prison at Yuma on November 21st. Sutton, who had been born in Missouri, was described as aged twenty-seven, five feet four and one half inches in height with hazel eyes and light hair. Sutton could read and write. Brophy had been born in Tennessee, was twenty-four years of age, five feet six inches in height with light grey eyes and light colored hair. He too was literate. Sutton was registered as prisoner № 18 and Brophy as prisoner № 19. Both men were released on May 23, 1882 after having served their sentences. Brophy was not heard of again but Sutton took on a new crime partner – Miguel Lavadie.

Sutton and Lavadie robbed a drunk named Louis Baker who, the day following the robbery, died of congestion of the brain from a blow to the head received during commission of the crime. The two prisoners were held to answer after Lavadie made a full confession. Both men managed to escape several times but were caught and returned to jail each time. Sutton was convicted and returned to prison.

This was the second stagecoach robbery involving undercover detective John Mantle, sometimes spelled Mantel or Mentel. The first instance of his undercover efforts resulted in the arrest and trial of Charles Bush in San Francisco, the robbery taking place at Indian Wells, California. Mantel never returned the four hundred fifty-seven dollars taken from Sheriff Bowers near Wickenburg nor the money belonging to the Post Office, and retained twenty-five dollars stolen in the Indian Wells robbery which belonged to the editor of Prescott's *Weekly Miner* newspaper. Mantel was released from custody each time on order of the U. S. Attorney General. After the trial in Yuma he went to California and was not heard of again in the Territory.

April 19, 1878

Bill Reed, a smallish man about five feet three inches in height, was only sixteen years old when he signed on to drive stagecoaches for the California & Arizona Stage Company. He had four years three months experience on the night of April 19, 1878 as he supervised the loading of passengers and through-mail from Prescott onto the stagecoach at Wickenburg. The coach rolled out as the clock struck nine.

There was no shotgun guard nor an escort. It was dark, because the moon had not yet risen, so the lamps on the coach were lit. The four horse team easily pulled the coach over the level road northward for three quarters of a mile, then turned due west toward Ehrenberg.

The Arizona desert west of Wickenburg is generally flat but at the four mile mark is a small hill four hundred yards north of the Vulture Mill. The horses had just reached the crest at half past nine when three men stepped out of the darkness from the right – the driver's side. The men were afoot and no animals were in sight. One man was near six foot tall and brandished a six shooter. The shortest robber was five foot three inches in height and wielded a short shotgun. The medium sized man, about five feet six inches, waved a rifle at the driver and ordered him to "Stop that stage!" All three were masked with a white cloth over their neck, head, and hat.

The medium sized man did all the talking and ordered the passengers, A. Angles and William Linchan, out of the coach. Reed held the team steady as he watched the robbers relieve his two passengers of two hundred dollars and sixty dollars respectively. The passengers were then marched to the front of the stagecoach where the small man could cover them and the driver with the shotgun while the other two highwaymen continued searching for plunder.

The medium sized robber ordered the driver, still on his seat, to give up the express box first and then the mail bags, and Reed complied. The tall and medium robbers took the box and sacks behind the coach and cut the mail bags "right across." When they were through they brought the bags and the express box around and placed them back into the coach's boot. Reed later testified that he hadn't been able to see if any mail had been removed nor if there had been any contents taken out from the box, but it was learned that there were two bars of Peck bullion from Tucson worth three thousand three hundred seventy-two dollars and gold bullion from the Crook mill valued at one thousand five hundred twelve dollars sent express.

The passengers were ordered to get back into the coach and the medium sized robber told Reed he intended to tie him up overnight. The robber quickly reconsidered and told Reed, "You can go if you think you can go on without trying to get back to Wickenburg."

When Reed agreed the robber warned him, "If you try to get back to Wickenburg you're a dead man."

Reed drove on. The robbery had taken nearly an hour and during that time the moon, in its first quarter, had risen. By its dim light Reed could see the robbers from as far as a third of a mile beyond, and at that point he saw them still standing on the crest of the hill watching him. He continued on to Musquit Station. After the stagecoach was out of sight the robbers rode northwest toward Date Creek, possibly to throw trackers off their trail.

In the vicinity of Date Creek the dispatch bearer for the McCrakin Company was stopped by two mounted men, who ordered him to throw up his hands. Just as he refused a third party appeared upon the scene with such suddenness he frightened the two highwaymen who, in their flight, dropped a package containing distinctive jewelry. The package was picked up by the dispatch bearer and taken to Wickenburg. Perhaps it was fortuitous or part of a carefully laid plan, but the dispatch bearer would report that the men who stopped him were headed in a northwesterly direction; while the package would implicate the pair in the stagecoach robbery.

Wells, Fargo and Company offered their standing reward of three hundred dollars each for the arrest of express robbers besides a portion of the treasure recovered as salvage. Governor Hoyt offered a reward of five hundred dollars for the apprehension of the parties who robbed the mails and treasure box.

Stage line superintendent J. W. Evans, who had been in Wickenburg at the time of the robbery, tracked the robbers. On April 24th U. S. Marshal Standifer received a dispatch from Evans that he had struck fresh sign in the area of Date Creek but then had tracked the robbers back towards Wickenburg. Evans next went to Prescott to speak with the passengers, trying to "get some clew to the stagecoach robbers," and then continued on their trail eastward.

Evans returned to Prescott after an unsuccessful hunt for the robbers. He had been joined by a detachment of the United States Cavalry and several Indian scouts, who tracked the robbers almost to the New Mexico boundary line. The pursuit was abandoned, however, when it was supposed that the robbers were in Sonora or Texas.

Evans had no information as to the identities of the robbers so, when three men were arrested in Gillette, he stopped looking for the persons responsible for theft of the U.S. mails and express on April 19th. Evans concerned himself with other stagecoach robbers and stage line matters until September 2nd, when a stagecoach was robbed twenty miles west of Maricopa Wells. Later that month he would arrest one of the perpetrators of the later robbery and be astonished when his man – James F. Rhodes – confessed that he and two accomplices had held up the stagecoach on April 19th, and then told all of the details.

James F. Rhodes, a Freemason, had come to the Arizona Territory shortly after his release from the Nevada State Penitentiary in December 1874. By February 1878 Rhodes was working at the ranch of brother Freemason John William 'Jack' Swilling north of Gillette. Jack, a six footer like Rhodes, was one of the Territory's most active pioneers and he often employed men who seemed down on their luck, as Rhodes had been when he approached Swilling.

Jack later learned of Rhodes' bad character, dismissed him and ordered him off the ranch. Jack explained that he had been suspicious of Rhodes for some time, explaining, " it was generally supposed that Rhodes and others were up to something. They were figuring around there, and Rhodes had got a gun of mine and he was armed."

Swilling's wife wanted Jack to get away from the saloons in Gillette, where he drank excessively to dull the pain from several old but severe injuries, and she convinced him to go out and recover the remains of pioneer Jacob Snively for a Christian burial. Another old Hassayamper named George Monroe, who was five feet three inches tall, and a new comer to the territory named Andrew Kirby, who was five feet seven, agreed to accompany him. The party of three left at mid-day April 16th and traveled several days, arriving at Snivley's Holes about four o'clock on the afternoon of the 18th, and soon took up the remains. A camp was set up near the grave, but it commenced to rain during the night so the men arose to get an early start. On rising Jack noticed three sets of foot tracks passing very near where they had slept, and remarked to Monroe, " ... There is some develment going on in this section and, if there is any develment done they will blame you and I and Andy Kirby for it, because this track is similar to ours. They passed as close to us as eight feet and they did not wake us up."

Rhodes' party had followed the Swilling party to ensure they did not turn back. After confirming that the Swilling party was in camp at the Holes, the party of robbers traveled fourteen miles northwest to the hogback which lay four miles west of Wickenburg and there awaited the arrival of the evening stagecoach and robbed it.

Swilling often bragged of involvement in all sorts of adventures when drinking, and a few days after his return boasted that he and his party had "jumped" the stagecoach on April 19th. They were arrested and examined in Yavapai County, but there was not sufficient evidence to hold Swilling, Kirby and Monroe for the grand jury. They were then rearrested on the federal charge of robbing the U. S. mails. Swilling and Kirby were taken to Yuma and jailed while Monroe remained free on bail. Swilling died in the Yuma jail in August and Kirby was released soon after Rhodes arrived in Yuma.

Rhodes was examined on November 15th for the robbery on April 19th. Seven witnesses testified before the grand jury, including William Reed, the stagecoach driver who was robbed; Joseph W. Evans, the deputy U. S. Marshal who arrested Rhodes; W. Whipple; Charles Evans; Andrew Kirby; Pablo Salsido; and Thomas Napper.

Because Rhodes had cooperated in exposing the truth about the April 19th robbery and confessed, he was allowed to plead guilty to robbery of the mails, a lesser offense than "robbing the mails by jeopardizing the life of the carrier," which usually carried a life sentence. On November 16th Rhodes was sentenced to nine and a half years at hard labor; and that same day the two fugitives, Rodepouch and Mullen, were indicted *in absentia* for "robbing the United States mail by putting the life of the carrier in jeopardy on April 19, 1878."

On November 17th Rhodes became the twenty-fifth prisoner delivered to the Territorial Prison. Rhodes was held at the prison outside Yuma, rather than being transferred to Detroit, at the suggestion of Evans and the U. S. District Attorney "as it is more likely that he will be needed to testify against his accomplices." However, after three years at the Territorial Prison awaiting their arrest, Rhodes was transferred to the Detroit House of Corrections. He arrived there on December 18, 1881, at which time he was fifty-seven years old and in poor health. On June 30, 1884 Rhodes was pardoned and nothing more is heard of him.

Acting Governor John J. Gosper was anxious to put an end to robberies in the Territory. In late November 1878 he offered a reward of two hundred fifty dollars each for the capture of Louis Rodepouch and John Mullen. The governor had two hundred fifty handbills printed and by mid-December Marshal Dake had mailed all the circulars. These brought two sightings, one in Topeka, Kansas and the other in Olympia, Washington, but the fugitives remained at large.

Neither Louis Rodepouch nor John Mullen were ever tried for robbing the stagecoach and U. S. mails on April 19th, 1878.

August 15, 1878

On a Thursday night at about 11:00 o'clock p.m. the west-bound stagecoach was jumped by three masked men armed with shot guns and two others unmasked, all Americans, five miles west of Maricopa Wells. The passengers on board were Dr. J. H. McKee of Los Angeles, two discharged soldiers of the Sixth Cavalry, and Sgt. Baber of the Signal Service. The suspicions of the passengers were aroused before the stagecoach was stopped, which gave them the opportunity to hide their valuables except for a few dollars each.

The robbers ordered the driver to throw out the express box and mail, but the through-mail pouch escaped their attention. The robbers cut open the mail sacks but did not take any mail.

The passengers were ordered out of the coach with their hands held high and were searched thoroughly. The robbers broke open the express box with a king bolt and, finding in it several hundred dollars in greenbacks, felt good enough to give back the passengers' pocket money. The robbers allowed the passengers to gather up the mails, put them into the wagon, and then board. Two robbers who had remained in the background, unharnessed and led one of the stagecoach horses away. Then the driver was ordered to proceed. The robbers were slightly disguised, and acted like new hands at the business.

Notice of the robbery was delayed because the telegraph line between Yuma and Tucson had been down most of the time over the past three weeks. The repairmen said that it had been purposely broken in many places, and it was suspected the robbers might have been responsible. Two of the robbers were never identified but a third was arrested at the end of September for a stagecoach robbery on the 2nd of that month.

September 2, 1878

The westbound stagecoach from Phoenix to Yuma was robbed about twenty miles west of Maricopa Wells on Monday, a bright moonlit night. Barney Lee was driving with passengers J. H. Onstott, a Chinaman, a blacksmith and a stock tender, with the two latter being employees of the stagecoach company. At nine o'clock p.m., when near the Chimules, the stagecoach was stopped by three armed Mexicans, one of whom spoke very fair English. The passengers were ordered to get out and raise their hands, which they did until these were tied behind them. The coach and everyone on it were then taken a short distance from the road.

The driver and passengers were carefully searched, but not stripped. Onstott had a pocketbook with seventy dollars and some checks in his vest pocket which he managed to take out and throw into a bush while marching from the road with his hands tied. From him the robbers took eight dollars, a silver watch and his blankets; from the Chinaman they got one hundred ninety-six dollars; and from the stock tender twenty-six dollars. They broke open the express box with an axe, but it was empty. They cut open the mail bags and scattered the contents, but found nothing of value. They took three bars of silver bullion, all the stagecoach horses, and started South. Driver Lee and the passengers walked to Happy Camp, where they had to wait two days until another stagecoach came along.

A party of thirty Papago Indians was put on the robbers' track the next morning, properly stimulated by cash in hand and an offer of contingent rewards. The tracks were of six horses and one mule, being the three horses ridden by the robbers and four animals taken from the stagecoach. The robbers were followed to a camp, but from there part of the tracks continued to the southwest and part turned off to the northwest. The pursuing party was also divided in two to follow both set of tracks.

Deputy U.S. Marshal J. W. Evans followed the trail heading southwest. He penetrated about two hundred fifty miles into Mexico and for eighteen days was in rapid pursuit of two robbers, at one time being within a few miles of them when a heavy rain obliterated their trail. He was assisted by the Prefect of the northern district of Altar, who furnished him with a detachment of cavalry. However, even with assistance, he was unable to overtake the robbers. Immediately after Evans return from Mexico he was put on the trail of "the Mexican who spoke very fair English," and learned that the man he was following was James F. Rhodes.

Deputy U. S. Marshal Evans and Special Mail Agent Mahoney first heard of Rhodes at Rio Miembres, New Mexico after the robbery, and found that he had left there for Arizona. Evans went to New Mexico while Mahoney remained in Arizona to follow any clues telegraphed by Evans. Evans followed traces of Rhodes to Silver City, to Fort Cummings, toward Clifton, and back toward Pueblo Viejo, and finally to a point fifteen miles above Fort Thomas on the Gila River. Rhodes had broken up his share of the stolen silver bullion and had sold the pieces at various points, thus scattering sure traces of his course.

Evans tracked him to a cattle drive, the herd belonging to Van Smith. Evans rode up to the camp and asked for Stout, the name Rhodes was using, and the robber was pointed out to him. Evans approached his man, said "good morning," quickly covered him with his six-shooter and ordered him to dismount. That morning Rhode's back had hurt him so he had taken off his pistols and left them in the mess wagon, which left him no chance to resist. Rhodes was a large, athletic man but, being covered by Evans, he could not make a fight. Evans threw him a pair of handcuffs, ordered him put them on and to mount his horse again. The two men trotted down the road toward Fort Thomas before any of the other cowboys had an opportunity to know what was going on.

Evans arrested Rhodes for robbing the U. S. mails on September 2nd but then learned from his prisoner that he, with two others Rhodes identified as Louis Rodepouch and John Mullen, was responsible for the April 19, 1878 theft of U. S. mail near Wickenburg. Mahoney had started north for Camp Thomas but was met by Evans, with his prisoner, at Point of Mountain about eighteen miles from Tucson. Mahoney had not received Evans' telegram from Silver City, New Mexico asking the Special Mail Agent to join him in the arrest, owing to wires being down. At Tucson, Rhodes waived examination and was committed by U. S. Commissioner Neugass to await action of Grand Jury.

The September 2nd robbery had been committed in the Second Judicial District so Rhodes was scheduled to be tried at Yuma in November. Rhodes was lodged in the Yuma county jail and charged with having robbed the stagecoach, passengers, and mails on the Maricopa desert. However, Rhodes agreed to plead guilty to the charge of robbing the U. S. Mails on April 19th and was never prosecuted for the robbery of September 2nd, nor the robberies of August 14th in Pima County nor on August 15th near Maricopa Wells.

May 5, 1879

On Monday at 2:30 a.m., as the stagecoach from Maricopa was approaching Phoenix, and about three miles distant, the driver heard the command "Hail" and an instant afterward discovered in the darkness the muzzle of a shot gun within a few feet of his face. He then heard the command repeated in a style that meant business. The team was stopped and the express box demanded, which was handed over, when the order came to "drive on."

Mr. McClintock of the *Herald* and an agent of Hall's Safe and Lock Company were the only passengers inside but were undisturbed. The U. S. mail was not molested either.

Officers went out to the spot early the next morning, but found no trace that could be followed nor any clue that would lead to the discovery of the robbers. In the express box was a pass book, and the owner advertised for its return: "LOST – A pass book on the Hibernia

Bank Nº 63, 799 standing in the name of Palmer G. Wood. The book was stolen at the time of the stage robbery, May 5th, 1879. The finder will please return the same to this office, as it is of no use except to owner."

The road agent was not convicted of this robbery, but this was only the first in a series of four stagecoach robberies with the next three occurring on June 10th in Yavapai County, and on June 20th and July 11th in Maricopa County.

June 20, 1879

The southbound stagecoach, driven by line superintendent James Stewart, left Phoenix Friday evening at nine o'clock and was robbed three miles south of town. One man, armed with a rifle stopped the stagecoach. He did not disturb the three passengers on board but demanded the express box and mail sacks before ordering the coach to proceed.

Sheriff Thomas went to the scene the next morning and found that the robber had cut open the mail sacks at the point of the robbery. A quantity of letters were left in the road, gathered up and returned to town, but nothing of the express box could be found. Five registered packages, including one package from Prescott and four from Mineral Park, were found with the letters but four registered packages from Phoenix were taken.

From all appearances it was evident that this robbery was committed by the same highwayman who took-in the stagecoach May 5th at the same place. Sheriff Thomas tracked the robber from the point of the robbery to the river, a distance of about fifty yards, where all trace of him was lost. This was the third robbery in a series of four robberies by the same road agent, with the last occurring on July 11th, but this time he would bring along an accomplice.

July 11, 1879

The southbound stagecoach, which left Phoenix on Friday night at nine o'clock, was robbed by two men at a point seven miles below

Phoenix and about three miles from two former robberies of May 5th and June 20th. William Blankenship, who was acting as messenger, the driver and passenger William. S. Head of Verde were on board. The robbery took place on the open plain, the highwaymen being concealed by a fallen tree that lay parallel with the road.

Blankenship was riding with the driver, with a short express shot-gun lying across his knees when he saw something in advance of the stagecoach which he took to be men, thus putting him on his guard. As the stagecoach drove opposite the tree two men arose and the leader ordered the stagecoach to halt. No sooner had he spoken than Blankenship fired at him, but unfortunately missed. The robber immediately returned the fire and was followed by his companion. They succeeded in putting four buckshot into Blankenship's hands – two in his right and two in his left. Another buckshot grazed his cheek and still another went through his hair over his left ear. With four shot in his hands Blankenship raised his gun and fired a second time and is confident he hit one, as a loud oath was uttered with the firing of the charge. The robbers, having disabled the messenger, had won the battle so they ordered the driver to throw down the mail and express box, which was done. The stagecoach was then ordered to proceed. Upon meeting the up-stagecoach Blankenship changed coaches and returned to town for treatment.

Undersheriff McDonald rode to the scene that evening and followed foot tracks for about one hundred yards, where he found the express box and mail bags. The robbers had a rough time getting the box open, first trying to crush in the side and finally chiseling open a third of the top. The mail sacks had been cut open and the mail had been scattered about the area where the robbers' horses were tied. Two miles further west another mail sack was found. All the mail was gathered up and returned to Prescott.

The total plunder from the robbery included seven hundred twenty-four dollars consisting of two hundred seventy-five Mexican dollars, one hundred dollars in gold coin, a pair of buckles valued at forty dollars, a thirty-five dollar check, and the remainder in currency. There was also twenty-five thousand dollars in checks and drafts, but by July 25th these were recovered.

On Saturday Undersheriff McDonald returned from his pursuit after the robbers with Price Hickey and Frank Mayhew, who had been tracked from their home to the scene of the robbery and back. They were charged with robbing the stagecoach July 11th, but not charged in the three previous robberies, and bail was set at five thousand dollars each. Their hearing was scheduled for Sunday morning.

The examination before Judge Warfield occupied seven days. District Attorney Lemon was assisted by J. H. Mahoney, special agent for the Post Office and Wells Fargo's detective Bob Paul. Testimony revealed that neighbors had seen the two boys, Price Hickey and Frank Mayhew, go to the pasture for their horses and ride toward the scene a short time before the robbery. One witness noted that the horses were a grey and a dark horse, but not black. Mayhew rode a roan and Hickey a grey. One robber's horse had a distinctive defect in the left front hoof, and the track of Hickey's grey was identical. Hickey and Mayhew were held to answer, but released on bail of one thousand dollars and five hundred dollars respectively.

In October the Grand Jury considered all the testimony and evidence presented at the examination and listened to additional testimony, much of which contradicted the incriminating evidence. On November 1, 1879 the Grand Jury announced that they had dismissed the charges against Mayhew and Hickey, finding insufficient evidence to support an indictment.

Although the evidence against Hickey and Mayhew was overwhelming, legal manipulations and false testimony contradicting the incriminating evidence secured their release. No one was ever convicted of this robbery or the three previous robberies, but this close call with the law caused this pair of road agents to retire.

August 14, 1879

The stagecoach was robbed of Wells, Fargo and Company's express box on Thursday night, but the robbers made a "water haul." On the previous evening the stagecoach carried seventeen thousand one hundred sixty-five dollars in silver and one thousand five hundred nine dollars in gold shipped from Prescott and nine thousand dollars shipped from Wickenburg, besides a large amount of currency and coin in possession of the passengers.

The robbers were either not well posted or they were afraid to attack so formidable an escort as accompanied the Wednesday coach, which included Jilson riding as messenger and passengers C. C. Bean, C. W. Beach and Miss May Bean.

The robbers obtained nothing of value so were not pursued.

July 12, 1880

Monday morning at 2 o'clock the eastbound coach between Florence and Globe, while not far from Putnam's, was halted by three "road agents" thought to be Mexicans. They commanded the driver to throw out the express box, which was done. There was no money in the treasure box, but it contained packages valued at ninety dollars. The five passengers, who were not molested, were ordered to keep their seats and remain quiet.

Officers went on the trail but had not arrived at any conclusions as to who the guilty parties were. Wells Fargo detective Bob Paul joined in the pursuit. Nevertheless, the robbers were not identified and remained at large. The investigation by Wells, Fargo and Company continued.

After the robbery of the 12th it was decided to take no chances when valuable treasure was being moved. On July 13th the Globe stagecoach left with sixty thousand dollars in treasure aboard, guarded by detective Paul, three additional detectives and a deputy sheriff, all well armed with rifles and shotguns. In addition there were eight passengers, including three ladies.

On August 31, 1881 Deputy Sheriff J. W. Evarts brought Pony Deal to Tucson from Harshaw, charged with complicity in robbing the stagecoach between Florence and Globe. Deal was held by Sheriff Paul to await a demand by the proper officer. While Pony Deal was being arrested at Harshaw, his accomplice – Sherman W. "Little Bill" McMasters – was being sought in Tombstone.

On the evening of September 8th Marshal Virgil Earp telegraphed Sheriff Paul asking if he wanted McMasters or not, and while waiting for an answer engaged his man in conversation, but Paul did not answer Virgil Earp and instead telegraphed Wells, Fargo and Company's agent Marshall Williams, who did not immediately inform the city Marshal of the telegram.

The following day a friend of McMasters, known by the so-briquet "Nigger Jim," slipped into town and informed McMasters of Deal's arrest. McMasters then went to Safford street near the foot of Fourth to hide while Jim went to the corral to get McMasters' horse, so that the fugitive could escape.

When Earp was told by agent Williams to arrest McMasters he could not find him, and started towards the corral to have his horse watched. As he came near the corral he saw a man riding McMasters' horse and commanded the rider to stop. When the rider continued, Earp fired a single warning shot. This brought the man to a standstill, who asked, "Do you want me?"

The Marshal looked him over, and seeing it was not McMasters, replied "No, I made a mistake."

Jim rode down Allen Street to Third, across to Safford and up that street closely followed by the Marshal. When Jim reached Fifth Street Earp again called out for him to stop, which he did. Jim was then ordered to dismount, but refused until he was warned that he would be shot out of the saddle if he did not comply. Jim dismounted and the Marshal took possession of the horse.

Marshal Earp had hardly mounted the horse when McMasters jumped up and started to run. Earp fired five shots at McMasters but, being mounted, his aim was unsteady and the fugitive made good his escape. McMasters was soon followed by the Sheriff, but Behan could not overtake him. Jim then stole a pair of horses from the Superinten-dent of the Contention mine so that McMasters and he could escape.

Neither McMasters nor Deal were ever tried for robbing the Globe stagecoach. For more information on Pony Deal see the rob-bery of January 7, 1882.

Sherman W. "Little Bill" McMasters played both sides of the Earp and "cowboys" feud. He was suspected of being involved in several stagecoach robberies with Curly Bill Brocius' men, but was inside the billiard room with the Earps when Morgan was murdered.

He was on the train at Tucson as Morgan's body was being taken to California, and Frank Stillwell was killed. It has even been suggested that the five shots fired at him by Virgil Earp were intentionally wide of their mark, and it may have been on the Earps' recommendation that U. S. Marshal Dake offered McMasters a position as a deputy U. S. Marshal in mid-1882. Instead, McMasters declined the appointment and moved eastward, where he was killed during a gunfight in the Texas panhandle about November 1882.

The third robber was never identified.

September 13, 1881

The Gilmer, Salisbury and Company's stagecoach, driven by Richard Thompson, left Wickenburg for Prescott after midnight on Tuesday with Charles P. Stanton the only passenger on board. A short distance out from Wickenburg the stagecoach caught up with Carl Smith, a well known stock man of Peeples' Valley who walking home from the Vulture mine. They stopped and talked with Smith on the present Indian question and the driver invited Mr. Smith to get aboard the stagecoach noting that, as he was armed, it would provide mutual protection. Smith accepted and, after riding a short distance, laid down in the bottom of the coach to sleep but requested the driver to wake him if he saw any Indians.

The moon that night was about thirty degrees high, with two-thirds of its disk illuminated and the atmosphere was hazy with a few cumulus clouds, which provided excellent visibility. The coach was ascending "Six Mile Hill" north of Wickenburg when Stanton warned the driver of several men standing near the roadway ahead. As soon as he spoke a volley of several shots suddenly poured into the coach. No command to halt was heard.

The driver, at the report of the shots, exclaimed, "taken in, by God! Where are they!"

"Look there, to your right," replied Stanton, and in the place indicated the driver saw three men twenty yards distant, though there might have been more. They were charging toward the stagecoach.

Stanton, who was sitting on the front seat with the driver, instantly opened fire with his Winchester repeating rifle. Carl Smith, who was roused by the first shots, remained lying in the bottom of the coach with his head just over the sideboard, and from this position opened fire on the highwaymen with his six-shooter. The firing from the stagecoach was very rapid and the attackers fell to the ground.

The coach horses became excited at the sound of gunfire. As they reached the summit of the hill and were just passing over it the highwaymen discharged another volley into the coach, which was returned, and this second fusillade caused the horses to plunge and rear violently. The leaders jumped off the road and partly doubled on the wheelers but the driver, with the aid of his whip, instantly had them straightened out again and the horses broke down the hill at a fearful rate. The driver appeared to be falling out of the stagecoach, when Stanton seized him, and asked if he was shot.

"No, I am all right. I am bending over to watch for the big wash-out hole, but I think my leaders are shot."

Smith yelled out, "let them go till they drop, Dick, then we will cut them out."

The whole time occupied by the fight did not exceed a minute and a half. After traveling at this rapid speed about a mile the driver had the team under full control. He pulled up to examine the horses, who were still trembling, but could find no bullet marks on them.

They examined the stagecoach and found that four bullets had passed through it. One ball passed between the driver and Stanton's head, passing out through the top of the coach and over the seat upon which they were sitting. Another ball struck the bow, fastened to the seat upon which the driver sat and which supported the top of the stagecoach; this ball entered within four inches of the driver's back, and ranged diagonally through the coach tearing the canvas at the hind part on the opposite side where it passed out. The other two balls went through the stagecoach behind the entrance at such an angle that Smith would have been killed had he been sitting up. The bullet holes were from a .44 caliber weapon, indicating that they were fired from a Henry rifle or six-shooter.

It was never determined who the attackers were, but the evidence strongly suggested to the driver and passengers that it was Mexican road agents because Indians had never been known, in that country, to attack at night time and white men do not attack in a savage manner, they usually halt the stagecoach. But this was, invariably, the manner in which Mexicans attacked stagecoaches.

Shortly after the attack a way-faring Chinaman, who was resting on the road side, stated that some men on horseback rode rapidly past him in the direction of Wickenburg or the Vulture mine, further supporting the supposition that it was not Indians.

The robbers were never identified.

May 10, 1882

An unsuccessful attempt was made to rob the Vulture stagecoach on a Wednesday night. The stagecoach was about three miles out from Seymour en route to Vulture when the driver heard the order to "Halt!" and the horses suddenly came to a stand still. Mr. Liggett, who was on board, got off to see what was the matter and found that a wire rope, like that used on the incline at the mine, had been stretched across the road to form a barricade and stop the leaders. The driver, Al Livermore, called to Liggett to step on the rope to allow the stagecoach to pass, which he did, and as the stagecoach passed two shots were fired just as someone called out in a German accent "Jump out." All plans of the robbers failed and the wagon bounded on its course greatly accelerated in speed. Several shots were fired after it, but to no effect. Later it was found that Giant Powder cartridges had been planted across the road which, had they exploded, would have blown up the stagecoach and its passengers. The robbers were apparently after the payroll for the Vulture Mine.

The materials used in the attempted robbery led to the capture of one of the parties implicated in the act – George Nelson – who was arrested in the hills near Vulture by Constable Vidal on the following night. Nelson still had some of the incline rope with him when arrested. Nelson admitted his guilt and told the authorities that William Miller was with him.

Nelson and Miller, two German miners who were employed at the Vulture mine, had quit their jobs. Nelson was paid off on May 5th and disappeared shortly after, while Miller was paid off on May 7th when he also disappeared. At the same time a box of giant powder cartridges was missed, and also some wire rope from the shaft where Miller worked.

A telegram reached Phoenix at 1 o'clock to the effect that Miller was wanted and H. Pateman, of the Vulture mine, recognized Miller and pointed him out to officers. Deputy Sheriff Tom Rogers arrested Miller in front of the Bank Exchange Hotel and lodged him in jail. He denied any part in the robbery and claimed to have been out prospecting.

On May 18th George Nelson had an examination before the Justice in Vulture and, after proving an alibi, was discharged; but, Miller was still believed to be one of the robbers. On May 23rd Sheriff Rogers returned from Vulture City with all the witnesses necessary for the prosecution of Miller.

On June 8th Miller tried to escape from jail and would have succeeded had it not been for the vigilance of Tom Rogers and Louis Gazelle. They heard a suspicious sound in the jail and, on going in to investigate, found that Miller and another prisoner had succeeded in sawing through one of the iron bars. They were immediately moved to another cell. During the early morning hours of October 4th Miller and another prisoner made good their escape by weakening the iron bars of their cell using muriatic acid so that they could be broken and removed, and once outside it was but a moments work to scale the tumbled down wall and flee. A large bottle, which had contained the muriatic acid, was found in the cell. The acid had been smuggled to them in some way which was never discovered.

Sheriff Orme, with a posse, went in pursuit of the escapees but failed to capture them. J. B. Hume, chief detective for Wells, Fargo and Company, wrote to Mr. Pridham, Wells, Fargo and Company's agent at Los Angeles, and gave a brief history of Miller's career:

Miller, who broke jail at Phoenix on the 4th inst., was held for attempting to rob the Vulture stagecoach May 10, 1882. Miller had been working at the Vulture. He was held to answer before the Grand Jury, which met this month. He ran on the Southern Pacific trains in 1881, from Los Angeles to Deming, as newsboy under the name William Ehrke. On the night of August 14, 1881 he stole a bar of Contention bullion from the depot at Benson and buried it a hundred yards from the depot, and on the night of September 1ˢᵗ raised the plant and buried it in some other place where it still remains. The bar was worth thirteen hundred dollars.

He then worked as a brakeman. He was known among train men as 'Dutchy, the Peanut Butcher.' On hearing of his escape we authorized the agent at Phoenix to offer one hundred dollars for his capture. Wells, Fargo & Co. have a standing reward of three hundred dollars for the arrest and conviction of every person engaged in the robbery or attempt to rob their express.

William Miller was not heard of again in the Territory.

January 19, 1884

On Saturday night the stagecoach from Wickenburg was stopped and robbed by one man when but three miles from Prescott near the Swilling Ranch. The mail bags were demanded before the coach was allowed to proceed. These were cut open and the letters rifled. The robber was masked, wore a blanket over his clothing, and had his feet muffled. He was armed with a six-shooter.

Deputy Sheriff Tom Rogers went out in pursuit of the stage-coach robber. The first clue officers had was the discovery of a pair of mufflers worn over the boots which were made from a sheep skin. The tracks of the highwayman, which were seen from this point on his trail, showed a peculiar impression made from the track of his boots and led back to Gillett.

Suspicion turned to Fred Wolfangel, who had been in Gillett only about a week but left suddenly the day after the robbery. In searching through his room a blanket was discovered beneath the mattress which had a hole cut through the center to fit around the neck, and another hole in the side for his pistol arm.

Rogers and Marshal Mulvenon proceeded to Tiptop where they found Wolfangel. The tracks they found near the scene of the robbery exactly corresponded with his boots while the sheep skin mufflers fitted nicely. He was arrested, but denied any part in the robbery. He had no plunder on him nor among his property. He was taken to Prescott and lodged in jail while the officers worked at strengthening their case against him.

Wolfangel was released without an examination and was never tried for stagecoach robbery, suggesting that further investigation revealed he was not the robber. The robber was never identified.

November 17, 1884

On October 20, 1885 Tombstone's *Epitaph* reported that "James Crothers has been arrested in Aspen for a stagecoach robbery committed near Phoenix, Ariz. November 17, 1884. He was a pal of Joe Chambers, who is now in jail in Phoenix for the same offense."

James Carruthers, alleged accomplice of Joseph Chambers in robbing the stagecoach between Vulture and Phoenix, was acquitted. The *Weekly Citizen* of November 21, 1885 reported, "Joe Chambers, well known here as the foreman of the Kimball mine on Lynx creek last year, and recently tried at Phoenix with Carruthers on a charge of holding up the Vulture stagecoach last November, will be tried at Prescott this term on a change of venue, the Maricopa jury having disagreed on his recent trial."

Chambers was also acquitted on the stagecoach robbery charge and released. The robbers were never identified.

August 18, 1885

A dispatch from Phoenix dated the 18th reported that two stagecoaches had been taken in after midnight between New River and Gillette by two road agents. Both boxes of Wells, Fargo and Company were broken open, but only one letter and a waybill were taken. After robbing one of the stagecoaches, and cracking Wells, Fargo's box, one of the robbers coolly told the driver of the coach to tell Wells, Fargo's agent at Phoenix that he could in future save his boxes if he would considerately forward the keys with the stagecoach driver.

The stagecoach drivers were not molested, but the passengers on the southbound coach lost a small sum of money. The teams of both stagecoaches were taken as the robbers fled toward Phoenix.

On September 1st Tombstone's *Epitaph* said that: "... So skillfully were the robberies planned and so audaciously carried out that up to the present writing neither of the highwaymen have been arrested, although a supposed accomplice named Pennington is now in jail at Phoenix." Pennington provided sufficient evidence to implicate John Bennett as one of the road agents.

Bennett, a few years previously, had "jumped" a lot on the corner of Fourth and Fremont streets and erected a tin house, but was later evicted. Then for several years had followed the business of prospecting about Tombstone. A few months earlier Bennett had gone to Phoenix with a team sent over there by Briggs Goodrich and worked for him a short time, but he resigned and gave as a reason that he did not intend to work any more and that he would rather rob stagecoaches. His talk at the time was considered idle bravado. A reward of one thousand dollars was offered for his capture.

The Black Canyon robbers, Bennett and a man who gave his name as Tom "the kid" Day, were captured at Quijotoa on Saturday, September 12th and lodged in jail at Phoenix. The arrests were made by deputy U. S. Marshal E. M. Mills after A. Carrington, who was familiar with the men, pointed them out.

Bennett did not hesitate in acknowledging his complicity in the affair and boasting of the details. Tom "the kid" Day admitted that his true name was Collister. John Bennett and Tom Collister were convicted of robbing the U.S. mail.

Bennett received a sentence of fifteen years on one charge and another year on an additional charge, making sixteen years in all, to be served at the House of Corrections at Detroit. Bennett asked to serve his time at another institution – either Yuma, Laramie, or Topeka – but his request was denied.

Collister received a sentence of fifteen years, also to be served in Detroit. Deputy U. S. Marshal E. M. Mills, with deputies Hines and Kelly as guards, left for Detroit with the prisoners on December 18, 1885.

Thomas Collister, born in England, was twenty-six years of age when he arrived at the House of Corrections on December 21, 1885, and was reported in good health. He had been a machinist before turning to stagecoach robbery. He was Catholic, and could read and write. Collister had no wife nor children, listing his mother and father as his nearest relatives. He served his entire fifteen year sentence, less good time, and was released on October 2, 1896.

John Bennett, born in Wales, was twenty-five years of age when he arrived at the House of Corrections on December 21, 1885 and was reportedly in poor health. He had been a miner, he was a Catholic, and could read and write. He had no wife nor children, listing his mother and father as his nearest relatives. He found it impossible to complete his entire sixteen year sentence so on January 6, 1893, less than four years before the expiration of his sentence, he swallowed a lethal dose of aconite.

John Pennington, at age twenty-three years, cooperated with law enforcement and in return was convicted on the Territorial charge of highway robbery. He was sentenced to ten years to be served at the Territorial Prison near Yuma. He was registered as prisoner № 354 on December 13, 1885, also recorded as his date of release as he was deceased upon his arrival at the prison. Pennington's body was brought to Yuma where a coroner's jury brought in a verdict in accordance with the facts.

Pennington escaped from deputy Sheriff Blankenship while en route to Yuma by train. The deputy reported: "The train was east of Gila City, the prisoner apparently asleep in the seat behind me, when I laid my head on the seat and went to sleep. When I woke up, a mile west of Gila City, the prisoner was gone. I had the train stopped, went back to Gila City, and stayed till morning when I made preparation to pursue the escaped man. However, before I was off, a freight train came in bearing the remains of the dead man, which they found eight miles east of Gila City under a trestle work. He had jumped from the train and struck his head on the timbers, which killed him instantly."

These same men had robbed a stagecoach in Pinal County on August 7th, but were never tried for that crime.

November 7, 1887

The stagecoach from the Vulture mine was robbed on Monday at 11 o'clock p.m. when a few miles beyond Calderwood Station, which is about twenty-two miles from Phoenix on the Vulture road. An employee of the Vulture mine, accompanied by two Phoenix men, were returning from the mine and when they reached the point about where the robbery occurred a man raised up from the brush, gazed at the stagecoach, and then retired from view. When the incoming stagecoach reached this same point it was robbed by a lone individual who succeeded in obtaining forty dollars from the only passenger, named Ryan, while the driver contributed eighty dollars bringing the total loss to one hundred twenty dollars.

The following evening the passenger, who was an employee of the Vulture company and saw the man get up from behind the bush, told Frank Wells and Sheriff Halbert that the robber was in town and pointed out a man as the one he had seen. Frank Wells told the suspected road agent that he wanted to talk to him, whereupon the man got up hastily, went out with the officers, and made tracks straight for the county jail. Wells and Halbert arrested the man, whose name was Henley, and lodged him in a cell. Henley soon regained his composure and protested his innocence. He had a hearing before Judge Woods the following day and was held, but the investigation continued until the officers were satisfied that Henley was not the highwayman and he was released. The robber was never identified.

Circumstances suggest that William Bonner, the cowboy found dead on the 9th in the Tonto Basin, and who was believed to have robbed the two stagecoaches between St. Johns and Navajo Station on October 30th, swung south on his way back to the Tonto Basin, arriving before November 7th, and stopped long enough to rob the stagecoach between the Vulture mine and Phoenix.

November 3, 1888

The stagecoach which left Phoenix last Saturday morning for Prescott, when about sixteen miles out on the desert, and within one mile of the new town of Peoria, was stopped by a highwayman at ten o'clock in the morning. The passengers, three in number, were relieved of their superfluous coin, amounting to eleven dollars and fifty cents. The passengers were Judge Noyes, Mike Maloney, and an Italian who, with the driver, were "stood up in a row" and ordered to place their contributions on a designated stone by the roadside. The driver was then ordered to throw out the large mail sack and, on lifting it from the bottom of the coach in sight of the robber he said he didn't know whether he wanted it or not. The driver advised him to let it alone, and he replied that he would and ordered the driver to continue on.

The stagecoach had not proceeded more than a mile when it was met by Bud Gray, democratic candidate for sheriff of Maricopa County, and J. K. Murphy a deputy sheriff, who were told of the affair and who proposed to take up the trail and, if possible, capture the highwayman.

The description given tallied with that of the man who recently stopped the Jerome stagecoach and levied an assessment on its passengers. The robber was never identified. This was the second in a series of six robberies, with others occurring on November 10th and 16th in Maricopa County and on the 12th and 19th in Yavapai County.

November 10, 1888

This, the third in a series of robberies, caused the newspapers to say that a stagecoach robber was "infesting the stage line between this city and Prescott. A few days since he took in the Wickenburg route without getting anything. ..."

The robber was never identified.

November 16, 1888

The robber returned to Yavapai County but four days later was back in Maricopa County. The stagecoach between Mesa and McDowell was held up about sundown by the same dismounted man who had been "infesting the stage line" single handed, this time not more than three mile from Fort McDowell. Once again nothing of value was taken.

The robber first asked for the treasure, and was told that there was none. He felt the registered pouch and thought it was empty so handed it back, though it contained a very valuable gold watch. He then demanded the driver's money and pistol. When told the driver had neither, the robber said, "I have been holding up stages all over this country of late, and nobody has anything. I have been waiting for the paymaster but cannot find out when he will be along. I will see you again some day."

The driver described the road agent as five feet seven inches in height, with sandy brown or auburn hair, medium build, very quick and active in his motions, and the outlines of a very prominent nose through a dark mask extending to his chest.

The description corresponded with a stranger who ate dinner at the Fort that day and asked in course of conversation, "What time does the mail arrive?" Upon being advised to stop over in Phoenix, he said, "I am broke now, but expect to get some money between here and Phoenix." The man at the fort had a very good horse but, like the robber who halted the stagecoach, had no hat.

The robber was never identified. He would travel north into Yavapai County to commit his last robbery on November 19th.

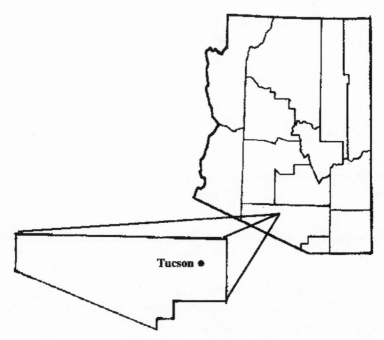

Stagecoach Robbery in Pima County

The first Legislative Assembly, which met in the fall of 1864, established four counties with Pima in the southwest, with its county seat at Tucson.

October 2, 1875

Eighteen miles north of Florence the stagecoach was halted by three men, two of whom leveled shotguns at the driver and passenger Mr. Bullock. They commanded the stagecoach to stop and required both men to throw up their arms, which they did. The third highwayman then searched Bullock and took all the funds found in his pockets, amounting to about one thousand four hundred dollars. The mails were not disturbed.

Mr. Bullock later reported that this was, by no means, all his money as he had concealed on his person considerably more greenbacks as well as a large quantity of bullion in his trunk. He had been to Tucson to the "Feast" and had been quite successful there.

It was later speculated that the attack was made for his special benefit, as he was known by many to have left Tucson with a large amount of money.

Prescott"s *Miner* newspaper commented: "This is the first and only time known where a stagecoach had been stopped and passengers robbed in the Territory ... ."

The robbers of the Tucson coach were never identified.

December 12, 1877

The stagecoach which left Tucson at two o'clock p.m. on Wednesday was stopped east of Desert Station by three armed men about eleven o'clock at night. The robbers permitted the driver to cast his experienced eye down the barrels of their well charged shotguns and then requested him to "disgorge." Under the circumstances the driver concluded to allow them to examine the express box, which they did, and then allowed the stagecoach to pass on without further molesting the driver or passengers. Mr. Frank Staples, Tucson's express agent, said there was not a cent in the box, so that the would-be robbers gained a crime without booty. Parties from Tucson started in pursuit at once, but the robbers were never identified.

December 22, 1877

The robbers failed to obtain any money in their December 12th robbery so by the 22nd they were ready to try again. The stagecoach from Tucson was halted about two miles east of Desert Station on Saturday night and again plundered. There were two passengers in the coach, E. Conkling, artist and correspondent for Frank Leslie's paper, and a discharged soldier whose name was not recorded. The robbers took the express box, and all the mail sacks and searched the passengers, but failed to find two hundred fifty dollars the soldier had on his person. Express agent G.A. Brown said that the express box contained about one thousand dollars and Collingwood & Co. lost about two hundred dollars in a registered letter. The amount that the robbers found in the mails was unknown.

Only two men were engaged in the robbery and, from their description, the location and their *modus operandi*, it was certain that they were the same parties who committed the former robbery. Acting Governor Gosper offered a reward of five hundred dollars each for the capture of the highwaymen and stated that, should they prove to be the same parties who stopped the coach previously, the reward of four hundred dollars each then offered would also be paid, making in all eighteen hundred dollars for the two and an additional four hundred dollars for the third man in the first robbery.

Parties went out, determined to give the road agents a hard chase, and it seemed the efforts had paid off. Both robbers were reportedly captured at Maricopa Wells on January 24th. It was also reported that when apprehended the registered mails were still in their possession. On the 26th U. S. Marshal Standifer and stage line superintendent J. W. Evans left to bring them back to Tucson. However, Evans returned to Prescott and reported that, "the men recently taken up at Burke's Station, on suspicion of their being stagecoach robbers, were entirely innocent and have been permitted to go about their business."

The robbers were never identified. Tucson's *Citizen* observed, "there would be a mild satisfaction in knowing that they were resting in the cold silent grave with their toes turned up to the daisies."

July 31, 1878

The stagecoach left Tucson on Wednesday at the usual hour of 2 o'clock p.m. Arthur Hill was driving and Veterinary Surgeon Wheatly, John P. Clum, and one Chinaman were the only passengers. At 5 o'clock p.m. with a light rain falling, they reached the ranch at Point of Mountain, eighteen miles northwest from Tucson. About ten minutes later the coach entered the sand at Point of Mountain and the horses necessarily slowed to a walk.

Suddenly a man accosted the driver in rather harsh tones, the driver replied and stopped the coach. A tall form in a mask appeared at the left side of the coach and covered the driver and passengers with a Spencer carbine and a six-shooter while commanding everyone to remain still at the peril of their lives. Clum had a pistol, but it lay on the floor of the coach. Wheatly had one also, but it was on the seat under a blanket. The attack was in open daylight but so unexpected that both men were surprised, and once under cover of the robber's arms they were compelled to obey his commands.

He ordered the men out of the coach and carefully went through them, and after the collection had been taken the robber remarked that one of the passengers "looked like a sick man." After scanning the coach for other valuables, and finding none, he ordered the driver to proceed which order was obeyed. However, just as the coach started forward the road agent challenged everyone to come back and fight him as soon as anyone felt disposed to do so.

The road agent was about six feet tall and well built. He had his pants tucked in his boots and wore small brass spurs, such as were used by the army. His face was covered with a muslin mask with openings for his eyes and a red mouth sewn on. His weapons were a Spencer carbine and a Colt's army size six-shooter, and when making the attack he held the carbine to his shoulder all the time and his pistol leveled in the fingers of the left hand so close to the gun-barrel and parallel with it that it appeared to be fastened to the Carbine.

A stagecoach had been robbed east of Silver City, New Mexico three months previously, with Col. Willard and Lt. West aboard. While that robbery was committed at night, the passengers were able report that the robber "had a pistol strapped to his gun," which led to the conclusion that the two robberies were committed by the same road agent.

J. P. Clum, reporter for Tucson's *Citizen*, wrote, "This editor has frequently read of the daring deeds of fierce highwaymen and several times within the last six months it has been necessary for us to describe the bold operations of these desperadoes, but never until day before yesterday have we had the good fortune to witness the *modus operandi* by which these members of the shotgun gentry extract the valuables from a stagecoach and passengers by the simple but magical persuasive power of cold lead." Clum also observed, "... the express box was empty and there was nothing of great value in the mails hence, as he only obtained thirty-seven dollars from the passengers, his booty was small and he will no doubt feel it necessary to rob another coach soon." The robber was not captured, but Clum was correct as the robber appeared two weeks later.

August 14, 1878

The stagecoach left Tucson on Thursday with two passengers and Arthur Hill, who had been the driver on October 31st, was again driving. John Miller, one of the passengers, was sitting on the outside and as they neared Point of Mountain he asked Hill to show him just the place where the coach was robbed previously. The driver replied that it was only a short distance ahead and he would point out the spot. When they reached the place Hill said, "There. The robber was hid behind that bush," and then in the same breath shouted, "and there he is again," as the masked robber sprang from behind the same bush.

The road agent pranced before the horses shouting, "yes, here I am again. Throw up your hands!" On command the mail sacks and express box were thrown out. The inside passenger was ordered out and searched, but lost only eight dollars. Miller was more unfortunate, as he was obliged to give up his pocketbook which contained about two hundred twenty-six dollars. The robber ordered the driver to proceed and the stagecoach arrived at Desert Station just about dark. Parties immediately left for Tucson to notify the authorities.

The next morning the Sheriff's posse took the robber's track, but failed to find him. The strangest bit of evidence from these two robberies was that two horses appeared to leave Tucson toward the scene of the crime but none returned. Finally a tracker named Juan Elias was put on the track. It happened on this second occasion that the robber's horse threw a shoe, creating the odd impression of an animal with three hoofs traveling in one direction and the fourth un-shod hoof in the opposite direction. Elias back-tracked the hoof prints to their source and found the robber's horse in the corral of David Nemitz. Elias examined the animal and found that the robber had developed a way to turn the horse's shoes around. The shoes had been made especially for this purpose, with four nail holes on each side of each shoe so accurately spaced that when the shoes were reversed nails could be pushed through the holes in the horse's hoof. All that remained was to turn the nails down and cut the clinchers.

Nemitz was arrested and bail was set at two thousand five hundred dollars, but Nemitz expressed an interest in telling all if he could be protected from the real stagecoach robber. Nemitz said that he had worked in James Carroll's corral but had recently left that employment and taken up residence south of James Lee's flouring mill several miles south of Tucson. He admitted that the road agent obtained his supplies of food and water and also kept his horse at Nemitz' home, but explained how he had become involved with stage-coach robber William Whitney Brazelton: "He called one day, asked a couple of questions and went away. He returned the next day and asked for a confidential conversation, which was granted. On the first visit I did not recognize the man, nor the second time until informed that he was a former fellow-laborer in the corral when Mr. Leather-wood owned it. I said, 'You look like a hard game,' and he replied, 'you bet I'm a hard game,' and then he told all about his robberies. I was then in the power of a man who placed little value on his own or anyone's life. I felt obliged to obey the robber's commands. Owing to the facts in connection with my own arrest and the search going on, I feared Brazelton would suspect me and kill me. If the Sheriff's posse failed to kill the robber my own death would soon follow, and I warned the Sheriff that the man would not be taken alive unless by artful strategy."

From all that Nemitz had told Pima County Sheriff Charles A. Shibell, the sheriff deemed it necessary to shoot Brazelton on sight, and so instructed his deputies. Shibell summoned Marshall Buttner, R. N. Leatherwood, Charles O. Brown, Charles T. Etchells, Jim Lee and Ika O. Brokaw as his posse. The plan was for the posse members to sneak out of town and assemble near the mesquite log where Brazelton was to meet Nemitz, who had agreed to provide the road agent with supplies for the evening's work.

Nemitz disclosed that Brazelton was preparing to commit another robbery that night and would be weighted-down with all his arms. When the robber arrived at the log he had upon his person two belts full of cartridges, two six-shooters and a Spencer rifle.

Brazelton approached the log cautiously and gave the signal, a cough, which was returned by a posse member. He then placed his hat on the log to signal Nemitz to come to him. Something alarmed Brazelton and he leaned over the log as if to look on the other side, where one of the posse members was concealed, and the silence was broken by the blast from a shotgun. A fusillade of pistol shots followed immediately and Brazelton exclaimed, "You S** of a B****," as he fell. He lay still in the darkness and the posse heard him gasp, "I die brave, my God! I'll pray till I die."

The posse remained silent, listening carefully in the dark for any sign that there was fight left in Brazelton. Finally they lighted matches and counted ten holes deposited in his chest between the robber's shoulders in the area of his heart and lungs. The ambush had been so sudden that Bill Brazelton had been captured and mortally wounded without the opportunity to fire a single shot.

The Sheriff searched the robber's body and discovered the hood, with red mouth sewn on as described in previous robberies, and in his pockets was some of the loot, including a pair of distinctive earrings and a gold watch. Ika Brokaw went to town and procured a wagon. "Brazen Bill" Brazelton's body was then taken into Tucson and tied upright in a chair and displayed at the courthouse until the inquest and burial the following afternoon.

Brazelton was described in the Prescott *Enterprise* as "the most successful 'single-handed' highway robber of modern times." The article continued, "Who he was and whither from will soon become clear, we suppose." J. P. Clum later reported, "Billy Brazelton was born in San Francisco. He was early left an

Courtesy: Arizona Historical Society/Tucson

orphan and made his home in an old boiler, the remains of a wreck on the Barbary coast. He attended the public schools of San Francisco, became a hoodlum and killed his first man in a row when he was but 15 years old. He robbed nine coaches in Arizona and New Mexico single-handed. Once he was closely pursued by a posse near Silver City, New Mexico when he managed to separate them and killed them one by one as they came up. He was dextrous with firearms and had no streak of yellow in him." In 1902 Clum stated that he had recently visited the grave of Brazelton a short distance from Tucson.

That would seem to be the end of the Brazelton saga, but Bill was not yet finished. Twenty years after Brazelton's death W. C. Davis of Tucson spoke of the stagecoach robber at San Jose, California, as reported in San Jose's *Evening News*:

> The Indians and Mexicans, particularly the old people of the latter race, will never go past a place after dark where any tragedy has ever been committed, or which has been given the reputation of being queer when it has been given out that any one has seen things. ... There is a place not far from Tucson where it is said they will not pass after dark, even if they have to make a journey of a mile to go around it. The incident which put a hoodoo on the spot occurred some twenty-five years ago. ... The spot where the highwayman met a tragic death was avoided after night fall by the Indians and Mexicans and even now some of the old timers, who remember the affair, will not go past the place in the dark, and will recite stories of how a phantom highwayman is seen standing in the road, just as Brazelton was halted on the night of his death.

August 14, 1878

The stagecoach leaving Yuma and the one that left Florence were both robbed about four miles apart by four Mexicans.

The coach from Yuma to Tucson was stopped first. The highwaymen drove it a hundred yards from the road and systematically went through the mails, express, baggage, driver Osborn, and W. S. Bell, the only passenger. Bell had sixty dollars in gold in his sock and two hundred fifty dollars in greenbacks sewn into his sleeve, which the robbers found. They then made him and the driver strip naked, but gave back the clothing they wore. They gutted the baggage and carefully searched the entire wagon, cushions and all. They took both horses and loaded on the clothing and the express box, which they had not known how to open

The robbers started up the road to meet the stagecoach from Florence, and met it within a few miles; then went through the same performance taking horses, clothing, express box, watches, and even pocket knives from driver Charles H. Kenyon and the only passenger, newly appointed deputy U. S. Marshal J. W. Evans.

After the robbers left, Kenyon went back a couple of miles and borrowed two horses from a party of campers, then drove on to Desert Station, arriving there about 5:30 a.m. Meanwhile Bell and Osborne had walked to Desert Station and were just about to start for Tucson to give the alarm when Kenyon and Evans drove into sight with the Florence stagecoach. All the men boarded and the whole party reached Tucson about 7:30 a.m.

Five hundred dollars was immediately subscribed to employ Papago Indians as trackers for the large number of citizens who had volunteered to go after the road agents. This party got off about noon, but was unable to find the robbers.

Deputy U. S. Marshal Evans was also out hunting the stagecoach robbers and later reported that the trail led toward Sonora, where the robbers' tracks were lost over the international border. The robbers were never identified.

September 16, 1879

The stagecoach going from Phoenix to Tombstone was robbed when about four miles west of Tombstone by two Americans with shot guns. There were seven passengers aboard and all were robbed, but the mail and express were not touched. The robbers got about one hundred fifty dollars before they left in the direction of town.

The *Arizona Silver Belt* said that the robbers were probably among the many tramps who had been loafing around Tombstone, but they were never identified.

May 21, 1880

Friday evening the stagecoach left Shakespear westbound, having on board Miss Ella Sheppard and a man whose name was not recorded. Chavis, the messenger, sat beside driver John Henry. At 9 o'clock p.m., when coming through Granite Pass nine miles from San Simon Station two figures suddenly arose, one on each side, and commanded the driver to halt. The order was accompanied by two shots, one from each of the bandits who were recognized as Americans.

The first two shots struck Chavis who grasped his rifle, which was on the back part of the seat, and he made a desperate effort to return the fire; but, before he could get in position he was shot again. Chavis fell over onto the front of the boot with his head and shoulders over the edge and, had it not been for Henry's coolness, would have certainly fallen over among the mules.

The driver was shot twice in the right leg, but that did not prevent him from reaching over and pulling Chavis back into the boot and holding him there with his left foot. Henry then gathered up the reins and started for San Simon with the right foot, in spite of his wounded leg, working the brake while the other held the messenger in the boot the entire distance. The coach arrived at 10 o'clock a.m., and was a sight with blood spattered all over it and the mail sacks.

On their arrival Chavis was taken out alive, but he died in a few moments. Henry was taken to the Post hospital, where he stayed several weeks to recuperate.

The robbers – murderers of Chavis – were never identified.

December 20, 1883

At a point six miles north of Canoa and twenty-nine miles south of Tucson at about 2 p.m. on Thursday, the stagecoach driver on Moreno's line observed ten "Tejanos", as he called them, by the roadside. Some were mounted, others were leaning under some mesquite trees, and their horses were feeding about. As the stagecoach came along one of them advanced, threw up his hand, and cried "Stop!" and the driver checked his horses.

"Have you got anything?" asked the robber.

The driver replied, "No, nothing."

The robber then looked into the boot and bed and saw they were empty and said , "All right," and waved the driver to proceed.

The driver started up his team and came right along. At Canoa he met Aguirre's stagecoach where he warned the driver, but the people on Aguirre's stagecoach saw nothing of them.

Mr. Samaniego said that "Tejanos" is a the term for cowboys rather than "Texans." The robbers were never identified.

July 23, 1885

The stagecoach between Crittenden and Harshaw was stopped and robbed six miles from Harshaw on Thursday at about 2 o'clock. F. M. Peterson, the stagecoach driver, was shot through the heart and his body was carried about a hundred yards away from the road. The horses were cut loose, the mail was robbed and the wagon dumped over the side of the road.

Peterson was a native of Sweden, but had resided in Crittenden for several years and had only been married three weeks. He had been one of the principal witnesses for the prosecution in the celebrated Billy Claibourn murder case. Petersen's body was brought into Crittenden for burial Friday afternoon.

A party immediately started in pursuit of the robbers but failed to overtake them.

The robbers were never identified.

October 17, 1888

The Jerome stagecoach, which arrived in Tucson at 4 o'clock Wednesday afternoon, was held up at 11 o'clock a.m. by one man at Summit, a short distance beyond Sanders' Station. The passengers, J. I. Gardner, Tom Urquhart, W. A. Smith, and Sam Goldwater of Tucson and a commercial traveler were ordered to alight, stood up alongside the road, and told to empty their pockets. The result was a sum of money amounting to about thirty dollars. The passengers were then ordered to "pile in and drive on," which order they obeyed. Neither the mail nor the express was disturbed.

This was the first in a series of six robberies, with the others occurring on November 3rd, 10th, and 16th in Maricopa County; and November 12th and 19th in Yavapai County. The robber was never identified.

August 10, 1892

Antonio Valdez, who for twenty years was well known in Tucson as a stagecoach driver, started out on his usual drive to Quijotoa Wednesday morning conveying the United States mail. He had proceeded but a short distance through the mountain ranges south of the city when he saw a buggy in front of him which had no top on it. The party driving seemed familiar to Valdez, so he urged up his horses to overtake the buggy, which shortly disappeared around a bend in the road.

When Valdez arrived at the location where he had lost sight of the party he was commanded to halt by a masked man. The horses, when they saw the robber, shied to one side and the road agent called on him to stop or he would shoot, so Valdez reined in his team. The robber demanded the mail sacks, which were given to him. He cut them open but there were only papers in the pouch and one single letter. The robber then ordered Valdez to drive on, and he lost no time in complying. The robber was described as a masked American who spoke Spanish fluently.

Valdez drove to the ranch of Mayor Maish, then started back to Tucson to give the alarm. At one o'clock p.m. U. S. Marshal Paul, Sheriff Brown, and Postmaster Corbett started in pursuit, but could not overtake the fugitive.

The robber was never identified.

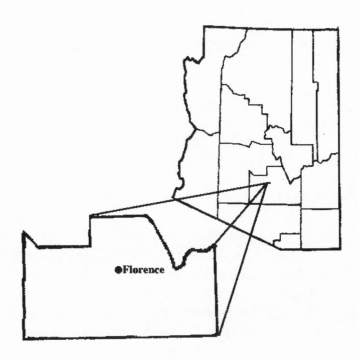

Stagecoach Robbery in Pinal County

In 1875 Pinal County was formed from the northwest corner of Pima and the southeast portion of Maricopa, with its county seat established at Florence.

February 13, 1879

The stagecoach from Tucson to Florence was robbed on a Thursday night. A telegram to the agent in Prescott said that the passengers were robbed, but did not indicate that any large amounts were taken. With the mails and express unmolested there was little motivation to pursue the robbers. The robbers were never identified.

February 19, 1879

The coach which left Tucson for Yuma on Wednesday afternoon was stopped by masked men five miles west of Picacho and robbed. The robbers secured twenty dollars, a gold watch and chain, and a pistol from the passengers. They took up the express box but it sounded so empty that they handed it back. The robbers then took one of the coach horses and left, but as the driver had four horses in his team the coach was not much delayed. The stolen horse came into Desert Station Friday morning. Again, only the passengers were robbed so no pursuit was organized. The robbers, probably the same as robbed the stagecoach on February 13th, were never identified.

August 10, 1883

The stagecoach was taken-in at the foot of the hill leading out of the Gila Valley, about one and a half miles above Riverside. The robbers had stationed themselves behind bushes on either side of the road and when the stagecoach passed between them, opened fire on the messenger and driver without a single word of warning. The messenger, Johnny Collins, was killed at the first fire, a charge of buckshot entering his chin and neck. The road agents continued shooting until Humphrey, the driver, called out, "For God's sake, stop shooting! You have killed one man. What more do you want?"

The robbers then shot one of the leaders and one of the wheel horses, after which they ceased firing and proceeded to examine the stagecoach. They found Felix LeBlanc inside the coach and ordered him to step out and drop his money onto road. As soon as he had obeyed this command they ordered him to throw the express box out of the boot. He made an effort to do so but the box was very heavy and the dead messenger was lying on top of it. Seeing that LeBlanc could not remove the box alone the robbers ordered Humphrey to assist him. The driver asked permission to remove the body of the murdered man from the boot, but one robber replied, "Let him lie where he is and get that box out at once, or we'll put holes through you S*** of B******."

By an almost super-human effort the two men dragged the box from the boot and threw it onto the ground. The robbers then handed LeBlanc a new hatchet and ordered him to break open the box. As soon he had accomplished that work the robbers ordered both men to march up the road in the direction of Cane Springs, and accompanied the order with a threat of death should they attempt to return.

The robbers took two thousand dollars in silver and five hundred dollars in gold from the box and packed it on one of the coach horses. They left six hundred twenty dollars in currency in the box, having overlooked it in their haste. Where their horses were hitched they dropped a pair of leather saddle bags, a belt full of Winchester cartridges, a package of tea, loaf of bread, and an old-fashioned dirk knife, evidently custom-made by some blacksmith.

LeBlanc and Humphrey continued up the road until they met the down-stagecoach at Cane Springs, about three miles from the scene of the robbery. There were several passengers aboard and McKenny was driving. When LeBlanc and Humphrey recited the tragic experience through which they had just passed, McKenny and the passengers concluded to camp at Cane Springs until daylight and, to make sure that they would be safe overnight, climbed up the side of the mountain some distance above the road.

At daybreak McKenny hitched-up and drove to the scene of the robbery and murder. The dead messenger was still lying in the boot face down and his gun lay in the road a few steps in the rear of the coach, where it had dropped from his lap when the fatal charge of buck-shot struck him. McKenny turned the broken express box over and found twelve dollars of the money LeBlanc dropped on the ground.

News of the robbery did not reach Florence until 10 o'clock Saturday. Sheriff Doran was at Pinal and telegraphed that he would meet the posse at Riverside. Undersheriff Scanland and Fred Adams left for the scene and, upon arriving, took the track of the fugitives with orders to follow it as long as a trace remained.

The robbers took a trail circling to the right from the place of the robbery and leading over the hills to the San Pedro road at a point about two miles above Riverside. When they came to the San Pedro road they stopped for the purpose of dividing the treasure into two packs and strapping it on to the stagecoach horse which they had taken for that purpose. At this point they dropped a nickel-plated shot-gun shell, Nº 12 Winchester fire.

They followed the San Pedro road and passed Dudleyville at a full gallop, one leading the pack horse and the other riding behind and whipping up the exhausted animal. Each man held a revolver in his hand. The boys in front of the Dudleyville store hallooed them and demanded the reason for their hurry, but they made no reply.

About five miles above Dudleyville the robbers turned out of the road into the timber, where their tracks could not be followed owing to the fact that the ground was covered with a thick growth of summer grass. The lawmen were certain that they had killed the stagecoach horse and buried the money in this timber because, when the robbers passed Mesaville five miles further on, they did not have the pack animal with them. They were still riding at a high rate of speed at five o'clock Saturday morning as they passed Perdue's place, and were noticed by both Mrs. Perdue and Mrs. Pearson, who was a guest at the house. The robbers could not be traced above Redfield's.

In the meantime J. P. Gabriel, who was at Riverside on mining business, commenced an investigation and learned that Red Jack left the stagecoach at Evans and LeBlanc's station and asked if two men had left a horse for him, and when he learned that they had not he raved about their treachery and said he would make it warm for them if they failed to keep their agreement. Red Jack left the saddle he brought with him on the stagecoach and started out on foot.

Gabriel believed Red Jack was involved in the robbery and decided to arrest him. The editor of the *Enterprise* agreed to accompany Gabriel and when they reached Putnam's found Sheriff Doran, who had just returned from inspecting the robber's camp in the mountains. Gabriel informed him of their purpose and Doran saddled up his animal while Putnam saddled a fresh jack for Gabriel. At ten o'clock the posse was off in the direction of the San Pedro River.

Some time after midnight they reached Dudleyville, where they learned that Red Jack had given one of Mr. Finch's sons fifteen dollars to take him as far up-river as Captain Cage's. Red Jack had said that he would reach Redfield's that night if he had to steal a horse to accomplish the journey. This seemed to confirm that Jack was a party to the robbery. The posse borrowed two Winchester rifles and a six-shooter from Alex L. Pam, owner of the Dudleyville store, and continued on. Just before daylight they arrived at Mesaville and found Undersheriff Scanland, Adams and Harrington, who had spent the night there. They promptly saddled their horses and joined the posse.

Fresh horses were obtained at Brown's so they could continue to Captain Cage's. At Cage's place they learned that Red Jack had paid ten dollars to a young man named Huntley to take him to Redfield's. At G. M. William's they secured another change of horses and by noon were at Frank Shield's residence for yet another change of horses. While waiting for dinner, Huntley came in and said that he had started to take Red Jack to Redfield's but that Frank Carpenter met them about one half mile above Shield's place. Carpenter and Red Jack dismounted, went out to one side, and had a confidential talk. They returned to Huntley and Carpenter gave Red Jack ten dollars with which to pay Huntley and gave his horse to Red Jack to continue on to Redfield's, while Carpenter went to Mesaville.

The posse divided – three men taking one side of the river with three on the other side – and pushed on to Redfield's. They reached their destination about seven o'clock p.m. and rode down upon the occupants unexpectedly. Two of the wanted men – Len Redfield and Joe Tuttle – were in sight and three suspicious looking strangers were camped in front of the house; but, Red Jack had passed through at one o'clock that afternoon.

The lawmen anticipated a lively fight at Redfield's, but were disappointed. The posse unsaddled their horses and went into camp, keeping a guard through the night to see that the fugitives did not escape or ambush the lawmen.

The next morning Sheriff Doran placed both Tuttle and Redfield under arrest and made a careful search of the premises. He found a number of suspicious articles, among them a United States mail sack. After the arrests it was decided that Gabriel would continue in pursuit of Red Jack, while the rest of the party returned to Florence with the prisoners and arrested Frank Carpenter along the way.

Carpenter, who was a nephew of Redfield, was found at Dudleyville and gave the latter completely away. Undersheriff Scanland had on his saddle the saddle-bags found at the scene of the robbery, and as soon as Carpenter saw them he turned to Len Redfield and said, "Len, these fellows have got your saddle-bags." Tuttle soon admitted that Red Jack, Charles Hensley and he were the men who had robbed the stagecoach, while Len Redfield and Frank Carpenter were only accessories.

With Red Jack and Hensley still at large the governor issued a reward proclamation:

GOVERNOR'S REWARD

Whereas, Stage robbing is becoming apparently
a permanent industry of the Territory and
is one which carries with it the destruction of life and
always is attended with danger to
the peaceful traveling public, and
Whereas, ... highwaymen did stop
the coach on the Florence road,
killing W. F. & Co.'s messenger, and
wounding the driver of said coach,
Now therefore, I, H. M. Van Arman,
Acting-Governor of the Territory of Arizona,
by virtue of the power vested in me,
do hereby offer a reward ...
For the arrest and conviction of
the murderers on the Florence road,
ONE THOUSAND DOLLARS
Should fatal consequences to the robbers
attend their capture, identification and proof
that they were guilty parties will be sufficient
to secure the payment of the reward offered.
Done at the City of Prescott, the Capital,
the 13th day of August, A.D., 1883

H.M. Van Arman
Acting Governor

Attest:
John S. Furman
Assistant-Secretary
Arizona Territory

In addition to the reward offered by the Territory, Pinal County offered two hundred dollars and Wells, Fargo and Company had their standing reward of three hundred dollars for each robber, though these additional rewards were for arrest and conviction only. This brought the total reward for each robber to one thousand dollars.

Joe Tuttle provided two confessions. Each confession implicated the principals and the accessories. He insisted that he had only fired one shot while Hensley had fired seven times, and described the entire plan of the robbery. They had sent Red Jack, known under the aliases of Jack Averill, Jack Elmer, and Jack Boreman, to Florence to watch the stage office and see when the treasure box appeared to be well filled. He remained there nearly one week and was observed at the stage office every day when the agent was loading the Globe stagecoach. On Friday, when he saw that it required two men to lift the treasure box into the boot, he suddenly concluded that he must go to Riverside on that stagecoach. He sold his horse, explaining that he was going to Riverside to obtain work in the mines.

In the meantime Tuttle and Hensley had established a camp in the mountains near Riverside where they could watch the road and see who was aboard the stagecoach. They were seen Friday afternoon under a large mesquite tree near the road in the large wash near Evan's station. A rifle and shot-gun leaned against a tree and their horses were hitched near by. When the stagecoach passed by this point Jack commenced singing for the purpose of assisting his partners in recognizing him. His presence on the stagecoach was the signal that the treasure box was full.

As soon as the stagecoach passed, the robbers mounted and followed at a distance until twilight came, then they pressed on and were only a few yards behind the stagecoach when the driver pulled up at Evans & LeBlanc's station for supper and a change of horses.

The two robbers rode by the station a short distance, turned out of the road towards the river, and rode along the river bank to avoid being seen at Riverside Station. When they reached the ford a hundred yards above Riverside they crossed the river and rode on a mile and a half to the point they had selected and prepared for the robbery. The branches on the bush, behind which one of them stood, were carefully parted and tied back to give the robber full command of the road without exposing himself to view, and from there they attacked the stagecoach when it came up.

Tuttle and Redfield had their preliminary hearing on Monday the 27th. The defendants were held to answer and remanded to the Sheriff, who lodged them in the county jail. The following Monday morning deputy U. S. Marshal J. W. Evans, accompanied by a posse of seven men, arrived at Florence with a writ of *habeas corpus* for Len G. Redfield. The town's people had been informed that among the posse was a close friend of Len Redfield named Bullis and Len's brother Hank. The writ, issued by Judge Pinney at Tucson, had been based upon affidavits setting forth that the life of Len Redfield was in danger from mob violence.

As soon as Evans arrived he served the writ on Undersheriff Scanland and placed his guards around the jail. Evans had planned to smuggle the prisoner out of town before dawn, but Deputy Scanland asked that Redfield be kept there until seven o'clock a.m. to give him an opportunity to telegraph Sheriff Doran for instructions. Evans agreed to the delay.

District Attorney Jesse Hardesty discovered Evans' guards at the jail and immediately protested against the procedure. Scanland then informed Evans that his guards must be withdrawn, as a deputy U. S. Marshal had no authority to guard a county jail. Evans assented and withdrew his guards. Hardesty then telegraphed Judge Pinney asking him to rescind his order. He also informed the judge that the town was arming and that any attempt to remove Redfield from the jurisdiction of the Sheriff could result in his being lynched. Judge Pinney did not reply.

Once Evans' presence and purpose became known the alarm was sounded and the citizens, aroused to the highest pitch of indignation, assembled. The presence of Len's brother and a friend "armed to the teeth" gave the impression that the posse would, at their first opportunity, overpower Evans and set the murderer free. So, it was finally determined after much debate that Len Redfield would not be permitted to leave the town alive.

Evans attempted to counter the rising bitterness by sending Hank Redfield and Bullis back to Tucson and by announcing that he would summon every citizen in town to assist him in removing Len Redfield from the jail and taking him to Tucson. Upon hearing this

Deputy Sheriff Scanland summoned every able-bodied man as his posse to guard the jail against any unauthorized actions by Evans.

When the citizens arrived guards were stationed around the court house and jail to repel any attack that might be made by deputy Marshal Evan's party. The main body of the citizens' force, which numbered about one hundred, filed into the jail yard where they took Undersheriff Scanland and jailor McKane prisoner and placed them under guard. The Deputy and his assistant were searched for the jail's keys and the key to the outside door was found in McKane's pocket. A search of the Sheriff's office was then made and the key to the inside lock was found.

The jail was opened and ropes were thrown over the braces between the joist. When the men went into Redfield's cell he looked around and calmly said, "Who is the leader of this gang?" Tuttle broke down completely when the men entered his cell and he placed his hands over his face and sobbed, "Let me talk; give me time to talk." Without delay, Tuttle and Redfield were quietly taken out into the corridor and hanged. As the rope was placed around Redfield's neck he remarked, "Well, boys, I guess my time has come." Although strangled they both died without a struggle.

After the men were hanged young Carpenter was bought out of his cell and told to look at his uncle and Tuttle, and take warning by their fate, that he was young and could turn from his course and make a man of himself. He was pale as a ghost when brought from his cell but seemed to recover when assured that he would not be hanged.

The crowd guarded the hanging men until a physician could pronounce them dead, then the committee disbanded and went about their business. An inquest by Judge Thomas soon followed, coroner Schoshusen being absent, and a verdict was found that the two men had been hanged by persons unknown.

The remains of Tuttle were buried just after sundown in the town's cemetery. Evans had telegraphed Hank Redfield at Tucson to inform him of the fate of his brother and to ask for instructions on what disposition should be made of the body. The answer was to send it to Tucson, and on Monday evening the body of Len Redfield was sent in one of Eugene Cabott's wagons.

On September 7th Wells, Fargo and Company paid Sheriff Doran six hundred dollars for the capture of Redfield and Tuttle.

The pursuit of Red Jack Almer and Charles Hensley continued. Red Jack and Hensley first traveled to a spring near King's ranch and then went on to a miner's cabin belonging to Hartzell and Dan Dougherty, which was located in the Rincon mountains thirty-five miles from Redfield's ranch. Hensley gave Dougherty ten dollars to go into Benson and buy ammunition and told him they would return the next day. Dougherty went into Benson and while there told his business.

Sheriff Paul was notified. He took Mr. Davis of Benson and followed Dougherty back to the cabin. There they contacted Dougherty and explained their purpose. Dougherty told them that the boys would be there the next day for the ammunition and fresh horses. One horse, Dougherty explained, was being shoed by an old man who had stopped at the cabin.

The Sheriff and Davis prepared to camp for the night as the old man went out to burn charcoal to heat the shoes, but soon came rushing back howling in fright. He said that Hensley had appeared suddenly and leveled a pistol at him.

Paul and Davis hurried in the direction from which the old man had come and saw Hensley running up a gulch. Although he was about two hundred yards away they fired several pistol shots after him, without effect. Red Jack was further up the gulch lying under a cliff. When Red Jack heard the shots, and saw Hensley running, he got up and ran.

Paul and Davis followed them into the rocks, where the trail was lost. They then returned to the fugitives' camp to inventory the articles captured, which included Hensley's coat, Red Jack's hat with a copy of the reward notice in it, seventy-five Winchester cartridges, an ample supply of provisions, and one horse.

On Monday, September 24th Pete Mathews, a prospector in the Rincon mountains, went down to Pantano and telegraphed Sheriff Paul that he had seen Red Jack and Hensley in camp the day previous in a canyon a mile and a half from Page's ranch. The lawmen struck the camp at first light on Tuesday and drove the men out of their blankets. The fugitives managed to flee a second time, but again were forced to abandon all their provisions and equipment. Red Jack and Hensley headed for a Mexican ranch eighteen miles above Redfield's, with Sheriff Paul and J. P Gabriel close on their trail.

On Tuesday, October 2nd George Martin, Wells, Fargo and Company's agent in Tucson, received news of the fugitives, immediately notified Sheriff Paul, and hired a locomotive to carry the posse to Willcox. The Sheriff took with him deputy Alfredo Carrillo, T. D. Casanega and George McClarty. They went first to Hooker's ranch, twenty-two miles northwest of Willcox, and got there about midnight. Paul sent Carrillo to Camp Grant the next morning with instructions to meet him at the Percy brother's ranch ten miles northwest of Willcox. At Percy's Paul got information that led him to believe the fugitives would come there. There were two strings of wagons near Percy's house – four wagons in each train positioned about thirty feet apart. The fugitives were to get provisions from the tailboard of one wagon.

Paul deputized Jim Percy to hide under one wagon with him and John McCluskey and John Laird to hide under another, creating a crossfire. It was a stormy night, a little after nine o'clock, when Red Jack and Hensley approached the tail-board and Sheriff Paul called for them to stop.

Both men ran while shooting toward the sound of Paul's voice, and the whole posse fired a volley at their flashes. They heard the men fall, but when shooting by the fugitives continued the posse returned fire. Paul called a cease fire as soon as he was certain the men were mortally wounded. Just then Laird was shot in the calf of the right leg, the bullet passing through the boot-leg making a wound two inches long. After about an hour without a shot being fired McCluskey and Otto Moore went around to where they had left their horses tied to the telegraph poles. As they got their horses they heard one of the men fleeing.

Paul sent for Carrillo, Casanega and McClarty, who got into camp about two o'clock a.m. At daylight they recovered Red Jack's body, an empty pistol by his head. Red Jack had first fallen within twenty feet of the wagon but had crawled another twenty yards to where Hensley was lying. Red Jack had received a charge of buck-shot in the pit of his stomach from McCluskey's shotgun, and had a rifle ball through the right cheek-bone just under the eye. The men could hear him groaning for five hours before he fell silent, but it was too dangerous to approach him in the darkness. When searched he had not a cent in his pockets.

Hensley left behind his .44 Winchester model 1873 because the cock had been shot off in the fight, but took Jack's rifle. Hensley had crawled four hundred yards on his hands and knees to where he left his horse. He then followed the telegraph poles toward Willcox three miles and turned into the mountains; struck into a canyon and went over a ridge; then down on the other side into another canyon, right down in the bed, and followed it about three-quarters of a mile.

Paul kept a lookout ahead while the men trailed. The sheriff was ahead on the right hand side of the canyon when he saw Hensley's horse, bridled and saddled, standing between the posse and a pile of rocks. Paul called to Carrillo, McClarty, Otto Moore and a vaquero named Jimmie, who were on the left hand side, to circle around. Casanega and McCluskey stayed with the Sheriff as he focused on the rock pile and called to Hensley to surrender.

The first they knew of Hensley's whereabouts was his shot from about sixty yards distant, where he had hidden behind a scrub oak. He was down on the right side of the gulch laying on his belly and shooting right up the hill toward Paul, and all that could be seen was the smoke of his gun. The boys on the other side could see him plainly, however, and the shooting became general and continued until Carrillo called out, "Don't shoot, he's deader'n hades."

Paul yelled out a warning to Carrillo, "Don't go near him, he might shoot you."

Carrillo charged the fugitive and pried Red Jack's rifle from Hensley's hands. He then examined the body. Hensley was lying on his belly and, when rolled over, was "perfectly white, there being no blood left in him." Carrillo said that if they had not found Hensley, he would have died of his wounds in a short time. Hensley had been shot right in the center of the breast and in the left groin there was a wound from the night before, clotted with blood.

Paul estimated that the fugitives had fired more than thirty shots during the wagon train battle and Hensley had emptied Red Jack's sixteen-shot Winchester rifle in the canyon fight. When searched Hensley had only fifty-five cents in his pockets.

Judge Nichols sent out a wagon and brought both bodies to Willcox for an inquest. The judge reported that the two men had been riddled with bullets.

Frank Carpenter, last living member of the gang, apparently took the advice of the vigilantes too seriously. On November 22, 1883 the *Gazette* reported on Carpenter"'s death:

> Frank Carpenter, who was recently admitted to bail in Florence on the charge of being an accessory to the Riverside stagecoach robbery, and has been living on his ranch some twenty miles from Benson, died on Tuesday last from nervousness and fear. The hanging of Redfield and Tuttle has so worked on him that he imagined every person he met was going to hang him, which so affected his mind that he died of fright.

With the principals and accessories dead all that remained was to collect the reward. Sheriff Paul went into Florence in August 1884 and presented his claim for six hundred dollars for the capture of Red Jack and Hensley. The Board of Supervisors paid accordingly.

December 31, 1883

The northbound stagecoach leaving Florence for Globe on Monday was stopped by a highwayman between Florence and Little Cottonwood – about four miles from the latter place. He gave the usual command to the driver to throw out the express box, which was done, and then ordered the driver to turn back. The passengers were not molested.

The highwayman was described as five feet eight inches in height, rather sparely built, with short brownish chin whiskers and mustache, sallow complexion, angular features, and he wore a dark suit of clothes and a hat with a broad brim. He was not masked, but nevertheless the robber was not identified.

January 1, 1884

On Tuesday evening at about 5 o'clock p.m. the Globe-bound stagecoach was held up by an unmasked man when twelve miles from Florence. The robber took Wells, Fargo and Company's box, which contained less than one hundred dollars. There were no passengers, nor was there a messenger aboard to guard so small a treasure.

The robber was never identified.

November 14, 1884

Friday morning at about daybreak, at a point one mile east of the tollgate on Pinal mountain and about eleven miles from Globe, the incoming stagecoach from Florence was held up by three men. Wells, Fargo and Company's treasure box was rifled.

The driver, Ed Thornton, was ordered to halt and in the uncertain light before dawn discovered two men covering him with their weapons, one was armed with a revolver while the other covered him with a rifle, and a third man stood in front of the horses. They ordered him to throw off the box, which he did with some difficulty as it was covered up with express goods and mail sacks. After determining that Thornton had no money on his person they permitted him to drive on.

When the stagecoach reached Globe, Thornton reported that the two armed robbers were Mexicans, but had not been able to get a good look at the third man. Sheriff Pascoe and J. J. Vosburgh, the express agent, started for the scene of the robbery. On their return that evening Sheriff Pascoe said that the express box was found near the scene of the robbery, entirely empty, and intimated that he had obtained a slight clue - three men of forbidding appearance armed with guns and revolvers were seen on the streets of Globe on Thursday, and it was thought these were the robbers.

Wells, Fargo and Company's agent said that the highwaymen had made a "water haul," as the treasure box contained no money. With nothing of value taken, there was no motivation to pursue the robbers.

February 2, 1885

It was about 7:30 in the evening when stagecoach driver Charlie Miller reached the rocky point east of Pinal, and just as he reached the top of the hill a man stepped out from behind a clump of bushes and ordered him to halt. Thinking it was a joke of some of the freighters who were camped only a short distance away, he paid no attention to the order. The robber, seeing this, ordered him to halt again and pointed his gun at him.

Miller saw his mistake and, being unarmed and also seeing that there was no other salvation for him, stopped the stagecoach. The robber ordered the driver to throw out the box and dismount, and then ordered two passengers to get out and throw up their hands. As soon as these preliminaries were accomplished the robber instructed one of the passengers to get up on the driver's seat and hold the team with one hand while raising the other.

The robber ordered Miller to break open the box. Miller requested permission to get an old hatchet that he had in the boot, and permission was granted. Miller proceeded to demolish the box, though with great difficulty.

Another bandit, who had previously kept himself concealed behind some bushes, threw the driver a flour sack and ordered him to fill it with the contents of the box. The first highwayman then ordered the passengers to board and the driver to turn the stagecoach around and proceed in the direction from whence he came.

Miller drove down the road a short distance, then waited a few minutes before turning around and driving into the City of Pinal, arriving there about 9 o'clock p.m.

George A. Brown, express agent in Globe, said that there was one package in the box containing four hundred dollars in gold and several other packages. The robbers did not try to go through the passengers nor the mails, but seemed contented with what they got from the express box.

There was a standing reward of eight hundred dollars for the arrest and conviction of each robber – three hundred dollars offered by Wells, Fargo and Company, three hundred dollars offered by the county, and two hundred dollars from the U. S. government for the conviction of parties delaying or molesting the United States mails.

The robbers were not captured.

February 23, 1885

On Monday the stagecoach, driven by Charles Miller, with four San Francisco drummers including George Borrdaile, M. W. Griffin, L. Siebenhauer, and Mr. Elscacer, left Florence for Pinal and Silver King. Everything went well until they reached the spot about one and a half miles east of Pinal, where the stagecoach was taken-in on the 2nd, when suddenly two masked men stepped out from behind some bushes and ordered the driver to halt, at the same time drawing a "bead" on him and the passengers with their arms.

The robbers ordered him to throw out Wells, Fargo's treasure box, to come down and break it open. They ordered the passengers out and required them to hold up their hands while Miller took a rock and broke open the box. The robbers threw Miller a sack and told him to fill it from the contents of the express box.

They watched as he filled the sack and, seeing that the treasure box did not contain much of value, they inquired if he had anything else of value on board. He replied, "nothing but mail," whereupon they ordered him to throw out the sacks and they cut them open. Finding nothing in this to suit their fancy and, seeing they would get nothing for their trouble unless they went through the passengers, they ordered the drummers to unload their pockets, which amounted to about one hundred forty dollars, three gold watches, one silver watch, and several pocketbooks. After the collection was made they ordered the passengers to board and the driver to turn around and drive back about a mile, when he might turn again and drive into Pinal. The tired, wet and broken crew arrived in Pinal about 9 o'clock in the evening and gave the alarm, and also telephoned Silver King.

Henry Jarrard and Andrew Dorsey, after the robbery of February 2nd, had spent money pretty freely and had no visible means of making any such amounts as they were throwing away, which raised suspicions among the officers. Posses from both Pinal and Silver King went toward the old "Pike" cabin near the foot of King Hill, where Dorsey and Jarrard lived. Deputy Sheriff William Willey and Thomas Buchanan of Pinal reached the cabin first at about half past 9 o'clock, knocked at the door, and found the two men in bed. They admitted Willey and Buchanan, who took a hurried glance at the room and occupants, and asked if they had heard anyone pass or if the stage-coach had gone by. Jarrard answered that they had heard several people pass but did not know whether the stagecoach had passed. Willey then borrowed a candle and went out and examined the road for tracks. At that time the plunder was on a shelf in plain view and would have been discovered by the officers had they not been in such haste. Willey returned the candle to Jarrard and he and Buchanan mounted their horses and started on the road toward Silver King. As soon as they left, Dorsey and Jarrard hid the treasure inside the cabin.

Willey and Buchanan had gone only a short distance when they met Jeff Bramlett and Jack McCoy, who were going to Pinal at the request of Judge Whiteside to inform Deputy Sheriff P. Boscha of the robbery. Willey and Buchanan accompanied the pair to Pinal.

Boscha persuaded McCoy to get his team out of Lewis' stable and take him up to the "Pike" cabin. They were accompanied by Bramlett and, upon their arrival, arrested Jarrard and Dorsey on sus-picion and took them, with Jarrard's wife, to Silver King. They locked the cabin door securely behind them. Dorsey and Jarrard were kept separate at Silver King until morning. They were independent and impudent and no amount of "working" could get them to incriminate themselves.

In the morning Boscha and Bramlett went back to the cabin and began to dig and rummage around for evidence. Boscha struck a soft place in the ground under the bed and at a depth of about a foot unearthed a box containing a portion of the plunder. Bramlett then found two empty pocket-books in a rat-hole under the stove, but they were unable to discover the rest of the spoils.

Boscha went to Silver King, returned with Dorsey, and con-fronted him with the evidence of his guilt. Dorsey confessed, but did not know where the remainder of the plunder was hidden. Conse-quently, Boscha had to go after Jarrard and, finding that the "jig was up," told where the rest of the property was cached. All the plunder that was missing was eighty-five dollars, and this was found in a pocket-book hidden in the back part of the stove.

The prisoners had a preliminary examination before Judge Whiteside at Silver King on Tuesday and he held each on two thousand dollars bail to await the action of the Grand Jury. They could not furnish the bonds and were lodged in jail.

In early March deputy U. S. Marshal H. D. Underwood of Tucson went to Pinal to gather additional evidence in preparation for the trial. He went through the U. S. mail which had been recovered and also served several subpoenas on witnesses to appear before the U. S. Grand Jury on Monday, March 9th. He took the empty mail sack, which the robbers had cut open, and detained the four passengers in Tucson pending the hearing.

In 1885 a Territorial law had been passed by which the crime of highway robbery could proceed through information as well as indictment, and Dorsey and Jarrard were brought to trial on information. They were convicted and on May 9th each man was sentenced to eleven years to be served at the territorial penitentiary near Yuma.

Andrew J. Dorsey was registered as prisoner № 293 on May 11th. Upon his arrival he was described as nineteen years old, five feet ten inches in height with brown eyes and black hair, and could read and write. He listed his father as next of kin. Dorsey's mother was Mexican and Dorsey, who looked Mexican and had changed his first name from Refugio to Andrew as a child, learned to speak Spanish fluently.

Henry Jarrard was registered as prisoner № 294 on May 11th. Upon his arrival he was described as twenty-five years old, five feet nine inches in height, with blue eyes and light hair, and was able to read and write. He had been married at Pinal to a fifteen year old girl only eight months previous to his arrest, and she was listed as his next of kin.

Dorsey's father filed a petition proposing that a trial upon an information, rather than by indictment, was illegal. He succeeded in obtaining his son's and Henry Jarrard's release on a writ of *habeas corpus*, issued by the Territorial Supreme Court on March 26, 1887.

Dorsey and Jarrard were brought from Yuma to Florence on April 14, 1887 to appear before Judge Levi Ruggles, who discharged them in accordance with the supreme court's decision. Papers were issued at once for the re-arrest of the two stagecoach robbers but immediately after the discharge, and before it was possible to serve him, Dorsey walked out of the back door of the court house and found a saddled horse provided by sympathizing friends. Dorsey escaped to Mexico where he lived until his re-arrest in 1891.

Henry Jarrard was re-arrested, tried, convicted and sentenced to one year eight months at the Territorial prison. He arrived at the prison on October 15, 1887 and was registered as prisoner Nº 471. On September 17, 1888, only eleven months later, he was pardoned by Governor Zulick.

The search for Dorsey continued for nearly five years. Great efforts had been made to intercept him in the United States, as it was believed he was responsible for a series of stagecoach robberies. However, by the time Dorsey was retried on the 1885 robbery charge the real road agent in those subsequent robberies – Santiago "Geronimo" Moreno – had been killed and the robberies correctly attributed to him.

Dorsey was located at Santo Domingo, one hundred miles west of Tucson. A requisition was issued by the governor of Arizona; and, Marshal Paul went to Mexico and caused Dorsey's arrest. Dorsey was taken to Nogales where he claimed citizenship in Mexico and insisted that his name was R. A. Dorsey and not A. J. Dorsey, as listed on the requisition. The governor of Sonora ordered Dorsey to Hermosillo to investigate the matter and to await proof of nationality and identity from the United States, which Marshal Paul secured and delivered.

Finally a telegram was received by Governor Irwin stating that Dorsey would be given up to United States' authorities forthwith. Once again Marshal Paul returned to Sonora, got his prisoner, and delivered him to the jail in Florence. In May 1892 Dorsey was brought to trial in the second judicial district on the 1885 stagecoach robbery charge.

On the last day of the month the case was dismissed.

August 7, 1885

Jesus Lujan was driving the stagecoach from Maricopa to Phoenix and, when about seven miles east of Maricopa at about 8:30 a.m., two men armed with guns arose from the side of the road and ordered him to "stop right there!" He complied and a demand for Wells, Fargo and Company's treasure box immediately followed. B. Heyman, a passenger who was riding on top, threw out the box. Four passengers, including B. Heyman of Tucson; A. L. Brown, a commercial traveler; a brother of Dr. L. Stearn; and a Mexican, were ordered to exit the coach and were covered by the gun of one robber.

A. L. Brown was detailed to unhitch the leaders and remove their harness while the Mexican was given a hammer to break open the box. This was quickly accomplished and the highwayman who seemed to be directing the job took the contents and emptied it into a flour sack, which he had with him. Two of the coach horses, valued at two hundred fifty dollars, were tied to a tree near by.

The robber stated that as the treasure box did not appear to contain any great amount of money he would need some silver from the passengers. Heyman contributed two and a half dollars, Brown four dollars, and the other two in about the same proportions. There were several valuable watches among the passengers but the highwaymen did not see fit to take them. When Stearn made his contribution he pulled out a pocket-book and, taking some silver therefrom, handed the amount over and the robber who was holding the gun told his companion to make him give up the pocket-book, but the latter replied: "No; we don't want it." The passengers were then allowed to get into the coach again.

The robbers mounted the horses they had taken from the stagecoach team and ordered the coach to move on, and then rode off in an easterly direction. There was one short heavy set and one tall man engaged in the robbery. The former did all the talking until after the job was performed, when the latter excused himself to the passengers for not having any champagne with which to entertain them.

The robbery was committed in Pinal County so A. Leonard Meyer notified the officers there of the crime as soon as the stagecoach arrived in Phoenix. Pinal County officers went in pursuit, but the robbers were not captured. These same robbers would stop and rob two stagecoaches in Maricopa County on August 18, 1885 and would be captured. The robbers' names were John Bennett and Tom Collister, and their accomplice was named John Pennington.

November 20, 1885

Robert Joyce drove the stage between Pinal and Florence. On Friday morning he prepared the stagecoach at Pinal and left at quarter to seven a.m. One and a half miles out on the Florence road was a reef of rocks which the stagecoach reached about twenty minutes after leaving town.

Joyce first heard a mumbling noise and immediately afterwards saw a masked man pointing a double-barreled shotgun at him. The man then clearly said, "Halt!" The robber was partly hidden behind the reef of rocks with only the upper half of his body visible, his mask appeared to be made of mosquito netting. The robber inquired if there were passengers or arms on board, but there were neither. He then demanded that the bullion be thrown down and Joyce threw out two Silver King bricks totaling three thousand five hundred ounces. There was U. S. mail on board but the robber did not ask about it.

Joyce then told the robber that he would have to go back to Pinal, but the robber ordered him to continue to the next house along the road threatening, "or you will be hurt." Joyce drove to the next house before turning around and returning to Pinal, arriving at half past eight a.m. He reported that he recognized the robber's voice, and had heard it many times, but could not identify the man.

Suspicion soon focused on William Taylor and circumstantial evidence suggested that James Slears had assisted in the robbery. Slears was seen saddling two horses just before the stagecoach left town and he did not return to town until after noon. Slears and Taylor shared a room with D. O. McDowell at Hunt's old saloon. McDowell, when questioned, said that both Slears and Taylor were prospectors who sometimes went out together, but usually went alone and at different times. Slears owned a double-barreled shotgun which he leaned against the head of his bed. McDowell was not sure if the shotgun had been in the room on Friday morning but said it was gone after that. Slears was arrested on Friday evening at Silver King on suspicion of being involved in the robbery, but by Saturday had escaped.

On Sunday at about 2 o'clock a.m. Taylor came to his room, gathered his gear, then woke McDowell to give him the key and say that he was going away. Taylor asked about Slears and was surprised to learn that he had been arrested. Taylor thrust his hand into his right coat pocket, as if he had a pistol there, and slowly backed out of the room. As he left he said he would see Slears, but William Taylor was not seen or heard of again in the Territory.

The bullion was recovered on Sunday under strange circumstances. Henry Pruett claimed that, being a strong believer in Christianity, he had a vision on Saturday night during which Christ told him where to find the bullion and on Sunday morning went directly to the spot. He found the bars thrown into a large bush by the side of the trail about one mile from the road.

On Wednesday the 25th at about eight o'clock p.m. Slears knocked on Sam Neighbors' door and asked him to go into town to buy him a bottle of gin. Slears made a point of telling Neighbors that he had not seen Taylor since the robbery, but said that he had been promised an interest in the bullion since Taylor had his rope. He also asked Neighbors to help recover his shotgun, which had been hidden in the rocks near the Lost Prize Mine. He warned Neighbors that if he recovered the shotgun to be careful as it was loaded, though he did not know the nature of the load in the shells.

Neighbors went to town, bought the gin, and returned directly home even though he sensed that he was being followed. He found that Slears had moved twenty-five yards from the house and was hiding behind a large pile of rocks. Slears asked Neighbors to go out on the road and bring in a friend who was waiting for him, and Neighbors agreed. A short distance down the road Neighbors encountered lawmen P. Boscha, L. K. Drais, and J. Thacker, who ordered him back to his house.

As soon as Slears saw the lawmen approaching he ran. Boscha ordered him to stop and fired a warning shot, but Slears continued to run and disappeared into the darkness. The fugitive fled directly to C. H. Wheelers' ranch on Queen Creek where he stole a horse and bridle to expedite his escape. Boscha and Preston found his track the next morning and started in pursuit.

J. McCoy, a livery keeper at Silver King, was told that the shotgun was hidden at the Lost Prize Mine, one mile northwest of Silver King. McCoy went to the mine and found the gun partly hidden under rocks seventy-five yards from the shaft. He delivered the gun to the officers.

Slears was arrested on Friday the 27th and brought before the justice court on Sunday. He pled not guilty to the highway robbery charge and was ordered held for the grand jury, but waived examination on the charge of grand larceny for stealing the horse and bridle. Slears was sentenced to four years at the Territorial Prison for grand larceny.

Slears was never indicted for stagecoach robbery. He arrived at the Territorial Prison on April 26, 1886 and registered as prisoner N°372. Upon his arrival he was described as aged thirty-four, five feet ten inches in height with dark hair and blue eyes. He could read and write. He disclosed no living relatives. Slears served his entire sentence, less good time, and was discharged on April 23, 1889.

November 28, 1885

The driver of the Riverside stagecoach brought in an empty mail sack on Saturday night.The driver said the coach was stopped by a lone highwayman between Willow Springs and Manlyville, small stations near the San Pedro River. The mail was demanded and the pouch was promptly handed out. The strap that fastened the pouch was cut and the robber dumped the mail, then handed the sack to the driver and told him to go on. The road agent was already rifling the letters before the driver could proceed.

The road agent made a "water haul," as the Riverside mail usually consisted of no more than a dozen way letters coming by way of Florence, and contained little of value.

The robber was never identified.

December 13, 1885

The stagecoach from Florence to Pinal was robbed Sunday morning at Cane Springs and the mail rifled. The registered pouch was not molested.

The robber was never identified.

January 23, 1886

The Pinal stagecoach was taken-in on a Saturday night and nothing of consequence was stolen. Two passengers were aboard but they were not molested.

The robbers were never identified.

October 2, 1888

The down stagecoach, which left Florence a little behind time on Tuesday, was held up at the lower end of the dry lake about five miles from Casa Grande. George Cumins was driving and carried no passengers.

As he was crossing the dry lake, about half past three o'clock, a big cloud of dust ahead warned him of the approach of some travelers, but as teams and horsemen were often met upon the road, this fact did not excite the least curiosity. He closed his eyes to keep out the dust, letting his team proceed slowly, until suddenly he was commanded to stop in broken English.

Cumins opened his eyes to look down the barrel of a pistol held closely to his head by a Mexican on horseback at the side of the stagecoach. Another Mexican stood guard in the road ahead of the team. The fellow at his side then demanded money and, after some delay and threatening gestures with the pistol, the driver tossed out the express company's treasure box, which contained very little money. The robber then demanded a key to the box, and could not understand why the driver did not possess it.

The robber more fiercely demanded money, so the driver gave him a dollar – all he had with him. This still did not satisfy the robber and not until Cumins surrendered the registered mail pouch from Globe was the robber satisfied.

He took the mail sack himself and gave the express box to the man who had been blocking the horses, and then told the driver to go on. The two men left in the direction of Sacaton.

Wells, Fargo and Company's agent Marshall and driver Cumins cut the trail near the scene of the robbery and easily followed it directly to the nearest point of the mountains. There they found the broken treasure box and mutilated mail pouch, with letters scattered about, nearly all of them opened. They gathered the mail and took it back to town.

Both robbers were Mexicans. One was dark complexioned about 25 years old and the other a boy of only twenty with light complexion and a smooth face. Neither wore any disguise. It was suggested that they were novices in the business, and might have acted on an impulse in "jumping" the stagecoach.

The trail led directly to the Montezuma ranch, fourteen miles west of Florence on the Gila River, where it was obliterated by the tracks of a large of herd cattle in that vicinity. Sheriff Fryer joined the pursuit, which had gained on the robbers as they headed toward Tempe, but the robbers eluded capture.

This was the first in a series of ten stagecoach robberies by the same twenty-five year old road agent later identified as Santiago "Geronimo" Moreno. He obtained a new partner, Guadalupe Redondo, for his subsequent robberies and, by June 2, 1891 when they committed their last stagecoach robbery in Cochise County, they had become "old hands at the business."

November 22, 1888

The down stagecoach to Casa Grande was held up by two Mexicans on Thursday afternoon at the dry lake at the same point it was robbed on October 2nd. They took a watch from the driver, Nelson Caplett, and also some cash and checks from A. S. Donau, the representative of L. Zekendorf & Co. of Tucson, the express box, and four sacks of mail. The men were not disguised and spoke fair English.

As soon as the stagecoach reached Casa Grande the driver telegraphed back to Florence and Undersheriff Hinson Thomas, in the absence of Sheriff Fryer, deputized George R. Morse and W. P. Bamrick and provided them with funds to hire several Indian trailers. They proceeded to search for the robbers.

A party of four possemen also left Casa Grande and the next day two of them returned with the empty mail sacks and express box, which they found half a mile from the scene of the robbery. The road agents had taken all the letters with them.

Morse and Bamrick followed the two robbers but lost their trail near a river crossing, where other tracks obliterated it. It rained on Saturday, which made further search useless, so they returned on Sunday night with information from the Indians that the robbers had taken refuge in the black mountains across from Sacaton on the Gila River.

J. H. Hull collected a purse to finance another search and on Monday morning a posse consisting of L. K. Drais, W. P. Bamrick, W. E. Miller, John Ruckelshausen, C. L. Scribner, John W. Rannells and Harry Williams started for Sacaton to search the mountains. They took all necessary accouterments for the expedition, obtained horses at the reservation, and hired Indian guides. They visited all the caves and places of concealment in the mountains, but failed to find any trace of the robbers, so they returned to town Wednesday morning.

This was the third in a series of ten stagecoach robberies by the same man. His last stagecoach robbery occurred on June 2, 1891 in Cochise County.

November 23, 1888

On Friday, November 23rd J. M. Hurley of San Bernardino, California, who had been visiting Florence to look after his property interests along the Florence Canal, started for Casa Grande in his buggy at about eleven o'clock. He was followed a little later by Mr. E. A. Saxe who drove one of his old stagecoaches, and still later the regular stagecoach left Florence for Casa Grande carrying the mail and express, but no passengers.

Upon reaching Oneida station, an abandoned ruin where the overland road crosses the present Casa Grande road about two miles south of the Halfway House, Hurley was stopped by a lone highwayman and relieved of fifty dollars in currency. The lone highwayman, an American about five feet nine inches tall wearing black pants, a vest and blue shirt, wore a mask with eye holes cut from an old blanket. He covered Hurley's head with a piece of blanket and kept him prisoner until his job was completed. Hurley talked with the man trying to note peculiarities in his voice and speech.

E. A. Saxe soon came along, was stopped, hooded and held prisoner, but he was not robbed. The stagecoach drove up at noon, was also halted, and the driver ordered to throw out the mail sacks and express box. These were opened by the highwayman and the money taken out. He then ordered Hurley to gather up the mutilated letters, return them to the sacks, throw them into the coach, and then ordered the stagecoach to proceed as he disappeared into the brush.

The stagecoach hurried into Casa Grande, where the driver notified the authorities. Undersheriff Thomas started J. P. Gabriel and J. D. Thomas from Florence to the scene of the robbery with instructions to make a capture, if possible. The rain of the previous night had, however, obliterated the trail.

Later that night a stranger walked into Casa Grande and remained there all night. He had been an object of suspicion a few days earlier when he had come up from Casa Grande on the stagecoach way-billed as Henry Brown. He got out at the stage office, took his roll of blankets, and disappeared. On Thursday evening he visited Sam Bostic's barber shop and was shaved, after which no one saw him again until he walked into Casa Grande on Friday evening. He was pointed out to Saxe, who at once positively identified him as the robber by virtue of the clothes he wore.

The stranger was arrested and in one pocket was found thirty five dollars in gold and silver; in the lining of his hat a number of greenbacks were discovered; and in the pocket of his vest a number of gold coins were found. He gave his name as Henry Miller, said that he had walked the entire distance from Florence to Casa Grande, and denied being the Henry Brown who came up Wednesday.

At Miller's examination Monday morning both Saxe and Hurley fully identified him as the guilty party, and Justice Marshall held him to answer before the grand jury. He arrived at the county jail on Monday night in the custody of J. P. Gabriel, A. Price, and D. W. Cummins.

On November 30th Henry Miller, alias Henry Brown, made a full confession of the robbery to Judge C. M. Marshall, the Judge who had held him to answer. Miller explained that he was out of money and could find no work. It was then that he conceived the idea of robbing the stagecoach, "inspired by the success of the California and other Arizona men of that stamp." He told the judge where he had concealed his gun and masks.

Constable Cummins of Casa Grande made a search at the point where Miller said he had hidden his gun, and under some bushes three hundred yards from the scene of the robbery he found the shot gun, a good double-barreled muzzle loader, and nine masks as the robber evidently had anticipated a stagecoach filled with passengers.

Henry Miller pled guilty and was sentenced to twelve years imprisonment. Miller was delivered to the penitentiary at Yuma on December 14th. The prison record reflects that Miller, prisoner N⁰ 556, was thirty-five years old, could read and write, had blue eyes and a light complexion, and had a noticeable limp in his right leg. He said he had a wife in Texas. He was put in charge of the broom factory, where he served his time as a model prisoner until he was pardoned by acting Governor Murphy on January 20, 1891. But, Miller's prison experience had not yet come to an end.

Miller was re-arrested in Los Angeles, California and returned to Arizona in April 1891 to be tried on the federal charge of "robbing the U. S. Mails." Miller's second trial was before Judge Kibby at Florence, and Miller was convicted and sentenced to ten years imprisonment at San Quentin. On June 11, 1891 U. S. Marshal Robert Paul went to Casa Grande to convey the prisoner to his new home, but Miller had escaped. Indian trailers succeeded in finding and recapturing Miller at the Gila River between Florence and the Gila Road. U. S. Marshal Robert Paul took Miller back to the rail depot at Casa Grande and then escorted him to San Quentin prison.

January 1, 1889

Tuesday afternoon at 4 o'clock the stagecoach from Florence to Globe, driven by Sam Childs, was halted twelve miles from the former city by a road agent armed with a Winchester, who commanded the driver to throw out Wells Fargo and Company's box. There were four passengers on the stagecoach, one of whom was District Attorney Graves of Gila county, who had four hundred dollars in his pockets. However, the robber did not molest the passengers. After the box had been tossed down the highwayman ordered Childs to turn the stagecoach around and drive back toward Florence.

As soon as news of the robbery reached town Undersheriff Scanland summoned a posse, composed of express messenger Banks, Charlie Decker, Billy Kellogg and the editor of the *Enterprise*. The posse arrived at the scene of the robbery shortly after daylight Wednesday morning. Evidence showed that the robber had taken a large rock and mashed the box into smithereens and then appropriated the contents, consisting of forty dollars in silver, some jewelry, and a box of fine cigars.

The posse took the robber's trail and followed him as far as the Swiss Boys' ranch, near the Owl Heads, but were unable to obtain fresh horses or feed and so were forced to turn back.

The robber struck straight across country and carefully avoided all ranches and people. He evidently knew the country well and had selected his route before committing the robbery.

The robber was never identified.

July 31, 1889

J. B. McNeil of Florence gave a package of money containing four hundred fifty-seven dollars to E. H. Williams, driver of the stagecoach between DeNoon and Silver King. Williams, upon his arrival at his destination, reported that he had been robbed between Pinal and the Silver King. His story, however, was not supported by the facts and he was arrested. Upon preliminary examination he was discharged for lack of evidence.

On August 14th J. B. McNeil received a note from Felix LeBlanc of Pinal intimating that, for a proper consideration, a strong clue to the perpetrator of the crime and probable whereabouts of the money could be had. George Evans was sent to Pinal to unravel the mystery. He spoke with LeBlanc, who revealed that Williams had approached a man at DeNoon and offered to divide the spoils if that man would "hold up" the stagecoach, but the party refused. LeBlanc demanded one-half of the sum recovered, which it was agreed would be paid. LeBlanc then revealed that the person who Williams had approached was H. B. Gilkey.

Gilkey gave Evans all the information he had on the matter. Evans approached Williams "... and taxed him with taking the money, and by adroit hints made him believe that he [Evans] knew more about the dark transaction than he really did." Williams, at first, assumed a defiant attitude but finally weakened and, upon a promise of being given an opportunity to escape, told Evans that the money was hidden at Silver King. Williams asked Evans to get his buggy so that they could drive to the stable at the Silver King, where a search of the manger uncovered the plunder. Only twenty dollars had been spent by Williams.

Upon his return to Florence Evans spoke with the District Attorney, who issued warrants for Williams as a principal and for LeBlanc as an accessory after-the-fact. J. P. Gabriel was sent after Williams and arrested him on Thursday the 15th at Kellogg's station, thirty-five miles from Pinal on the road to Phoenix. Williams was brought to Florence and placed in the county jail. Meanwhile, Deputy Boscha went to Pinal, arrested LeBlanc and also brought in Gilkey as a witness.

At the preliminary hearing on Monday, August 19th the case was laid out and the court discharged LeBlanc, but held Gilkey and Williams to appear before the Grand Jury. Gilkey was soon released on a writ of *habeas corpus*, as there was no charge against him.

E. H. Williams was indicted on a charge of grand larceny, tried, convicted, and sentenced to one year in prison. He was registered as prisoner N[o] 609 at the Territorial Prison on October 17, 1889. Williams, a dark complected German, was thirty-four years of age, five feet seven inches in height with brown eyes and dark hair. He could read and write, but had no particular job skills.

Governor Wolfey granted Williams a pardon at the time his sentence expired – August 15, 1890 – so that his rights of citizenship would be restored.

October 2, 1889

Wednesday's down stagecoach from Florence was held up by two Mexicans six miles north of Casa Grande, and all the mail and express matter was taken. Nelson Caplett, the driver, said he had traveled beyond the dry lake and saw in the distance two horsemen coming toward the road at right angles from the left, or the southeast direction. He intuitively concluded that he was in for trouble, but there was no escape and he kept on his course, the two men reaching the road just as he drove up. The older Mexican aimed his rifle and the younger one held his revolver on Caplett, who told them not to shoot as he was unarmed. When he raised his hands the older man lowered his rifle, but the young Mexican kept him covered with his pistol. Neither robber was masked. The younger outlaw used all the vile language at his command in abusing the driver and threatened him with dire vengeance if he dared to inform authorities. Caplett said that the younger man would have killed him if the older man had not intervened.

The robbers took out the mail sacks and express box and thoroughly searched the stagecoach for valuables, not forgetting to go through the driver's pockets which experience had taught him to keep empty. They also demanded something with which to break open the express box and were given an extra king-bolt, which seemed to satisfy their demands.

They cut the traces before they rode off to the northwest, and shortly after they disappeared over the ridge surrounding the dry lake Caplett heard their blows in breaking open the box. Caplett got down and lashed the single trees to the double-tree where the outside traces had been cut, and in this condition he made Casa Grande in about twenty minutes.

It was not known how much money was taken. There was only one package from Pinal but it was not known what the through-pouch from Globe contained. The express box was not a bonanza, but several packages of merchandise were stolen along with about five hundred dollars in currency.

The U. S. government had a standing reward of one thousand dollars for each mail robber and Wells, Fargo and Company had a standing reward of three hundred dollars each for express robbers, while the territory also offered a reward for the arrest and conviction of the robbers.

Deputy Sheriff Hickey and J. C. Loss at once made ready and returned with Caplett to the scene of the robbery. They followed the trail and found the empty box and, further on at the same point where the pouches were found on a previous occasion, they found the mail sacks ripped open and empty. From this point the trail went in the direction of Walker's butte. The robbers did not try to masque or obscure their trail and seemed confident that the lawmen could not catch them.

The robbers were well known at Casa Grande and at Florence because of the repeated robberies in the dry lake area. The officers at Casa Grande telegraphed officers at Tempe, where the robbers were thought to have relatives living, to look out for their arrival.

This was fifth in a series of ten stagecoach robberies by "Geronimo" and Guadalupe Redondo, the last being committed on June 2, 1891 in Cochise County.

February 6, 1890

The down stagecoach from Florence to Casa Grande, driven by George Cumins, was held up on Thursday morning by a Mexican between the McLellan wash near Mayhew's station and the Casa Grande ruins. The robber was masked and mittened in black and armed with a Winchester. The Wells, Fargo and Company's express box was demanded, broken open on the spot, and searched. The robber laid down his rifle to receive the box from the driver, which would have given passenger Hurley and the driver an opportunity to get the drop on him, but neither man was armed. After securing the treasure the robber returned the broken box to the boot, picked up his gun, and disappeared into the brush. Neither Dr. Hurley nor driver Cumins were molested.

The box contained little of value, but the manner of the robbery raised speculation that the man was "green at the business" as he failed to notice forty dollars in the box before returning it to the stagecoach boot and, as he examined the box, laid aside his Winchester.

His thorough disguise made identification impossible unless caught while fleeing. Deputy Sheriff Price went in pursuit but was unable to overtake the road agent.

March 20, 1890

The down stagecoach from Florence to Casa Grande, driven by George Cumins, was held up by two Mexicans on Thursday morning at 10 o'clock below the dry lake. One of the robbers was masked but the other was bare faced. Wells, Fargo and Company's express box and all the mails were demanded and the passengers were relieved of their valuables. One plucky passenger refused to give up his money and told the robbers to shoot if they wanted to, and his cool nerve saved him from molestation. The mail was carried away and the mutilated pouches and broken express box were later recovered and taken to Casa Grande. No organized pursuit was made.

Samuel Hughes was out to his ranch thirty miles south of Tucson the next day when two Mexicans rode up and asked for something to eat. One rode a light dun and the other a dark gray horse. One of the men was five feet ten inches tall, slim built, weight about one hundred ten pounds, with a light mustache and goatee. The other was about five feet tall with a dark complexion, more like an Indian than Mexican, and a dark mustache. Hughes described them to Sheriff Shaw, who said there was little doubt they were the stagecoach robbers.

This was sixth in a series of ten stagecoach robberies by "Geronimo" and Guadalupe Redondo, with their final robbery being committed on June 2, 1891 in Cochise County.

April 1, 1891

The Casa Grande and Florence stagecoach was robbed Wednesday, April 1st by a lone Mexican described as twenty-five years old with smooth face and dark complexion, who spoke good English. He was riding a light brown horse.

The robber, Jesus Arvisu, managed to elude capture for four months, but was arrested at Willcox on a misdemeanor charge. While in jail he was identified as the robber of the stagecoach in Cochise County on May 16, 1891. Within a week of his capture he was indicted by the U. S. Grand Jury, tried in the Circuit Court, convicted and sentenced to ten years imprisonment at San Quentin. He was never tried for stagecoach robbery in Pinal County.

December 20, 1891

Passengers Aeschllman, Young, Atkins and Lonergan were in the body of the coach with passenger Berry alongside driver Les Middleton. At half past 10 o'clock Sunday night, when about nine miles from Riverside and about one hundred yards from the summit, the coach was suddenly stopped by the stern command "halt, stop!" One man stood on the roadside about ten feet from the coach with one revolver pointed at the driver and another leveled at the coach.

The road agent said, "shell out the box," and Middleton replied that it was on behind. The robber then commanded, "throw it out and be damned quick about it."

Middleton got down and threw the box on the ground. The road agent asked if there was any bullion aboard and the driver replied that there wasn't. Middleton then asked if that was all he wanted, and the robber said it was and ordered the coach to proceed. He did not molest the passengers nor the U. S. mail.

Atkins was the only man in the party who had a pistol, but it was on the inside of his overcoat and he did not have an opportunity to pull it.

The robber was an unmasked white man, but it was too dark to see any identifying characteristics. He was wearing spurs, but a horse was not seen. Less than a month later a stagecoach would be robbed again under strikingly similar circumstances.

January 5, 1892

The stagecoach from Riverside to Florence, driven by Mr. Goff, was held up on a Wednesday evening when about eight miles beyond Riverside and within two hundred yards of where the robbery of December 20th occurred. The highwayman pursued the same tactics as in the first robbery. Only one man appeared and, after halting the stagecoach, ordered the driver to throw out the box and then demanded the bullion with an assurance which suggested knowledge that it was on board.

The driver reluctantly complied, and then the robber asked if there was any registered mail aboard. Goff informed him that there was a lot of mail on the coach, but that he did not know anything about the registered mail, and he was then ordered to drive on. A moment later Goff heard a shout and pulled up his team, when the robber ordered him to drive on, that he was not calling to him, which seemed to indicate that there was a confederate nearby in the brush.

There was little in the express box but two bars of bullion valued at two thousand two hundred fifty dollars was aboard. Wells, Fargo and Company offered a reward of three hundred dollars for each robber, and one fourth of the property recovered.

Sheriff J. H. Thompson and Deputy Pemberton of Gila County accompanied by two Indian scouts started that same evening for the scene of the robbery, where they were met by deputy U. S. Marshal Drais and Sheriff Truman of Pinal county. It became clear that there were two men involved and that these highwaymen had effectively obscured their tracks. This caused great difficulty in finding the trail until the print of a shoe from a pack horse was identified.

Sheriff Thompson led the posse which tracked the highwaymen. The trail led into the Pinal Mountains before it was obliterated by a snow storm but, before the trail was lost, the Sheriff noticed a wire hanging from a tree partly submerged in the upper Salt River. He investigated and found one of the bars of stolen bullion dangling just beneath the water's surface. There was blood on the wire and the Sheriff, already suspicious of a particular Globe badman, inquired of that town's doctor. The doctor confirmed that the blood on the wire was human and recalled treating King Ussery for a wound which could have been made by a wire.

Henry Blevins was known to be Ussery's friend and frequent companion, and had been with King Ussery when he robbed and maltreated John Gorman, the toll-gate keeper on the eastern slope of the Pinal mountains. On January 15th Sheriff Thompson brought Henry Blevins to Tucson after he was arrested by deputy Pemberton at his cabin on the upper Salt River. The general impression was that Ussery was the lone robber but that Blevins had been nearby and assisted Ussery in hauling and hiding the bullion.

Deputy Pemberton remained at Blevin's Salt River home to continue the investigation and search for the second bar of bullion. Pemberton had discovered a coal pit seventy-five yards from Blevins' house where the men had been burning charcoal, evidently preparing to smelt the bullion, which convinced Pemberton that the bullion was still near by. He had no luck in his search until he went to the slough two hundred yards from Blevin's house. He found footprints in the sand on the bank and upon a log lying in the water. He decided to sound the slough and, stepping onto the log with stick in hand, began poking it into the murky waters. He struck something hard and, feeling about, determined it to be the approximate dimensions of a bar of bullion. He thrust his arm into the water, which was only a foot deep, and recovered a gold bar later valued at one thousand dollars.

The search for King Ussery continued. A party rode into Florence at the end of January and claimed to have seen Ussery riding a brown horse and accompanied by Jack See. See left Gila county with Ussery and stayed with him as far as the Arizona canal, where they separated and Ussery continued on to Mesa City. Sheriff Truman summoned a posse and immediately started in pursuit. They followed his trail to Mesa City, but arrived eighteen hours behind Ussery.

See rejoined Ussery the following day with a bay mare for a pack animal and two horses, trying to give the impression they were heading for San Diego. Officers from Tempe joined in the pursuit, struck the trail eight miles south, and followed it southwest. However, the Tempe officers were not prepared for a long chase and gave it up, but the Florence posse continued the pursuit.

Ussery had actually stayed in the county, where he had family and friends who could shield him from the law and where he knew the country well. Sheriff Thompson learned of Ussery's frequent visits to his mother's home. He took Frank Prothero and traveled a circuitous route to arrive before daybreak outside the Ussery home. Wallace Ussery, younger brother of King, came out of the house and was easily subdued. Wallace was then bluffed into fearing bodily harm, so that he called to his mother to convince King to surrender. Within a few minutes King appeared at the door with hands raised, six-shooter in his belt, and he surrendered without resistance.

On May 7th Henry Blevins was found guilty of grand larceny for being an accessory after-the-fact in the stagecoach robbery and was sentenced to two years at the Territorial Prison. Blevins appealed on the basis that his trial had proceeded without a plea being proffered, and he was granted a second trial. On May 6, 1893 his case was resubmitted to the Grand Jury and on November 11, 1893 he was granted a change of venue to Maricopa County. He was again indicted, tried and convicted, this time receiving a term of seven years in the Territorial prison. Upon his arrival on November 1, 1894 he was registered as prisoner Nº 1007. He was forty-one years old, five feet nine inches tall, weighed one hundred seventy-six pounds, and had brown eyes and black hair. He was literate; and, listed his wife Addie as his nearest relative.

Blevins was discharged on February 10, 1895 to stand trial for stealing cattle from E. J. Edwards, a crime he had committed prior to his arrest on the stagecoach robbery charge. He was convicted and sentenced to five years at the Territorial prison. Blevins was returned to prison and registered as prisoner Nº 1097. On November 10, 1897 Blevins was unconditionally pardoned by Governor McCord and was not heard from again.

Ussery had his examination and was held for the next Grand Jury, bond set at five thousand dollars. On May 26th the Pinal County court dismissed the indictment against King Ussery. A new grand jury

was ordered for June 7th to hear the case again and, after being indicted in the second judicial district, he pled not guilty. He had subpoenas issued for three witnesses he claimed would prove his innocence, but the witnesses could not be found. He was tried and on
November 16th the jury returned a verdict of guilty. On November
22nd he was sentenced to a term of seven years imprisonment in the
territorial prison at Yuma.

King Ussery was registered as prisoner № 855 on November
23, 1892. At that time he was described as being twenty-two years
old, with blue eyes and brown hair. He was pardoned by Governor
Hughes on October 21, 1894.

Ussery was in trouble constantly over the next five years but
finally on December 25, 1899 he was on his way to serve a ten year
prison sentence for grand larceny, the property stolen this time being
a valuable race horse. As prisoner № 1580 he served nearly seven
years, which constituted his entire sentence with creditable time de-
ducted, and he was released upon expiration of his sentence.

King Ussery was not heard from again.

January 6, 1894

The stagecoach between Solomonville and Bowie, with a single
passenger aboard, was held up while en route to the railroad. A lone
robber with a rifle appeared in the road in front the horses and ordered the driver's hands raised. The mails and other valuables were
handed over. The sacks were opened and the promising packages,
containing about eight hundred dollars, were taken. Then the highwayman backed off and ordered the stagecoach to proceed. The passenger was not molested. The driver, on his arrival at Bowie, dispatched trailers and officers back to the scene. The driver thought
there was one robber but the passenger insisted that there were two
men involved. The trail showed but one.

Leslie Webb and Jack Felshaw were soon suspected of the
robbery, along with an old man named Abe Windsor. The investigation showed that Leslie Webb had purchased money orders in
Solomonville, payable to his brother Milo who lived in Deming, N.M.

Money from the Tucson depository had to be forwarded promptly to cover the money orders purchased, so the robbers decided to take-in the stagecoach carrying the money as well as anything else of value in transit, and then cash the money orders in Deming.

Webb rode in the coach carrying the money orders while Felshaw held up the stagecoach. Their efforts netted them two thousand five hundred fifty dollars in checks from the Indian agent at San Carlos, seven hundred eighty-five dollars in post office funds, and nine registered letters. The scheme to cash the money orders later failed as payment on the money orders was stopped by telegraph.

The three men were arrested on suspicion. At their trial they tried to avoid conviction by having John Jackson, another stagecoach robber who had already been sentenced to life imprisonment, take the blame for their offense. This failed when Windsor, under indictment for being an accessory after-the-fact, turned state's evidence.

Windsor confessed that Felshaw and Webb committed the robbery and that he had shared in the proceeds. He said that Webb told him that he had bought money orders in the amount of two hundred twenty-five dollars at Solomonville for his brother and that Windsor was to purchase money orders at Safford in the amount of one hundred twenty-one dollars payable to a firm in San Francisco.

Windsor revealed the hiding place of some of the plunder, including a part of the money from the mail bag. The serial numbers on the recovered bills matched those in the postal records, as it was required to record the numbers of money transported in the mails. Windsor, for his cooperation, was given a reduced sentence of thirty days in jail and fined one thousand dollars.

Felshaw was charged as the principal robber while Webb was charged as his accomplice. Faced with Windsor's testimony they confessed and the following day were convicted, each receiving a sentence of ten years to be served at California's San Quentin Prison.

August 26, 1894

The stagecoach from Casa Grande was stopped at the dry lake. That place was only a few miles from Casa Grande and at a point where the road passes over a small sand ridge before entering the dry lake. It was behind this small ridge that the robber concealed himself before he sprang from his crouching position, holding a revolver in each hand, and yelling his command to "Halt!." This startled the team into a run and the frightened horses plunged down the embankment and dashed across the lake.

Eugene Middleton, a passenger, was sitting on the back seat as the stagecoach passed the summit of the northern embankment when he noticed a saddled pony tied a few yards below. On the appearance of the robber Middleton sprang from the seat to the breaker beam on the opposite side of the stagecoach, but missed his footing and struck the ground. With the stagecoach disappearing in the distance, the robber turned his attention to Middleton and compelled him to "shell out." In one pocket Middleton had a ten dollar gold piece and ten dollars seventy-five cents in silver, which he handed over before the robber told him to go. The robber rode off in the direction of Florence.

Middleton also had one hundred fifteen dollars in bills, but he had wrapped the currency in paper and put the package under the coach seat, so that it was saved. Middleton described the robber as being some what under-sized, light complexioned for a Mexican and about thirty years of age. The road agent was angry because the stagecoach had escaped him and told Middleton that he would even up with the driver.

Sheriff Drais and a posse of four pursued the robber southward. The sheriff's horse failed and he turned over the posse to Sydney Bartleson. The posse was unable to overtake the robber, who fled into Mexico. Thirteen months later the stagecoach would be robbed again, but this time the officers were in close pursuit and captured Francisco Reina who admitted that he had robbed Eugene Middleton the previous year.

December 13, 1894

The Solomonville stagecoach, driven by George Gage, had just entered Big Hollow when a man raised up from behind a clump of mesquite bushes about ten or twelve feet to the right of the road and yelled, "hold up!" The driver stopped the coach and the man ordered him to, "get out on the ground and stand over there," indicating the spot with the barrel of his rifle. The robber stepped beside the wagon and tried to pull the mail sacks out, but was unable to do so. He then ordered Gage to climb into the wagon and throw out the mail. After he had possession of the sacks he turned to Gage and said, "now, you get out lively." Gage boarded and drove on.

Gage described the robber as a man of medium build with light mustache and small chin whiskers. He wore a canvas coat, black hat, and his legs and feet were wrapped in gunny sacks. He had a rag or handkerchief tucked under his hat, which draped over his face serving as a mask. Gage said that he had seen no horse; but, he was sure that the robber was a man he had seen sitting in a saloon at Bowie the night before.

Sheriff Olney and his posse, with Indian trailers, started for Big Hollow the next morning. However, the country in that area was sandy and it had rained the night before which obliterated any tracks. D. W. Wickersham and Will Boyd of Bowie found the mail sacks and recovered two registered packages, one from San Carlos and the other from Fort Thomas; missing was a registered package from San Carlos containing fifty dollars.

A man named Eastman, believed to be the one seen by Gage the night previous to the robbery, was followed and questioned by a deputy marshal. Eastman proved that he was in Willcox at the time the robbery took place. The investigators soon began to suspect that Gage may have robbed the U. S. mails.

George Gage had an examination before Commissioner Salterwhite. Sheriff Olney testified that after he questioned Gage he went to the scene and found that all tracks found were identical and at the place where Gage said he was confronted there were no tracks at all. Gage's tracks, where he had disembarked from the stagecoach, were plain to see. Gage was held to answer on a bond of one thousand dollars to await the grand jury, which did not meet until the second Monday in March. The owner of the Bowie and Solomonville stage line offered to pay the bond for his driver's release.

Gage continued to assert his innocence. After Eastman's alibi was proven Gage identified W. T. Boyd as the man he saw playing cards, and also identified his voice. Gage swore out a complaint against Boyd, a recently enlisted soldier, who was then arrested at Fort Grant and held in the jail at Tucson. There was not sufficient incriminating evidence to indict either man so Gage and Boyd were both released.

The robber was never identified.

October 3, 1895

The Casa Grande stagecoach was held up on Thursday near the dry lake by a lone Mexican. A. J. Doran was the only passenger and the highwayman ordered him to cut open the mail pouch. The contents did not look promising, and while the robber was carelessly moving the mail around with his foot, Doran suddenly grappled with him and attempted to wrench the pistol from his grasp. The driver of the stagecoach offered no assistance and Doran was not strong enough to cope with his adversary. He would have been shot but for the timely arrival of Mr. Drew. The highwayman quickly made his escape.

Shortly after the robbery, District Attorney Ellinwood sent a telegram to officers stating that the government was offering a five hundred dollar reward. William Stiles, known as excellent tracker, started south and employed the services of Felix Mayhew, who had been working in the mines. They rode rapidly toward the Quijotoa country, traveling about one hundred miles, and within the week had captured Francisco Reina. When arrested Reina had the revolver he had stolen, the knife used to cut open the mail bag, and two dollars and a half, having spent one dollar and a half of the plunder.

Francisco Reina admitted he was the same man who had robbed the stagecoach on August 26, 1894 when Eugene Middleton had fallen out and the coach left him behind to face the armed Mexican. Reina was examined, held to answer, and brought to trial for the robbery of October 3rd. Within little more than twenty-four hours after empaneling the jury, Reina was a life convict in irons on his way to San Quentin prison. It took the jury just four minutes to reduce their verdict to writing and present it to the court.

May 30, 1899

Pearl Taylor was born at Lindsay, Ontario, Canada in 1871. During her finishing school years she was plain and plump, so when a dashing gambler showed her his undivided attention she was easily infatuated. After several months she and Brett Hart eloped.

Brett and Pearl Hart moved about the Ontario countryside for several years, Brett plying his trade and both experiencing the financial ups and downs of the gambling profession. In 1893 they decided to attend the World's Columbian Exposition in Chicago where, Brett assured her, games of chance would make their fortune. Brett was ignored by big-time gamblers and finally settled on a job as a barker for a side show.

While Brett failed in his quest for financial security for his family, Pearl was more successful in her quest for entertainment, spending her days among the performers of the Wild West Show. When the Exposition ended Pearl parted from Brett, intent on seeing the old west for herself. Pearl left Chicago for Trinidad, Colorado and, it was rumored, her ticket had been bought by one of the show's cowhands who had taken a fancy to her. At Trinidad Pearl gave birth to a boy, whose father was never identified. The *Arizona Star* said of her life at that time, "She wrestled with the world in a catch-as-catch-can style making a living for herself and her baby son." Soon, however, she sent the boy to Canada to be raised by her mother and she continued her travels westward, working her way from mining camp to mining camp, taking whatever job presented itself. During these years she worked mostly as a cook or a house maid.

In 1895 Pearl and Brett met by chance in Phoenix and soon were together again. This time the relationship lasted several years and Pearl gave birth to a second child, a girl they named Pearl. However, during their separation Brett had developed violent tendencies and after a heated argument he beat Pearl, then quickly fled Phoenix and joined the army, never to be heard of again.

Pearl sent her daughter to Canada for her mother to raise and resumed her camp following. In the spring of 1898 she took a job at the Mammoth Mining Camp where she met Joe Boot, a miner, and a close friendship developed. When Joe announced that he was leaving for Globe to start a new job Pearl agreed to go with him.

Late in the summer of 1898 Pearl received a letter from her brother requesting money for her ailing mother. Pearl sent all her savings. When a second request came Joe chipped in and sent his spare change as well. But, Pearl suspected she would soon need more money and Joe suggested they start a hauling company to take supplies to the Mammoth Mine. When this venture failed they tried their hand at mining and struck a vein, but it played out quickly.

Finally the dreaded third request arrived and Pearl became frantic. She needed money to send her mother, but had none. It was then that Joe suggested they rob a stagecoach. Pearl reported that she was at first reluctant, but Joe was persuasive. After all, he assured her, it was just this one time to get enough money for her mother, and then they would settle down in another Territory to live a law-abiding life together. Pearl was finally convinced, and they made their plans over a campfire that evening. There seemed no reason to delay so before daybreak they set out.

Pearl cut her hair to resemble a man's and tucked the ends under her hat. She wore a man's gray flannel shirt, levis, and boots as her disguise. In her belt was tucked a well-oiled .38 caliber pistol. Joe sported a forty-five caliber six-shooter and a sawed-off shot-gun. They chose a point where there was a sharp bend in the roadway, which would require the driver to slow. There they took up positions to wait.

On May 29, 1899 at 2 o'clock p.m. they heard the stagecoach approaching and at that precise moment stepped out "with revolvers cocked and aim steady."

Joe called out, "Stop and elevate!"

Pearl, not to be left out, ordered in as gruff a voice as she could manage, "Raise 'em!"

Joe covered the driver and told Pearl to search the passengers. She ordered the three men out of the coach and systematically took their valuables: obtaining three hundred ninety dollars from a short fat drummer named O. J. Neal, a tenderfoot contributed thirty-six dollars, and a Chinaman gave up five dollars. Pearl then pranced back and forth, trying to seem desperate, but finally gave each man a dollar, "for grub and lodging." She ordered the passengers back into the stagecoach and sent them on their way. Joe and Pearl were new at the game and had not thought to ask for the mail sacks nor for the treasure box, an oversight that would later prove to Pearl's benefit.

Perhaps the robbers hoped that they would not be recognized, and the law would not know who to pursue, but that was not the case. As soon as the stagecoach driver pulled into Florence, Sheriff Truman was told the details. The driver identified the culprits as Joe Boot and Pearl Hart "who the driver recognized despite the fact that she looked like a young man." A posse was formed and the pursuit began.

Pearl and Joe had not made plans for their escape beyond connecting with the train at Benson. They realized that a posse would soon be on their trail, so they zig-zagged through the country for two days, getting lost several times only to happen onto a familiar landmark. During that time they barely avoided the posse on several occasions. Even the weather would not cooperate and they were drenched in a downpour. The pair was only twenty miles from their destination when they bedded down beneath a stand of trees – exhausted, wet and hungry. Soon Sheriff Truman's posse had them surrounded. The lawmen moved in quietly and collected their firearms, which had been placed close at hand, before awakening them.

Joe, seeing their situation, submitted but Pearl had other notions and fought ferociously. Sheriff Truman later commented of Pearl, after she was in jail, "One wouldn't think that she is a very tiger for nerve and for endurance. She looks feminine enough now, in the women's clothes I got for her, and one can see the touch of a tasteful woman's hand in the way she has brightened up her cell.

Yet, only a couple of days ago, I had to struggle with her for my life. She would have killed me in my tracks could she had got to her pistol ... ."

Pearl and Joe were lodged in the Florence jail but Pearl was soon transferred to the jail at Tucson, a wing of the county courthouse. Pearl managed to break jail at 3 o'clock a.m. on the morning of October 12th. The *Tucson Star* reported:

Early yesterday morning Pearl Hart, the woman stagecoach robber, escaped the county jail, and at this writing has not been captured. Pearl Hart was a prisoner of Pinal County officials, but was taken from the Florence jail and brought to this city, as the accommodations at the Pinal County jail are not suitable to women prisoners. Since her confinement here Sheriff Wakefield and his deputies have used every precaution for her safekeeping, and they naturally feel much chagrined over her escape. Since her confinement in the Pima county jail, Pearl Hart has occupied a room directly over the rear room of the county recorder's office. This room adjoins the small room containing the stairway leading up to the tower of the building. A door open from the small room on the second floor of the courthouse, at the head of the stairs leading down to the main entrance. Between the two rooms mentioned there is nothing but a lath and plaster partition. The door leading into the tower from the courthouse is generally locked, but on the night of the escape it apparently was not. It is evident that after everything was quiet someone entered the courthouse, walked up the stairway and entered the tower room through the unlocked door. It was the work of but a very few minutes to cut a hole through the wall into Pearl Hart's room. She held a sheet to catch the plaster that fell on her side. After the hole was cut through she put a table underneath, and placing a chair upon that, crawled through the hole. From the size of the aperture it is evident that Pearl Hart must have required considerable help in getting through. After joining her accomplice in the escape it was only necessary to open the door and descend the stairway into the street As there is no night watchman for the courthouse outside the jail, it was an easy matter to gain the street without detection. In all probability, horses were in waiting and the pair made a beeline for the border. It is claimed that she may have left the city on the westbound passenger train but this is hardly a possibility as the risk of detection was too great. To those who have seen Pearl Hart either in her proper attire or the masculine dress she commonly wore, it can readily be imagined how difficult disguise would be. Ed Hogan, serving sentence for drunk and disorderly conduct, is also missing and the theory is that he assisted Pearl in her escape. He had but ten more days to serve and had been given some liberty as a trusty. When the jail was locked up on Wednesday night Hogan was missing and it is presumed that he hid himself in the city until about midnight and then returned to the county building to assist in the escape, an understanding having been reached during his confinement as the method of escape...

Sheriff Wakefield pursued the escaped bandit as far as Bowie and then returned to Tucson. Even though the pursuit in the Arizona Territory was discontinued, Pearl was free only a short time. She and Hogan were soon captured by Sheriff Scarsborough of Deming, New Mexico at an "outlaw hangout." Pearl was reportedly starting a gang "of which she was to be the bandit queen" and Hogan was to be her first subject.

In early November Pearl and Joe were tried for stagecoach robbery. Joe pled guilty and was sentenced to thirty years at the Territorial Prison. He arrived there on November 11, 1899 and registered as prisoner № 1558. His record reveals that he was born in Ohio and upon his arrival was described as twenty-eight years of age, five feet four inches tall, one hundred forty-five pounds, with brown eyes and black hair. His previous jobs included sailor and cook. He could read and write and did not drink or use drugs, excepting tobacco. Joe worked hard at the prison, gaining the confidence of the prison staff, so was given the job of driving food to

Yuma Territorial Prison
State Historic Park

the outside work crews. On February 6, 1901 Boot drove his loaded cart through the front gate and continued on to freedom. Joe Boot was never heard of again in the Arizona Territory.

Pearl was found not guilty on the territorial charge of stage-coach robbery by a vote of eleven to one for acquittal, even though she had acknowledged her guilt in writing. The judge "roasted" the jury and had Pearl arrested immediately on another charge – stealing the pistol of the stagecoach driver. A jury was immediately empan-eled and she was tried, convicted of that crime, and sentenced to five years at the Territorial Prison.

Pearl arrived at the prison on November 17, 1899 and regis-tered as prisoner № 1559. She was described as aged twenty-eight years, was five feet three inches in height, one hundred pounds, with grey eyes and black hair. She was reportedly literate, drank alcoholic beverages and smoked tobacco. She also admitted to the use of mor-phine and claimed no legitimate occupation.

Pearl occupied the specially constructed women's quarters in the southwest corner of the prison, a cave-like cell carved into the cliff. The cell was as large as an ordinary bedroom and she had a "houseyard" in which to take her constitutional whenever she was inclined. The prison secretary reported that during her incarceration "her record was excellent, and she devoted her entire time while in durance to making lace and fancy work which had a good sale among visitors here." She also wrote poetry, some of which was published.

In mid-1902 Pearl's sister, Mrs. C. P. Frizzle of Silver City, New Mexico, arrived in Yuma for a visit. Mrs. Frizzle was an actress and playwright and had written a play entitled "Arizona Bandit" in which Pearl was to play the leading role. The play was scheduled to be put on the stage as soon as Pearl was released from prison, which was then anticipated to be in early 1904.

On December 15, 1902 Pearl was pardoned by Governor Brodie on recommendation of the Board of Control and Superinten-dent Griffith. The pardon was granted on condition that Pearl remain outside the Territorial boundary until the expiration of her sentence.

A later disclosure suggested that Pearl had become pregnant while in prison, and the suddenness of her pardon was the result. There is no record of a third child being born to Pearl, so the claim may have been a ruse to gain her early release or merely a misunder-standing on the part of a prison official. As soon as she was free she left on the train for Kansas City, where her mother and sister then lived. Arrangements had been made for "The Arizona Bandit" to play the Orpheum circuit.

After a brief career on the stage Pearl managed a cigar store in Kansas City but, once again, got into a bit of trouble and moved to New York City. She returned to Arizona shortly before the start of World War I. There she met and married a rancher named Calvin Bywater and they settled near Globe. Pearl Hart Bywater died on December 30, 1955 at the age of eighty-five.

The Last Stagecoach Robbery

A few sources identify Pearl Hart's robbery of a stagecoach in May 1899 as the "last in America." Many other sources, more conservatively, claim it to be the last such event in the West. Perhaps it is wishful thinking that the only recorded stagecoach robbery by a woman should climax this thrilling era of frontier crime.

But, Pearl Hart's robbery wasn't the last in America nor last in the West. In fact, it was not even the last in Arizona. The most that can be said of Pearl Hart is that she, with her paramour Joe Boot, committed the last stagecoach robbery in Pinal County.

Stagecoach robbery began in neighboring Nevada a decade earlier than in the Arizona Territory, though somewhat later than in California, and road agents continued to be active in the business until December 1916 when Ben Kuhn took in a mail coach near Jarbridge, Nevada during a terrible blizzard.

Will even later events surface as more research is completed? Only time, and thousands of hours of dedicated searching, will tell.

Pearl Hart, after her arrest, posed several times for pictures. Here she is dressed in men's clothing, as she was during her stagecoach robbery. She is loaded down with two pistols and a "gun" -- a rifle, although during the robbery she had only a six-shooter. Pearl thrived on attention and publicity, and this staged photo was intended to enhance her criminal persona.

Courtesy: Arizona Historical Society/Tucson (# 28916).

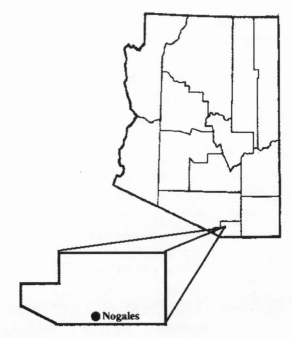

Stagecoach Robbery in Santa Cruz County

In 1899 Santa Cruz County was formed from the southeastern portion of Pima County, with its county seat established at Nogales.

August 25, 1902

On Monday afternoon Mr. Crepin and Nat Crocumb were going from Patagonia to Washington Camp in a buggy. Three miles from Washington Camp they were stopped by Hyram "Harry" Whipple, who was heavily armed but not disguised. Whipple was well known to everybody in that part of the county, so it was quite a surprise to the men when he demanded their money. Not quite comprehending the meaning of the road agent Crepin said, "I have little money with me but, if you need some, come to Patagonia and I will lend you all you want."

"I don't want to borrow it, but I do want what you have with you. This is no joke. I mean business. Get out and deliver," Whipple commanded.

The two gentlemen climbed out of the buggy and delivered what money they had, amounting to nine and one half dollars. The young highwayman proposed also to take their watches and chains, but they argued him out of that idea. While they were still on the ground another team drove into sight down the road.

"Who is that coming up the road?" asked Whipple.

"That is Dick Farrel," was the reply. Farrel was driving the stagecoach.

"He is just the man I want to meet. Nothing would afford me greater pleasure than to rob my old friend, Dick Farrel. You gentlemen get into your buggy and drive on while I proceed to hold up Mr. Farrel."

Crepin and Crocumb did as Whipple directed. Farrel drove into Washington Camp close behind the two men in the buggy and reported that Whipple had stopped and robbed him of eight and one half dollars and his gold watch. Sheriff Tom Turner of Santa Cruz County was soon hot on the trail of Whipple and had him in custody in no time.

Whipple had his examination the following day and was held for the grand jury. Whipple was indicted, but his trial was postponed until the beginning of the new year. Once the trial commenced it took only a few days to convict him, the delay being due mostly to the confusion over which crime to charge him with – the highway robbery of the two men in the buggy or the stagecoach driven by Dick Farrel. Finally the trial was conducted for the stagecoach robbery and Hyram "Harry" Whipple was sentenced to seven years imprisonment at the Territorial prison.

Hyram Whipple was registered as prisoner № 1957 on January 9, 1903. He was thirty-three years of age upon his arrival at the prison and was described as having blue eyes and dark brown hair. Hyram was literate, married, and had two children, but did not list his living relatives on the prison record.

Hyram "Harry" Whipple served his entire term, less good time, and was released on October 8, 1907, never to be heard of again in the Arizona Territory.

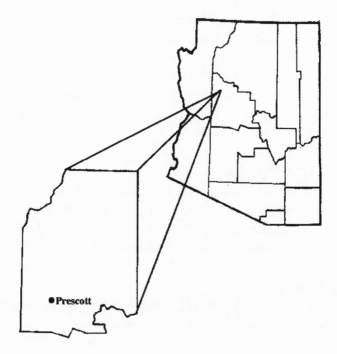

Stagecoach Robbery in Yavapai County

The first Legislative Assembly met in the fall of 1864 and established four counties with Yavapai County in the northeast, which established its county seat at Prescott. Yavapai is often referred to as the mother of Arizona's counties because it contributed to so many. The northern portion became Coconino County in 1891, but by then there were no more stagecoach robberies in the northern area. However, several robberies occurred in that region before it became a separate county.

January 5, 1877

On December 7, 1876 the stagecoach from Prescott to Wickenburg was attacked near Kirkland Creek at 10 o'clock p.m. The dispatch said, "The robbers commenced firing at the horses and driver, killing one horse, but as the horse did not fall until they were about five hundred yards from where first fired upon, the robbers did not follow the coach. The driver and passenger left the coach, went to Kelsey's and got assistance, returned to coach, found everything untouched and the horse dead." The attempt to stop the coach had failed, so the road agents could not be identified.

A month later the out-going stagecoach, driven by Jesus Lujan, was stopped at Woolsey Hill between Skull Valley and Tonto Springs, which was some twenty-eight miles from Prescott and the same place as the attempt of December 7th. Joseph Wiley Evans, superintendent for the California & Arizona Stage Line, was the only passenger.

The robbers had placed a rope across the road to stop the horses. At about 6:30 p.m. the leaders stumbled across the rope, at which time a robber called out "Stop! How many passengers have you?" The driver was then ordered to come down and take control of his leaders while the passenger was ordered out of the coach. The robbers had their faces covered with cloth.

Evans was commanded to throw up his hands, but when he held up only his right arm he was requested to show the other. Evans had only one arm so, upon making that fact apparent, was excused. Evans' pistol had been laying on the seat near his right hand but the command to "throw up," accompanied by the presence of a loaded rifle pointed at his head, came so suddenly that he had no chance to use the pistol and was obliged to let it lie on the seat where he had placed it.

One of the robbers searched the coach for express and mail matter while the other shielded himself behind a rock with a Spencer rifle pointed in the direction of Lujan and Evans. The robber at the coach picked up Evans' pistol from the seat and remarked that he would not mind swapping with him, but laid the pistol down again. They secured their plunder and then directed the driver to go on, with the remark that he or Evans might return in an hour to gather up the papers.

After going only a short distance Evans crawled back over the top of the coach, descended by the back boot, and dropped to the ground while the stagecoach remained in full motion. He walked back to the scene of the robbery with the intention of surprising the two men at their nefarious work. However, as he approached the scene he examined his pistol and, to his chagrin, found that while pretending to consider a swap of firearms the robber had removed all the cartridges.

The driver stopped the stagecoach, after driving some distance to find a spot to turn around, and drove back to the scene. Evans was already there and they examined the ground as well as they could in the darkness, finding the mail bags cut across and many of the letters torn open. They threw all they found into the coach and Lujan continued on to his destination.

Evans walked to a house in Skull Valley, procured a horse and made the best time he could over the new Miller road to Prescott, where he routed out U. S. Marshal Standifer, and the two started back on the main stage road toward the scene of the robbery. When but a short distance beyond Blair's ranch the two lawmen met two men on horseback leading a mule packed with a camper's outfit. This occurred between two and three o'clock in the morning and, thinking this a suspicious circumstance, the lawmen detained the two campers and took from them several packages of bullion, checks, and letters. They arrested the two and brought them to town where they were lodged in jail.

The *Miner* newspaper sent a reporter to the jail the following morning and he obtained a statement from the parties under arrest, who both said they had come from Nevada. One man, who gave his name as M. V. Alexander but would later correct it to Milton Alexander Vance, was described as medium height, sandy complected, with sandy whiskers. Vance at first said he had never been in Arizona, but afterwards qualified his statement by saying that they had been camped near Tom Sanders' house, west of Granite Creek, since New Year's Day. The other man was nearly the same size, also had a sandy complection and gave his name as Thomas Berry. Berry said he was well known in this Territory, having resided at Greenwood which he left a year and a half earlier. They said they had been to Hull's ranch at Mint Valley to see about ranching some horses, some of which they had brought from Nevada and some they had traded for.

Vance said that they had spent most of January 4th in the mountains near the American Ranch trying to find a spring, known to be a short distance beyond Lee's house, where they had planned to camp;

but, finding that they could not make their horses stay there, they had saddled up and rode toward Prescott. He said that while attempting to break camp a stranger, who had sandy whiskers, rode up and asked them to take a package to town and leave it at the express office. As they were going to town anyway they consented and the man handed Vance a small package, which afterwards proved to be the small bar of gold bullion, and he put it in his pocket. When the stranger handed him some larger packages, which could not be put into his pocket, Vance put them in his saddle bags and thought no more about it until he met Standifer and Evans. They were searched and when Standifer, instead of handing the bar of bullion back to him put it in his own pocket, he began to suspect for the first time that "he had got himself into a scrape."

A preliminary examination of the parties was held on January 12th. The circumstances of the robbery were described and various witnesses were called to verify that the items taken from the two defendants were the same items stolen from the stagecoach, and all items were identified.

Judge H. H. Cartter refused to believe that a complete stranger would willingly give up his plunder, and held them to answer before U. S. Commissioner Wilkerson on the U. S. charge of mail robbery. Both defendants waived examination before the Commissioner and were remanded to the custody of the Sheriff, bail set in the sum of twenty thousand dollars each, to await an appearance before the next U. S. Grand Jury.

The county jail was notoriously insecure so both men were taken to the Territorial Prison at Yuma, to be temporarily held until the Grand Jury met. During their stay Berry saw his first opportunity to escape. On June 6th Berry cut his irons and made a rush away from the guard, disregarding the many bullets fired at him. Berry claimed to be an old foot-racer and counted on his fleetness to ensure his escape, but forgot about the loss of wind and condition consequent upon months of imprisonment, so he was quickly recaptured.

On July 1st the robbers were returned to Prescott by stage-coach. During the trip Vance made his first attempt to escape by trying to wrench a pistol from the hands of U. S. Marshal Standifer.

Vance was overcome and admonished by the Marshal to "keep your seat and I will take you in on time." They were safely deposited in the guard house at Fort Whipple, but were moved back to the county jail for trial.

The trial proceeded on August 24th with the empaneling of a jury by Judge Tweed. Vance was represented by Drum and Bruner while Berry was represented by Aram and McCusker. Hugh Farley, Assistant U. S. District Attorney managed the case for the people. The trial and deliberation took less than a week and the men were convicted of robbing the U. S. mails.

The Judge, in passing sentence, waxed philosophically about the magnitude of the crime connected with robbery of the U. S. mails "which contain correspondence of great variety and sacredness, which are supposed to be protected according to their sacredness and value. It remains but for me to pronounce the sentence of the law, which is that you ... are guilty of robbing the United States Mail, from the carrier thereof, by use of dangerous weapons and of putting his life in jeopardy in effecting such robbery, and that you be punished there-fore by imprisonment at hard labor for and during the term of your natural life."

Within the week Vance made his second attempt to escape, this time with his cell mate – wife-murderer J. A. Lewis. The logs which served as the floor of the county jail were quite rotten. The prisoners obtained an old knife-blade with which they succeeded in removing a section of the floor large enough to admit the body of a man, and had dug away the dirt with their hands in order to get a hole open to the outside. They had succeeded in getting through to day-light when guard Kogstead, whom they mistakenly supposed was asleep, told them they had gone far enough.

The two convicted robbers were again moved to the guard-house at Fort Whipple in the hope that it could contain them. On August 18th they managed to escape together.

A reward of five hundred dollars each was offered by U. S. Marshal Dake and the proclamation was published in the Territory's newspapers on August 29th:

STAGE ROBBERS ESCAPED!
$500 Reward!
The undersigned Marshal of the Territory of Arizona
will pay $500 for the capture and imprisonment
or return to him at Prescott, Arizona Territory,
of the convicted mail robbers, Milton A. Vance
and Thomas Berry, or either of them. The prisoners
escaped from the military guard house at Fort
Whipple, A.T. on the night of the 18th of August 1878.
MILTON A. VANCE is an American by birth, about 37
years of age, 5 feet 9 inches in height, light complexion,
keen brown eyes, round build, heavy set, weighs about
160 lbs., with dark hair.
THOMAS BERRY is of Scotch or Irish descent, 5
feet 11 inches tall, brown hair, grayish blue eyes, heavy
beard, about 35 years of age, and has a rather sleepy
appearance, and weighs about 185 pounds.
The above reward will be paid to any person or persons
who will capture and give necessary information of
imprisonment of either, or both of the above described
criminals.

Berry gave the authorities a merry chase about the Territory for many weeks, riding a horse he stole from Mr. Hughes during his escape. It was Mr. Hughes' persistence in trying to get his horse back, however, that proved Berry's undoing. Hughes recaptured Berry near the Salt River and returned him to Prescott, again to the county jail.

Berry decided to share the details of his escape: "Under a close guard, ironed down with sixteen pound shackles, we were put to policing around officer's quarters, digging ditches, laying water pipe, making roads, tearing down old buildings, putting up stables, white washing, etc., to do all of which we necessarily got to handle tools, and whenever the opportunity presented itself we concealed such as would assist us in making good our escape... We were about thirty days making good our liberty. The cell we occupied was about 2 ft. 6 inches wide and 7 ft. long. The floor is laid on sleepers 4 x 6 inches, and raised about 5 inches off the ground. We worked our way to the west end of the building under the floor, where we found the same about 18 inches off the ground, which gave us ample room to work and a place to throw the dirt and rock from the hole we were excavating. The wall runs beneath the surface 2½ feet and is about 3 feet thick. When we had about completed the tedious undertaking of digging our way out, we procured some hardtack and bacon ..."

Vance continued to elude the authorities for more than two months after Berry's capture. Finally, on October 25, 1878, Vance was in irons at St. Joseph. Vance had written a letter from "Hole in the Ground" which led to his discovery and arrest.

On January 11, 1879 Berry was confined in the Yavapai County Jail at Prescott when he managed to escape again, this time with three others not including Vance. Berry made good his escape at about seven o'clock p.m. Some one had furnished another prisoner, who occupied a cell in the southeast corner of the building, with tools. He sawed off one of the iron bars of his cell window leaving room for a pretty good sized man to pass through. The prisoners were all turned into the corridor for their evening meal when they withdrew and crawled through the window. Three days later the *Miner* reported, "All of the escaped prisoners have been heard from and will be returned to their old quarters in the County Jail in due course of time."

Perhaps this last escape motivated the authorities to dispose of these troublesome inmates, as a month later the same newspaper announced that, "The Yavapai County Jail is now pretty well cleared of criminals, only six having quarters therein, three of whom are United States prisoners and subject to removal almost any day ... ." Two of the three U. S. prisoners were Vance and Berry who were soon taken to a penitentiary outside the Arizona Territory.

April 12, 1877

The stagecoach arriving at Wickenburg from Prescott Wednesday morning was attacked by robbers five miles south of Prescott. The express box was taken but the mail was not touched. The passengers scrambled to hide most of their valuables, but they were unmolested. The robbers, after obtaining the box, ordered the stagecoach to drive on.

U. S. Marshal Standifer went to the scene of the robbery on Thursday morning but found no trace of the robbers. He found the express box broken open and entirely empty, and near it a package of brass couplings for a water pipe addressed to Mr. Peralta at Wickenburg. This package and fifty-eight dollars in currency was all the box contained.

The robbers were masked closely and, consequently, were never identified.

September 27, 1877

The California-bound stagecoach left Prescott on Thursday morning at 6 o'clock a.m. Twelve hours later it was stopped by a lone highwayman eight miles beyond Antelope Station, just where the road leaves the mesa going South and enters the wash.

The road agent first commanded the driver to stop, get down from the box and hold the leaders by the bits, all the while covering him with a shotgun. His next command was for passenger Dan Thorne to throw out the express box and break it open with an axe, which the robber provided, and hand him the contents. Passenger Gus Ellis was then ordered to throw out the mail bags. Ellis and Thorne were then required to cut them open and hand over the letters and packages. The stagecoach also had on board as passengers Hon. E. G. Peck with his wife, children, and his aged father and mother, but they were not molested.

The complete contents of the mail bags were unknown but there was six hundred dollars in the mail belonging to the Post Office Department. The express box had one package of gold dust and bars valued at thirteen hundred dollars, one package of small bars valued at four hundred seventy dollars, a letter valued at one hundred dollars, and other letters and papers valued at one hundred fifty dollars. Two bars of Peck bullion worth four thousand dollars were returned to the coach.

The robbing was done in broad daylight so the passengers saw that the robber was masked with black gauze in such a way as to entirely hide his features. He was described as stout built, about five feet ten inches, dressed in laborer's garb, and quite prompt in his manner.

As soon as the coach reached Wickenburg the stage agent contacted the authorities and Wells, Fargo and Company. The usual rewards were offered and pursuits begun, but without results. The *Enterprise* commented on the lone highwayman, "... showing it, in one respect at least, to have been a remarkable job for one 'agent' – as it is certain one did the 'business' alone."

The same robber, "Brazen Bill" Brazelton, would take in stagecoaches near Tucson, Pima County on July 31st and August 14th, 1878.

October 6, 1878

The stagecoach, a buckboard, left Prescott for Yuma on Sunday evening at 8 o'clock p.m. When it reached a point about nine miles west of the sink of Date Creek it was "jumped" by two men. Lieutenant P. G. Wood was the only passenger. He had curled up on the seat and had just got to sleep when he was awakened by no gentle voice, and prevented from foolish demonstrations by sight of a gun drawn down on him. He and the driver were blindfolded and forced to sit down beside the road, while the robbers gathered the plunder together. Lt. Wood and the driver were made exceedingly nervous, while sitting blindfolded, by the accidental discharge of one of the robbers' guns.

Lt. Wood was robbed of five hundred eighty-five dollars and a watch bought from Morgan, the jeweler at Prescott; a .36 caliber Smith and Wesson six-shooter, nickel plated with black handle; a pen knife, and an old buckskin wallet. The thieves even took a ten-cent piece and tobacco out of the driver's pocket. They took three bars of silver bullion from the Peck mine valued at five thousand one hundred sixteen dollars which was said to be the first instance where silver bullion had been taken on that road, and only the second in the Territory. The treasure box was taken though it had little of value in it. The mails were not disturbed. The Lieutenant described the horse of the younger robber as a light bay mare, and was certain he could identify the robbers if he saw them again.

The Governor immediately offered a reward of five hundred dollars for each of the two stagecoach robbers while Wells, Fargo and Company offered their standing reward of three hundred dollars each and Marshal Dake gave his assurance that for "any extra expenses reasonably incurred in their capture, he would use his best endeavors to have put by the Department of the Government."

Henry Adams with three men and William Gilson with two men started from Date Creek on good horses and well armed, intending to pursue and capture the robbers. Several days later Marshal Dake sent men in all directions. A party of Indian scouts was sent to the scene of the robbery to act as trailers and trackers, and to try to find the bullion if cached.

On the evening of the 9th William Gilson came to Prescott and reported that it was impossible to track the robbers, as they had calculated cooly and prepared to elude their pursuers. He said that the point chosen for the robbery is one where bands of horses, mares and colts are running at large and making tens of thousands of tracks in all directions. The robbers intentionally were riding barefoot horses so that it was impossible to designate their tracks from the others.

Deputy U. S. Marshal Joseph W. Evans happened to be at Date Creek when the stagecoach was robbed and immediately took the field in pursuit; and, Dan O'Leary went out with a group of Wallapai Indians and "scoured very rough country without, however, doing more than satisfying himself that the stagecoach was robbed by two Mexicans."

In February 1879 U.S. Marshal Dake received new information on the robbers and, with deputy R. H. Walker and J. N. Thacker from Nevada, was again on their trail. Dake and Thacker went by way of Wickenburg and Rawhide, always just behind their prey. By the time they arrived at Signal Deputy R. H. Walker, who had arrived in town just in time to grab the two fugitives, had them lodged in jail. One of the bars of the bullion, valued at two thousand dollars, was recovered. The three lawmen took the robbers back to Prescott and arrived on the evening of the 26th.

Juan Ruibal and Nicanora Rodrigues were taken before Judge Cate on February 27th. Testimony revealed that Jesus Molino had been

Ruibal's partner in the robbery, while Rodrigues had only assisted in selling the bullion and had not taken any part in the robbery. The defendants waived further examination and were held to answer before the next Grand Jury. Ruibal was held on ten thousand dollars bail and Rodrigues was held on a bail of three thousand dollars.

The Grand Jury indicted Juan Ruibal for highway robbery and, upon being arraigned, pled guilty. The District Attorney asked the court to make the sentence as light as the enormity of the offense would permit as Ruibal "had divulged many things and made the officers but little trouble since being arrested." The court agreed and sentenced Ruibal to ten years at the Territorial Prison near Yuma.

Juan Ruibal was registered as prisoner № 38 on July 11, 1879. He was described as fifty years old, five feet four inches in height, with black hair and eyes. He listed no particular occupation. On March 27, 1883 Ruibal died while still in prison.

Efforts continued to bring Jesus Molino to jail. The authorities received word of the fugitive in the eastern portion of the Territory and Walker and Pierce were sent to capture him. They traveled over eight hundred miles but came back without their man. The *Miner* reported, "The information that was given here in regard to Molino being in that section was altogether hearsay, and the parties alluded to were found to bear good names."

Molino was never tried for stagecoach robbery and was not heard of again in the Territory.

November 11, 1878

The Yuma bound stagecoach, driven by Thomas Owens, was stopped on Monday at 2 o'clock p.m. by two highwaymen when about six miles north of Date Creek station, a location between Kelsey's and Gilson's. They took and shook the express box, but concluded the sound did not indicate sufficient treasure to warrant the trouble of breaking it open. When they learned that no bullion bars were on board, they were so disappointed that they ordered the stagecoach to drive on. Mr. Asher and wife were the only passengers on board and were not disturbed.

On November 30th the *Daily Miner* reported that Hume and Paul, Wells, Fargo and Company's detectives, "brought in and lodged in jail yesterday afternoon two strangers whom they charge with stopping the stagecoach near Date Creek on the 12th ... [Hume and Paul] feel quite confident that they are the roosters who made the attempt and that they are young in the business."

The detectives scheduled a hearing before Judge A. O. Noyes but District Attorney Paul Weber carefully examined the evidence against them and did not consider it sufficient to justify the expense of an examination. He asked that they be discharged.

Additional evidence implicating the two men was not forthcoming, and no other robbers were ever identified.

November 14, 1878

The outgoing stagecoach was stopped about fourteen miles south of Kirkland Valley by four men. Bullion was demanded but the driver informed the treasure seekers that the mills had all shut down and that he had none of the "desired and fascinating substance" aboard. The robbers searched, found no bullion, and allowed the coach to proceed.

The robbers were not pursued.

June 10, 1879

A lone highwayman stopped the outgoing stagecoach on Tuesday when about three miles from Prescott. There was one passenger and the driver aboard at the time, but as the robber had them covered with a double barreled shotgun they were powerless and were compelled to hand over the treasure box. The mail was not disturbed nor the passenger molested. They were then ordered to proceed. The stagecoach continued to LaFranchi's ranch, when the driver sent word to town that the stagecoach had been stopped and Wells Fargo and Company's empty treasure box captured.

LaFranchi, in coming to town, saw the highwayman near Simmons' ranch and notified Tom Simmons of that fact. Simmons immediately made efforts to capture him, but he was unsuccessful as the road agent escaped into the brush and rocks.

The robber was described as a medium sized man with black whiskers. He had a barley sack over his head during the robbery, which disguised his face perfectly. Several officers of the law went out but were unable to find the road agent, as he had made a hasty retreat into town.

This was second in a series of four stagecoach robberies. The same road agent would take in stagecoaches in Maricopa County on June 20th and July 11th, 1879. The highwayman would rob three stagecoaches singlehanded but bring an accomplice on his fourth, and final, robbery. The road agents would be captured, tried and acquitted, and the close call with the law would cause Price Hickey and Frank Mayhew to retire from the business.

November 19, 1879

The outgoing coach of Gilmer, Salisbury & Company, driven by Billy Osborne, was stopped fourteen miles west of Prescott and four miles east of Dixon's station on Wednesday evening by two highwaymen. On board were passengers, Mr. Rothchilds of San Francisco and Mr. Walters of Phoenix. The passengers were not molested and nothing was taken from the stagecoach except Wells, Fargo and Company's express box, which contained about two hundred fifty dollars. The robbers were armed with a shotgun and a rifle, which they brought into direct line with the persons of the driver and passengers, commanding them to "throw up." The order was obeyed, the treasure box delivered, and the stagecoach was allowed to pass.

Sheriff Joseph R. Walker received information on the following Saturday that the two men who robbed the outgoing stagecoach were living at the lower end of Thompson Valley, and immediately set about for their capture. He secured the services of Marshal Dodson, Tom Simmons and Al Seiber and about noon Sunday left for Thompson Valley where they arrived at the residence of Mr. Alred.

On Monday afternoon the robbers came to see Alred about driving cattle to Phoenix. The sheriff and his posse immediately commanded the two men, Thomas Francis, *alias* Wilcox and David Williams, *alias* Jenkins, to surrender. As quick as thought Francis started to run his horse while trying to pull a revolver at the same time, but before he could accomplish either he was shot out of his saddle and fell dead.

Williams, taking in the situation, slowly raised his hands and allowed the sheriff to disarm him. He was ironed, brought to town, and lodged in jail at 2 o'clock Tuesday morning to await his examination. At his hearing David Williams, alias David Jenkins, disclosed that his true name was William Morgan. Sufficient evidence was produced to hold Morgan for the grand jury, which indicted him.

Morgan was tried at the November term and convicted. Judge Silent, in passing sentence, said "It is the intention of this Court to stop the practice of highway robbery, so far as it is in its power so to do. You have been found guilty of that crime and this Court will impose the full penalty of the law. The sentence of this Court is that you be confined in the Territorial prison of Arizona for and during the time of your natural life."

William Morgan was the 47th prisoner to be admitted to the Territorial Prison near Yuma. He arrived on December 15, 1879. Morgan, a bricklayer by trade, was a Welshman aged forty years, five feet eleven inches in height with blue eyes and sandy hair. His sentence was listed in the prison record as "life until death," but he was pardoned by the Governor on August 7, 1885 upon recommendation of the Prison Board of Commissioners.

November 27, 1879

William C. Ayers drove the regular stagecoach southward from Prescott at 8:30 p.m. Mr. William Thomas of Gillette, an ex-foreman of the Tip-Top mine, was the only passenger on board. Ayers had commenced the ascent of a short steep hill two miles north of Gillette when he saw three Mexicans running toward the stagecoach shouting to one another "*Pronto! Pronto!*"

When they reached the lead horses they divided, two running down the right side of the coach. The one in advance rushed to the stagecoach door and, placing his pistol so close to Thomas as to burn his clothing, began to fire at him. The rearmost man on the right covered Ayers with his revolver and caught hold of the wheel lines. In English he ordered Ayers to stop driving and get down, and then called in Spanish to the man on the left, who was blazing away at the driver with his revolver, to cease firing.

The man on the left ceased firing at the driver, ran to the window of the left stagecoach door, and also began firing at Thomas – one man firing in at each door. After discharging his pistol several times the man on the left side drew a bayonet and repeatedly stabbed Thomas until he fell to the floor of the coach.

The two shooters left Thomas, came forward to the driver and took his revolver, watch and money. While they were doing this Thomas opened the coach door and fell out onto the road. He recovered in a few moments from the shock of the fall, got on his hands and knees and, crawling to one side, laid down. He was then robbed of all his valuables. Ayers asked the men why they had killed Thomas, and they replied: *Este Hombre es no bueno!* [that man is no good!].

The road agents then ordered the driver to take Thomas' trunk from the boot, get the key and open it. They sorted through the contents of the trunk, removing some items. They unhitched the coach horses, loaded their plunder on one and leisurely mounted the others before riding off northward. The four stolen horses were bays, branded with an isosceles triangle on the left hip.

Thomas had several frightful gunshot wounds and stabs in his breast and abdomen. Ayers made the wounded man as comfortable as possible and hurried into Gillett, where he secured a team and rode back to the scene. He brought the stagecoach, with the wounded man inside, into Gillett. Thomas died of his wounds at 2 o'clock p.m. on the 28th, the day following the attack.

On November 29th the fleeing Mexicans were reported in the vicinity of Fort McDowell with twelve men in pursuit. On December 1st it was reported that the posse had been close enough for the robbers "to be turned from their course by the pursuing party two or three times and the last heard from them they were directing their course towards Cave Creek in Maricopa county." On December 6th

Sheriff J. H. Behan, with a four man posse, were in such close pursuit that they had forced the robbers to abandon two of the coach horses.

Deputy Sheriff Waters met Al Seiber when he returned from the chase and learned that after robbing the stagecoach and shooting Thomas, then capturing the stage horses, the robbers took a southeasterly course and crossed the Verde six miles above McDowell. They followed the same course and struck the Salt River ten or twelve miles above where the Verde enters that stream. Here they went into an Indian camp and all tracks were lost, save the tracks of four horses which led in the direction of Sonora. Seiber and the others returned to McDowell for supplies and assistance, and while there were thrown off the course they intended to follow by a false report that the road agents had been caged near the Tempe settlement on the Salt River. They later learned that the robbers, after reaching the Indian camp on the Salt River, hired Indians to carry them into Sonora.

Robert N. Paul, Wells, Fargo and Company's detective, had followed the trail of the three Mexicans for several days immediately after the murder but had lost the track and was compelled to give up the pursuit. He continued to keep a sharp lookout and his efforts were finally compensated. On February 3, 1880 he learned that one of the robbers had been in Tucson and had just left with D. F. Harshaw for Davidson's springs. Paul at once hitched up his buggy and overtook his prey about twenty miles out on the Patagonia road. The fugitive, a Mexican named Demetrio Dominguez, was driving Harshaw's team when arrested and had in his possession a watch taken from Thomas. The watch was a four ounce, stem winding silver watch of ordinary description except that the stem, rings and hinges were of gold. The watch had recently been repaired in Prescott and the jeweler was able to describe and identify it. Dominguez was brought back to Tucson and lodged in jail.

The defendant waived examination before Judge Fleury on the 13th and the prisoner and was held to answer before the U. S. Circuit Court, bail set in the sum of two thousand five hundred dollars. At trial he was convicted after being identified as the murderer by the stagecoach driver, and was sentenced to be hanged.

Sheriff Thomas was intent on conducting a proper execution, and ordered a special set of stout straps with which to pinion his prisoner. One strap would bind Dominguez' arms close to his body at the elbows, a second strap would bind his wrists to his body at the hips, a third strap would bind his knees, and a fourth strap would bind his ankles. The straps were intended to prevent any contortions of the limbs at the time strangulation took place, should it happen that his neck was not broken by the fall.

In anticipation of his execution, Dominguez wrote out his confession: " ... I was cutting wood for the Gillett Mining Company when two men came to my camp ... they told my partner that night they wanted to go and rob the Prescott stage, and when they said it my partner rebuked them for it. After that the men remained for one hour longer. My partner then went to Gillett to buy provisions ... when they saw that I was alone in the camp, [they] proposed that I go with them and assist in robbing the stage ... [they] said that if I refused to go they would compel me to accompany them and at the same time they came up on each side, and one drew a revolver and the other a bayonet, and wanted to kill me. I was afraid they would do so and went with them to rob the stage ... When we had attacked the stage a man was killed ... The man who did kill him was Fermin Fiembres ... What I did was to unhitch the horses. The other man who attacked the stage was Umecino Moraga ... Fermin Fiembres lives in Suaqui Grande, Sonora and Umecino Moraga lives in Babraera, Sonora."

On the day set for execution Demetrio Dominguez was taken to the place near Phoenix in a carriage with an escort of twenty-five men, to prevent a rumored rescue by friends. He was hanged one year to the day after the murder of William Thomas and his remains were immediately buried not more than fifty feet from the scaffold.

Fiembres and Moraga, named by Dominguez as his accomplices, were never apprehended.

May 10, 1881

John Hance waited with his stagecoach, holding back a six horse team with a firm hand on the ribbons. The Atlantic and Pacific

Railroad passenger train rolled slowly to a stop at end of track on the east side of Canyon Diablo. Four canvas mail bags were removed from the train and hoisted into the rear boot, two of them unusually heavy, the leather cover was strapped down and the coach was immediately underway. The mail coming in from Winslow by train would now continue to Flagstaff by stagecoach. There it would be transferred to another stagecoach, along with the through-passengers, which would connect with the railroad at Needles, California.

After dropping out of the stone walls of Canyon Diablo the scenery dwindled to dirt banks. With black cinder country behind, Hance drove his team steadily upwards onto a bench of the San Francisco Peaks and into pine forests and cooler temperatures. The team was winded and taking a breather as it approached a flat divide when three unmasked men on horseback appeared on the right, two more on the left, six-shooters in hand. A burly red-bearded robber ordered the coach to halt, and Hance complied.

Hance laughingly informed the men that they had erred, as there was no money box on that trip, but the leader told him to be silent and signaled the two men on the left toward the rear of the coach. They unstrapped the leather cover and pulled two mail bags out onto the ground, leaving the other two untouched. Hance awaited further orders, fully expecting the men to go through him, the coach and the passengers, but was surprised when ordered to proceed.

Upon their arrival at Flagstaff the passengers told their story. Hance, smug over the situation, laughed as he told the agent how these robbers had made a "water haul", and that only a few people would be inconvenienced by not receiving their mail. The agent took him aside to explain the real situation, that those two mail sacks had contained one hundred twenty-five thousand dollars in gold and silver bars and coins, secreted in two five gallon whiskey kegs to fool highwaymen. Hance knew on the spot that the robbers had been provided specific information, and knew why they had not searched for nor taken anything else.

Posses went out immediately, but soon returned empty-handed, and requests for military assistance were ignored. But, Captain E. C. Hentig, 6th Cavalry, Company D of Fort Apache was already out on a scout through Sunset Pass to the Coconino Plateau. He heard of the robbery while on the trail and continued on toward Flagstaff by way of Canyon Diablo. Hentig's orders did not prevent him from pursuing the robbers, so he had his two Indian trailers look for their tracks. Although the trail was more than a week old, the Indians crossed it and followed it up a mountain to the eighty-five hundred foot level at a place later named Veit Spring. By mid-afternoon the Indians had found a log cabin, five men, and five saddled horses, as if they were about to depart.

Captain Hentig deployed his men into position around the cabin. The fugitives were at the corral preparing to mount when Hentig realized that one of the five men was the burly robber with red hair and whiskers who had been described to him. Certain these were the robbers he called for their surrender and ordered his men forward.

Startled, but determined, the robbers made a fight of it for several minutes; but, finally, all five robbers lay dead where they had stood game, without a single casualty among the soldiers. The robbers were buried in a mass grave on the spot.

A diligent search could not turn up the plunder.

May 2, 1882

Tuesday at half past ten p.m. Johnny Collins, the driver on the north-bound stagecoach, was stopped at the foot of Black Canyon Hill by a polite invitation to "pull up the ribbons and fork over." The robbers went through the express box but, getting nothing, they relieved Johnny of his gold watch and took a few dollars from a male passenger, but did not molest Mrs. Snider who was also aboard.

Taking the leaders from the team, they started up the hill to meet the down-coach, driven by J. Towbride, which had stopped at the pass on the graze a few hundred yards above. As before the highwaymen made a "water haul" on the treasure box, but got a pistol from the driver, a silver watch and a little change from J. A. Wright, and one hundred fifty dollars from Grinsfelder, a commercial traveler. Tom Childs, who went along with the treasure box as messenger for Wells, Fargo and Company, was caught napping and lost his pistol and Henry rifle. Another passenger, F. L. Hazelton, dropped his watch and wallet behind the seat and only "yielded up" a few dollars in change. After completing the job, the knights of the road took two horses from that team and sauntered off with the remark: "Boys, you will find plenty of horses around here in the morning."

There were four highwaymen, and their manner and action indicated that they had experience in the business. The robbers were never identified.

August 26, 1882

Stewart's Black Canyon stagecoach left Prescott at 8:30 on Saturday morning with passengers, Captain C. G. Gordon of the army and I. E. Solomon, treasurer of Graham county, and Dr. Lord aboard. They were stopped by two masked men about half past nine in the evening at a point three miles north of Gillett.

The passengers were required to hold up their hands while the road agents relieved them of whatever change they had. The express box was pulled out, thrown onto the roadway, and broken open. A small amount of money, all that was inside, was taken. The entire party was detained at the place until the northbound stagecoach came along, which was but a short time, when the same procedure was again conducted. This northbound stagecoach had on board Dr. F. K. Ainsworth of Prescott, Tom Wilson, Charles Hurley, G. H. Mandeville and J. H. Kirk, who, like the former passengers, were relieved of what money they had.

The plunder consisted of one hundred ten dollars taken from Dr. Ainsworth, fifty of which he was bringing up as a matter of accommodation for G. W. Curtis of Gillett; three hundred five dollars was contributed by Captain Gordon; sixty-three dollars was taken from I. E. Solomon; and thirty dollars was taken from Dr. Lord. The treasure box from the southbound stagecoach was a "water-haul" but the northbound treasure box contained three days of express, and it was speculated that the contents were probably of considerable worth. This speculation was supported by the actions of the robbers, who returned the watches and checks to their owners and gave each man one or two dollars for breakfast, depending on how much each had contributed.

The moon shone brightly enough to enable the passengers to describe the robbers. One man was about five feet eight inches tall, with slight build and square shoulders. He was dressed in dark clothes and hat and was armed with a repeating rifle and a revolver. The second man was about the same height, but a little stouter built, and he had chin whiskers which were a little gray. He had on two belts with one six shooter in each and a repeating rifle.

Wells, Fargo and Company had a standing reward of three hundred dollars each for the capture of any and all express robbers in the Territory; and, in addition, Governor Tritle offered a reward of three hundred dollars from the Territory for the arrest and conviction of each robber; and, the Board of Supervisors for Yavapai county offered six hundred dollars, making in all eighteen hundred dollars for the arrest and conviction of the two men.

The robbers were never identified.

March 17, 1883

Saturday night at about half past one o'clock one of James Stewart's Maricopa and Prescott mail stagecoaches, driven by George Thompson, was being hauled up a hill a short distance south of Bumble Bee station when a road agent "armed to the teeth" hailed the driver. Thompson stopped the team and obeyed the orders of the man, who had the drop on him. All that the fellow demanded was the express box, which Thompson reluctantly surrendered. Judge French was the only passenger on that stagecoach but he was not molested.

The robber made a water-haul, as there wasn't a cent in Wells, Fargo's express box.

The robber was never identified.

April 12, 1883

On Thursday as the stagecoach was coming down the Black Canyon route, a man was noticed in the road. The passengers, deputy

U. S. Marshal Evans and James Dodson, City Marshal of Prescott, both well armed, speedily dismounted and ran ahead. There was a sharp turn in the road and when the officers got to the spot where the suspicious individual was last seen there was no one on the road. The tracks of two men were followed into the brush.

No one was ever charged with a crime. Later two men would be arrested and charged with the robberies of June 27th and July 1st in the same vicinity. Defendant James Larsen would testify, "Chambers has been with me since about the 4th of April last." There were no other robberies in the vicinity of Gillette during that period, which suggests that this was the first attempt made by these two men.

June 27, 1883

It was a Wednesday evening as Amos Niccolls maneuvered his Gilmer & Salisbury Company stagecoach out of Gillette north-bound for Prescott. At half past 10 o'clock p.m., when the stage-coach was about two and one half miles from town, two robbers stepped from the left, the side farthest from the driver and an indication that they were novices. One robber sported a shotgun and the other a Winchester. They were both described as being "not too tall and heavy set." Both of the men had covered their faces with hand-kerchiefs.

The robber with the rifle pointed it at the driver and did all the talking, first ordering the driver to stop and then ordering him to "throw off that box!" The driver complied and threw down Wells, Fargo and Company's treasure box. The robbers did not ask for the mail sacks nor did they molest Mr. Brown, Miss Burfind or the young boy who were passengers in the coach. The driver was then ordered to proceed.

The box was broken open about thirty yards from where the stagecoach was stopped and twenty-two and a half dollars was taken. A shawl in the treasure box was left behind.

The robbers walked back to Gillette, partly over the hills and partly on the road. Their identities, however, remained a mystery un-til after their next stagecoach robbery on July 1, 1883.

July 1, 1883

On Sunday evening Amos Niccolls drove the Gilmer and Salisbury Company's stagecoach south out from Gillette bound for Bumble Bee Station. At half past eleven, when about three miles from Gillette and just before reaching the Agua Fria River, the stagecoach was stopped by one heavy set man sporting a gun. There was moonlight so, even though the driver was not sure whether the robber had a rifle or shotgun, he was sure it was a long barreled weapon that the robber pointed at him.

The robber ordered the driver to throw down the treasure box, which he immediately did. The box contained five hundred sixty-nine dollars and seventy cents, one small package valued at nine dollars, two waybills, and two metal charms valued at five dollars each. The mail sacks were not called for, nor was the single passenger molested. The driver was then ordered to drive on.

A description of the man was telegraphed throughout the Territory, and it was certain he was one of the two men who had robbed the stagecoach at the same place the previous Wednesday. Suspicion quickly focused upon the blacksmiths at Gillette – James Larsen and Joseph Chambers. They fit the description of the men and had recently acquired a quantity of money they could not explain. Larsen was arrested upon a warrant on July 2nd and admitted his guilt. He dug up the charms, one a distinctive Masonic emblem, from the floor of his blacksmith shop and gave them to Deputy Sheriff McDonald upon the deputy's promise to go easy on him. Based upon Larsen's confession Chambers was arrested on July 3rd.

The two men were examined and each was held on five thousand dollars bail, to await the action of the Grand Jury. The men were indicted on October 15th and soon thereafter tried and convicted.

Larsen's was sentenced to a ten year term in the Territorial prison at Yuma. Upon his arrival as prisoner № 192 Larsen, a Dane, was described as thirty-one years of age, five feet ten inches in height with light brown hair and brown eyes, and he was literate. James Larsen, after serving four years of his sentence, was pardoned by Governor Zulick on July 1st, 1887.

Chambers received a sentence of six years, but obtained a new trial and was acquitted. He would be suspected of another stagecoach robbery occurring on November 11, 1884.

August 10, 1883

On Friday evening the Ash Fork stagecoach, driven by O. Mercer, when out six miles from the railroad en route to Prescott, was stopped by three masked men. The three passengers, two gentlemen and a lady, were invited to alight and the robbers proceeded to relieve the men of their cash, which amounted to about fifty dollars. The lady was not molested. The driver was requested to hand over the treasure box, which was empty.

The governor issued a proclamation covering two stagecoach robberies occurring on August 10th. The information regarding the Ash Fork robbery follows:

> **GOVERNOR'S REWARD**
>
> Whereas, Stage robbing is becoming apparently a permanent industry of the Territory and is one which carries with it the destruction of life and always is attended with danger to the peaceful traveling public, and Whereas, On Friday, the 10th of August, 1883, near Ash Fork, in Yavapai county, three masked highwaymen did stop and rob the coach and passengers and Wells, Fargo & Co.'s treasure box, Now therefore, I, H. M. Van Arman, Acting-Governor of the Territory of Arizona, by virtue of the power vested in me, do hereby offer a reward of
>
> **TWO HUNDRED DOLLARS**
>
> For the arrest and conviction of each of the persons who committed the robberies on the Ash Fork road ... Should fatal consequences to the robbers attend their capture, identification and proof that they were guilty parties will be sufficient to secure the payment of the reward offered.
>
> Done at the City of Prescott, the Capital, the 13th day of August, A.D., 1883
>
> *H.M. Van Arman*
> Acting Governor

On September 27th three robbers were jailed and made a full confession of the crime. They said the whole amount they obtained was about twenty-one dollars. The robbers were efficiently tried, convicted and sentenced to terms at the Territorial Prison.

Joseph S. Owens, the 214th prisoner at the Territorial penitentiary, was received on December 19, 1883 to serve a sentence of four years. He was described as twenty-one years of age, five feet eleven inches tall, with blue eyes and brown hair; and, he was literate. He was pardoned by Governor Tritle on March 6, 1885.

George Allen Kirby was received on December 19, 1883 as the 217th prisoner at the penitentiary, sentenced to eight years. He was described as twenty-nine years of age, five feet eleven inches tall, with brown eyes and brown hair; and, he was illiterate. He was pardoned by Governor Zulick on June 21, 1887.

Seely Owens had also been sentenced to a term of eight years. He was described as twenty-eight years of age, five feet ten inches in height, one hundred sixty-five pounds, with dark hair and eyes. He had an ugly knife scar on his right wrist which also disfigured a finger on that hand.

The four o'clock stagecoach for Maricopa carried six prisoners consigned from Yavapai County to the Yuma penitentiary, including the three stagecoach robbers. The prisoners were under the charge of a single guard, deputy sheriff Vanderburg, who took his post on top of the stagecoach. When the stagecoach arrived at Maricopa Seely Owens, who was shackled, was absent having thrown himself from the stagecoach along the way. Owens spoke fluent Spanish, and it was supposed he had fled south of the border as he was neither seen nor heard of in the Territory again.

October 9, 1883

On Tuesday night the Prescott to Wickenburg stagecoach, driven by Joe Boley, when within two and a half miles of Prescott near Willow Creek, was confronted by a lone bandit who surprised the driver by calling out his commands from behind a bush beside the road. The robber concealed his identity with a gray blanket, with eye holes cut in it, placed over his head and reaching to his knees. His gun was a single barrel, but it could not be stated for certain whether it was a shot gun or rifle. He ordered Boley to throw out the mail bag and "be damned quick about it," and then went through the passengers. After the road agent had made his collection he ordered Boley to proceed on his way.

On arriving in town Boley reported the hold-up to Sheriff Henkle. The following morning the Sheriff, Deputy Sheriff Vanderburgh, and an Indian trailer visited the scene of the robbery and followed the trail of the robber into the rocks, where he had stopped to rifle the mails one hundred yards from where the stagecoach was stopped. They recovered the mail sack, which the robber had cut across before rifling the contents, paying no attention to anything except registered letters from which he obtained one hundred ten dollars. The Indian then tracked the robber back onto and across the road and in a southeasterly direction. The robber walked about in all directions as they followed his trail this way and that.

The tracks of the robber appeared large and, upon close examination, it was determined that the robber had "muffled up" his feet by wrapping his boots in heavy cloth, the wrinkles of the cloth and the string tied around the mid-step were visible in the footprints. After about a half mile the cloth over the heels wore off and distinctive boot prints became visible. After another half mile the entire bottom of the cloth wore away and the full boot track was visible. Three-quarters of a mile further on the posse found the ashes from a fire and found evidence that the robber had burned the cloth which had covered his boots. Now the tracks were plain to see and they proceeded with determination in one direction, which the lawmen followed toward town. At one point the trail was over newly plowed ground leaving clear deep imprints, and a short distance beyond the field of soft earth the tracks led directly to the front door of Elisha Givens' house in west Prescott, near Black's old feed yard.

Vanderburg saw that Givens wore boots with a sole and heel similar to the robber's and said "we want you!" Before any mention of the stagecoach robbery, Givens responded, "If you want me for robbing the stage, I can prove my whereabouts last night."

Givens was then arrested, his boots taken and compared to the tracks in the soft, plowed earth. The boot soles were quite peculiar – they were one-half solid with stamped leather from an old saddle skirt, the heels had been patched with shingle nails, and one heel was hollowed out in the center. The boot soles were fitted into the tracks and were impressed next to other existing tracks for a visual comparison. The hollow and the nails, in number and placement, as well as all other unique characteristics matched perfectly and the size was exact.

Givens had his examination and was held for the next Grand Jury. He was indicted and at his trial called witnesses who, he said, would testify to his whereabouts on the night of the robbery. Most of his witnesses, however, denied having seen him though some did place him in Prescott before or after the robbery. Givens also suggested that the Indian tracker who had pointed him out held a grudge against him because, when squaws were begging for produce the previous year, he had given them second quality melons and squash.

The jury could not reach a verdict in his first trial so he was remanded for a second trial. The judge gave an instruction regarding his alibi stating that Givens, to be exonerated, had to prove where he was at the time of the commission of the crime. Still, the jury could not reach a verdict. Givens was turned over to the U. S. Marshal for prosecution on the federal charge of robbing the U. S. mail.

Prosecution in the United States circuit court was successful. Judge French pronounced, "The judgement and sentence of the court is that you Elisha Givens are guilty of robbing Joseph Boley, a carrier, agent and person intrusted with the United States mail of said mail and that you be imprisoned in the Detroit House of Correction at Detroit, Michigan for a period of nine and one half years ..."

Elisha Givens had been born in Terre Haute, Indiana in 1821 but had been ranching in Mint Valley, Santa Clara County, California before he moved to Prescott in 1879. He was a carpenter by trade. He was of medium build with distinctive white facial whiskers. His health was quite poor when he arrived at Detroit's House of Corrections on January 28, 1884. It may have been his age or the condition of his health that earned him an early release, as he was pardoned on January 7, 1885.

January 13, 1884

On Sunday night as the southbound stagecoach on the Black Canyon route, driven by Charles McCool, reached a point between the canyon and Gillette when it was halted by one man with a shot gun. As soon as the driver halted the robber gave the order to "throw out that box," which was complied with. Then came the order "throw out the mail," and that was complied with also. "Drive on" came next and the coach continued on. There was one passenger on board, Mr. Frank Durand, but he was not molested.

Mr. Charles Charlebols, who was in the butchering business at Tip Top and Tempe, was riding immediately behind the stagecoach on horseback and halted with it, but was allowed to go on without being molested. The robber hesitated for about a minute after halting the stagecoach when he discovered Charlebols but concluded, as no demonstrations were made against him, to rob the stagecoach. However, it was a "water haul" as the extent of the find in Wells, Fargo and Company's treasure box was two bottles of patent medicine, and there was little more in the mails.

An Indian trailer went out with Deputy Sheriff Mulvenon, a Yavapai County officer, but soon returned and reported that the trail led toward the Tonto Basin. The Indian said that three men were engaged in the crime.

With nothing of value taken there was no further interest in pursuing the robbers so they were not captured. However, the man seen was a member of a party of three robbers, and they robbed stage-coaches on April 21st, June 1st, and October 19th, 1884.

April 21, 1884

The stagecoach from Phoenix to Prescott was robbed on Monday by one man at Soap Springs south of Gillette. The lone high-wayman made a demand for Wells, Fargo and Company's treasure box, molesting neither mails nor passengers. His demand was complied with by the driver, who then drove on. The express box was perfectly empty.

With nothing of value taken, no one injured, and little in the way of description to work with no effort was made to pursue or identify the robber. However, the man seen was a member of a party of three robbers, and they robbed stagecoaches on June 1ˢᵗ and October 19ᵗʰ, 1884.

June 1, 1884

The stagecoach southbound from Prescott was held up by two men when ten miles north of Gillette on Sunday night. The mail and express box were taken and the only passenger was robbed of two hundred dollars and a watch. One of the robbers searched the driver's pockets, but the robber resisted and would not submit until being fired at, his face being blackened by gun powder.

The Governor issued a reward proclamation:

$500 REWARD FOR STAGE ROBBERS

Whereas, it has been made known to me that the stage carrying the United States mails over the road from Prescott to Phoenix and Maricopa via Black Canyon was stopped at a point about ten miles north of Gillette, Yavapai County, Arizona, and the passengers and express carried by Wells, Fargo & Co., and the United States mail robbed, on the night of June 1ˢᵗ, A.D. 1884, by two highwaymen, to me unknown:

Now, therefore, by virtue of the powers in me vested as Governor of the Territory of Arizona, I do hereby offer a reward of Five Hundred Dollars for the arrest and conviction of the parties engaged in said robbery.

In witness whereof, I have hereunto set my hand and caused the Great Seal of the Territory to be affixed this second day of June, A.D. 1884.

F. A. Tritle
Governor of Arizona

Attest:
H. M. Van Arman, Secretary

The robbers were not captured but continued to rob stagecoaches on the Black Canyon Route. Their next robbery occurred on October 19ᵗʰ.

October 19, 1884

The south bound stagecoach was robbed on Sunday evening by two Americans two miles south of Bumble Bee. The Wells, Fargo and Company's express box was delivered on command. The Sheriff's posse went in pursuit.

The two men who robbed the stagecoach on the 19th were part of a gang of three, and all three robbers were run to ground and arrested. The posse followed the highwaymen and, after a running fight in which some close calls were made, they were surrounded and captured in New Mexico with the help of some Navajo Indians.

The prisoners were en route to Phoenix by train when one of the three men managed to escape. Frank Weedin was necessarily released from his shackles, and taking advantage of his liberty jumped from the train. A frightened lady jumped into the line of fire, making it impossible for the officers to shoot. Sheriff Orme immediately leaped from the train and fired five shots, one of which struck Weedin in the thigh. Indians were soon placed on Weedin's track, but he made desperate efforts to escape, having previously declared to the officers that he would rather die than return to Phoenix. Weedin was never seen nor heard of again in the Territory.

The other two men were delivered to the jail at Phoenix. They were held for the grand jury, indicted, tried, convicted, and sentenced to life terms at the Territorial prison.

Frank Howe, *alias* Thomassen, was thirty-four years old when he arrived at the Territorial prison. He registered as prisoner Nº 268 on November 7, 1884. He was described as five feet six inches in height with light complexion and blue eyes, though the sight in his left eye was entirely gone. His brown hair was prematurely graying. His ears grew noticeably close to his head ending in extreme tips. He was pardoned by Governor Zulick on July 25, 1888.

Oscar White was thirty-four years old when he arrived at the Territorial prison. He registered as prisoner Nº 269 on November 7, 1884. He was five feet seven inches in height with sandy complexion, red hair, and brown eyes. He was pardoned by Governor Zulick on July 25, 1888.

June 4, 1886

On Friday afternoon at about four o'clock the Prescott coach en route to Phoenix, when at a point ten miles south of Bumble Bee and still seventy-five miles from Phoenix, was stopped by two masked men who covered the driver with their guns. There was only one passenger, a lady who, upon seeing the red handkerchiefs which the road agents had tied over their faces as a mask, screamed and fainted when she took them to be Apaches. The driver went to her assistance and, while engaged in this occupation, one of the robbers held the horses while the other cut open the mail sack and helped himself to such contents as seemed to contain valuables. The road agents had expected to find express money, but were disappointed as the stage company had discontinued sending out messenger boxes except when under the care of well-armed messengers. No attempt was made to take money or valuables from the lady.

After satisfying themselves that there was nothing worthy of their time and attention they ordered the driver to proceed. The amount of registered mail between Prescott and Phoenix is very light so the amount of money obtained was very small.

The robbers were never identified.

November 12, 1888

A stagecoach robber was infesting the stage line between Tucson and Prescott. He appeared on the Black Canyon route but was frightened off before he had an opportunity to hold up the stagecoach.

The robber was never identified but would appear again on November 16th in Maricopa County and on November 19th, 1888.

November 19, 1888

Governor Zulick was coming down on the stagecoach Friday when they saw a man answering the description of the Black Canyon road agent. He had crossed the country to the McDowell road but, after his exploit there, crossed back again to the Black Canyon route. He had been frightened off once before and this time had deemed it advisable to let Governor Zulick's stagecoach continue unmolested as well.

Deputy Sheriff Jim Murphy, with Frank Prothero, trailed the lone highwayman into Yavapai County, but had not caught him by the 28th. He had not been having success with stagecoaches and tried another approach.

A Mexican named Carmen Valenzuela was driving a span of good mules towards Phoenix on the Black Canyon road when he was approached by a young man heavily armed with both revolver and rifle. The man asked Valenzuela whether his mules were good pack animals, and then let him proceed.

Valenzuela camped on the Arizona Canal on Friday night, nine miles north of Phoenix. Some time in the night the Mexican missed his mules, and being somewhat suspicious searched for the animals but could not find them. He rode all the next day but failed to discover anything but the tracks of the thief. He then came into town to ask for the assistance of the sheriff.

The road agent was not identified, but the increased attention seemed to have driven him from the region as he did not appear again on the Black Canyon route.

September 26, 1889

A road agent held up the stagecoach between Peeple's Valley and Stanton on a Thursday evening. The passengers were relieved of their cash, but the U. S. mails and express were left undisturbed. A man believed to be a Mexican was suspected, but nothing was immediately done to bring him to justice. A month later a terrible murder occurred on the Walnut Grove Road.

The same man suspected in the stagecoach robbery had been in Peter Verdier's store in late October and returned late on the evening of November 1st. He began to argue loudly with the storekeeper. The only other person at the store at that time was the Mexican woman who cooked for Verdier, who was in the kitchen when she heard several shots. She hurried to sound the alarm and the men who responded found Verdier outside the store with two bullet wounds in his body and his throat cut from ear to ear. The murderer, who was known to reside in Meager, had fled.

A trailer was employed by Charles Genung and they were soon after the murderer, who was working his way toward Weaver. The fugitive had hidden himself in an old tunnel in a canyon above Weaver.

Genung was watching the canyon when he saw the fugitive making his way out, shot gun in hand. Genung called to him, but the man turned and ran, and Genung fired. A rifle ball passed through the man's shoulder and he fell face downward. When he was captured, the murderer begged to be killed.

The shot-gun in his possession belonged to Verdier. He had a demi-john and a Valise taken from Verdier's store and a pair of pants taken from the stagecoach which had been robbed on September 26th. He had eighteen dollars on his person, all the money that had been in Verdier's store.

On November 9th at about three o'clock a.m., Charles Genung arrived at Prescott from Weaver with the murderer of Peter Verdier. He had already confessed to the murder. The prisoner, a Papago Indian named Andreas Lopez, was suffering very much from his wound but by December 12th the *Prescott Courier* reported that Lopez had entirely recovered.

On June 12th the following year he pled guilty to the charge of killing and robbing Verdier, thereby escaping the hangman's noose by cooperating, and was sentenced to ninety-nine years at the Territorial Prison. He was never tried for the stagecoach robbery.

Courtesy: Arizona Territorial Prison Historic State Park

Andreas Lopez, the 679th prisoner received at the prison, was assigned to cell № 8 until moved to the consumption ward. Upon his arrival on July 9, 1890 he was described as twenty-one years of age, five feet eleven inches in height and one hundred fifty-seven pounds, with black hair and eyes. He could neither read nor write. He had, or soon contracted, consumption in the prison and died of that disease on August 8, 1893.

June 28, 1893

George Miller drove the mail stagecoach on the Castle Creek Springs route. One day he came into the Prescott post office from his trip to Phoenix, but didn't produce the usual mail sacks and instead began hemming and hawing when questioned.

"What's the matter? Where is the mail?" asked the postmaster. "Were you held up?"

"Yes, that's it. I was held up," said Miller. "Two men came out of the bushes and one of them stood in the water ahead of me and made me hold up my hands. Then the other went through me. They took my money and my watch."

"We'll have to get some trailers and go after them in the morning," said the post master.

"Oh, its no use," said Miller, hastily, "they stood in water, so there will be no track."

The next day officers went to the scene and, beside the road, found the gutted mail pouch. The Indian trailers declared there were no tracks about of any highwayman.

Upon further investigation it was learned that Miller had spent several hundred dollars in a house of ill fame while on a spree the night before leaving Phoenix. His watch also turned up there, left by Miller. A warrant was issued and Miller was pursued.

Miller was captured at Holbrook by Deputy Sheriff Owen of Apache County. The fugitive was brought to Flagstaff and turned over to Deputy Ruffner of Yavapai County, who took him to Prescott for trial. Miller had a hearing where it was determined that he had gone through the mail bags and stolen about forty dollars.

Miller was held to answer and his trial was set for August 1st. No time was spared in trying, convicting and sentencing Miller to sixteen months imprisonment at San Quentin Prison, as he was tried on the federal charge of robbing the U. S. mails.

Eight days after the trial began he was on his way to prison the custody of deputy U. S. Marshals Newstadter and Merritt.

August 24, 1894

The regular stagecoach, driven by J. W. Jackson, left Prescott Friday morning en route to Verde Station, having passengers Messrs. Peff, Shinge, Ross, Jay, and F. X. Garrett on board. When they reached Point of Rocks a man with a flour sack over his head and a trusty Winchester ordered them to raise their hands. The lone highwayman commenced his work and secured a little over one hundred fifty dollars for his labor. The robber ordered the coach to proceed.

Jackson soon returned to Prescott to notify the officers of the robbery and also to swear out a complaint before Judge Fleury. Deputy Sheriff Potts was sent out to the scene. The officers had no leads and the robber could not be identified as the flour sack which he wore over his head during the robbery completely disguised his features.

September 11, 1894

The stagecoach from the end of the railroad pulled out of Congress about 8 o'clock Tuesday night for Phoenix with passengers J. C. Martin of the *Prescott Journal*, C. M. Funston of the *Coconino Sun*, A. J. Doran of Florence, Dr. J. V. Vickers, E. M. Park and C. Hartzhorn. When about two miles from Congress two highwaymen with gunny sacks thrown over their heads, with eye holes cut in them, sprang into the center of the road and with revolvers leveled on the stagecoach compelled the driver to stop his team.

"Get out, you S*** of a B****!" yelled the robbers to the passengers, and they got out.

"Line up and throw up your hands," and both commands were obeyed.

"Now pass out your valuables," and the passengers began to pungle. A. J. Doran handed over a gold watch, chain and Masonic charm, the whole valued at two hundred dollars, and about twenty dollars in currency; J. C. Martin gave up a silver watch and chain, and a little change; Mr. Funston told them he was a poor newspaper man and needed his watch in his business, so they allowed him to keep it, but took ten dollars in silver from him; Mr. Hartzhorn gave up eleven dollars and hid two gold watches and one hundred forty one dollars in bills and gold; Dr. Vickers gave up one dollar and ten cents but saved two hundred dollars and his gold watch.

After ordering the passengers back into the coach the thieves disappeared in the brush. The highwaymen were Americans, but so well disguised that only a poor description could be provided.

Sheriff Lowry and deputy Floyd of Congress were notified of the robbery, organized a posse, and started in pursuit but could not locate the road agents.

Trailers from Congress reported that the robbers had come back into that camp and suggested that they were hiding there, but they could not be identified.

September 2, 1895

On Monday night an attempt was made to hold up the Black Canyon stagecoach. Z. C. McCullough was driving for J. B. Hocker on the Black Canyon line between Mayor and Canon, a stage of the Phoenix to Prescott route. John Q. White, a painter and paper hanger, was the only passenger and had boarded at Bumble Bee. At about 10 o'clock p.m., just as the stagecoach rounded the hill top at Black Canyon Hill south of Bumble Bee, a man was noticed standing near the road side.

"Halt! Halt!" yelled the would be robber, but the wagon brake was screeching and the men did not pay particular attention until a rifle ball from a Winchester passed near their heads.

The shot excited the mules, which did not stop running until they reached the foot of the steep hill three-quarters of a mile further south of the attempted hold up. It was a daring ride over one of the roughest roads in Arizona, but the driver sat steady and steered the runaways around the complex curves and over steep grades, while the lumbering stagecoach jostled from side to side.

Nothing more was seen of the robber and the stagecoach reached Phoenix at noon with mail and passenger intact.

The robber was never identified.

April 26, 1898

On Tuesday the stagecoach en route to Crown King was stopped by a lone highway man between Spence's and Zent's stations and eighty dollars in cash was taken from Charles Hooker, one of the proprietors of the stage line, who was driving. The mail sack was rifled. There were two passengers aboard, one white man and one Chinaman, but they were not molested.

The robber was never identified.

January 2, 1901

The Castle Creek stagecoach was robbed on Wednesday afternoon a short distance from Hot Springs Junction while on the way to the springs. The driver, an Italian, was so preoccupied by other matters after meeting the robber that he took no note of him and could provide no description. The bandit secured nothing but a package of fifty dollars in silver addressed to Manager C. M. Colhoun of the springs, but did not molest the mail bag.

The driver hurried back to the junction and the pursuit was begun immediately. No tracks could be found beyond the place of encounter. Sheriff Munds of Yavapai County suspected William Loyal Curtis, so when Curtis arrived in Phoenix he was followed and the home of his wife on South First avenue was surrounded. Curtis' wife was still known as Mrs. Knapp, at that time, as her marriage to Curtis was not generally known.

Curtis broke out from the rear of the house and escaped. He was afterward heard of in northern Mexico, where the authorities sought him. He avoided detection for nearly a year when, under an understanding existing between Captain Mossman of the Arizona Rangers and Col. Kosterlitzki of the Rurales for the apprehension of all people along the border who ought to be apprehended, Curtis was discovered at Cananea working as a teamster for the Greene Consolidated Company.

Sheriff Munds obtained a requisition to extradite William Loyal Curtis and went to Sonora, Mexico. There were many formalities to be gone through, and formalities were performed very slowly in Mexico, so it was not until later that year that Curtis was returned to Prescott. He was charged with robbing the stagecoach between Hot Springs and Hot Springs Junction.

The Curtis case had been submitted to the Territorial Grand Jury, but they chose to ignore it. Judge Richard Sloan resubmitted the case to a new Territorial Grand Jury, but once again Curtis was not indicted. The foreman of the second Grand Jury wrote, "... We find, however, that Curtis has been indicted by the United States Grand Jury for each of these offences ... [and] has been arrested upon a warrant issued upon the indictments ... and is now held in custody by virtue of such warrant."

William Loyal Curtis was never tried on the federal charge of robbing the U. S. mail on January 2, 1901 as he had left the mail sacks unmolested on the stagecoach; nor was he tried for the territorial charge of highway robbery because two grand juries, based upon a mistaken impression, failed to indict him.

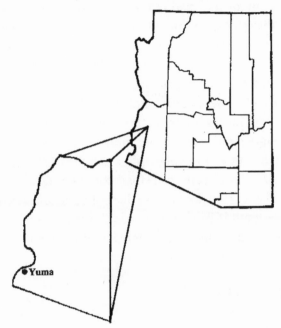

Stagecoach Robbery in Yuma County

The first Legislative Assembly, which met in the fall of 1864, established four counties with Yuma in the southwest. It established its county seat at La Paz and in 1871 moved it to Arizona City, which was later renamed Yuma.

January 30, 1878

The regular stagecoach driven by Nathan Powell left Yuma on Wednesday en route to Tucson. There were no passengers on that trip, but there was a treasure express box aboard. Powell was walking his horses after dark, less than two miles from Filibuster station and about forty miles east of Yuma, when two Mexicans suddenly sprang into the road, one on each side of him. The one on the left grunted something, when Powell flopped the whip over him. At that instant the fellow fired his pistol, the ball passing through Powell's left arm causing a painful wound but not breaking any bones. The swish of the whip and crack of the pistol started the horses into a run.

The other foot-pad ran after the stagecoach a short distance and fired two shots, but missed. Fortunately Powell kept possession of the lines and guided the team safely into the station. Powell returned to Yuma on Thursday's stagecoach to get medical care and was expected to recover quickly.

Hugh Henderson of Antelope had been warned of these two men by a Mexican who knew them to be bad characters. They had been at Henderson's station the morning of the robbery. One wore boots and the other wore moccasins, and the tracks in the road where Powell was jumped were made by that kind of foot gear. Many of the men in the area knew the men, so there should have been no trouble in identifying them if caught. One of them had been shot through the mouth which gave him a distinctive wobble-jawed expression. However, the robbers were never captured.

November 1, 1897

J. C. Kellum returned to Yuma from Harrisburg, one hundred miles northwest of Phoenix, on a Monday night. He brought with him a seven thousand dollar bar of bullion, the product of a mine in which he had an interest. Instead of going by the regular stagecoach, he decided to follow it a short distance away in a buckboard, accompanied by two guards.

A few miles south of Harrisburg the stagecoach was stopped by two Mexicans, who demanded the bar of bullion. The hold-up was hardly accomplished before Kellum's buckboard came up. Sizing up the situation, the guards jumped to the road and opened fire upon the robbers. The latter returned several shots as they retreated into the darkness.

The robbers were never identified.

October 27, 1903

The era of stagecoach robbery ended as it had begun, with a controversial crime in which a particular victim and specific plunder seemed the target, rather than the stagecoach on which she rode.

Miss Telford was returning to Los Angeles by way of Yuma on the stagecoach from Ehrenberg. She had been to Quartzsite and was carrying a "large bar of bullion, the result of a clean-up" at the Valensuella mine, where she had recently inherited an interest. The stagecoach was held up by two armed men who demanded the bar of bullion, showing that they were aware of its presence in the stage-coach. The other two passengers in the stagecoach were not mo-lested nor did they ask for the express box or mail. No resistance was attempted as the robbers showed their determination by firing several shots through the top of the coach.

Miss Telford asked that the story not be published as this might encourage others to hold up the stagecoach and would tend to frighten the robbers, so that it would be more difficult to apprehend them.

The robbers were never identified.

Proclamation of Pardon
Territory of Arizona, Executive Department

To all to Whom these Presents Shall Come Greeting:

    Whereas, application for pardon for restoration to citizenship has been made to this Department by _____ a convict in the Territorial Prison; who was tried and convicted of the crime of _____ at the _____ term, A.D., _____ of the District Court of the _____ Judicial District in and for the County of _____ and was sentenced therefor to imprisonment in the Territorial Prison for the term of _____ Years .

    Whereas the application for pardon is recommended by a large number of the most respectable citizens of _____ County, and

    Whereas a number of the grand jurors who found the indictment and trial jurors who tried the case, and the District Attorney who prosecuted the case unite in stating that they are familiar with the circumstances of the case, and believe that justice requires that he should be pardoned.

    And it appearing that he has been an industrious, trustworthy convict, and that he was a man of good reputation in the community in which he lived prior to his conviction, and having heretofore been paroled, during which time his habits and conduct have been exemplary, and believing this to be a meritorious case where executive clemency should be extended, in order that the ends of justice may be subserved.

    Now, Therefore, I _____ by the power and authority in me vested do hereby grant unto the said _____ forthwith.

IN TESTIMONY WHEREOF, I have this _____ day of _____ set my hand and caused the Great Seal of the Territory to be affixed. Done at Yuma this _____ day of _____.
By the Superintendent _____

Stagecoach robbers, and most Territorial prisoners, were released before their sentence was completed. When they did complete their sentence they might still receive an unconditional pardon to restore their constitutional rights, particularly their right to vote.

PERSPECTIVES, PROCLAMATIONS, and PUNISHMENT

The Problem in Perspective

The editor of Yuma's *Arizona Sentinel* newspaper predicted early in 1877, "What with the influx of capital to the Territory and the increasing travel, opportunities and inducements are augmenting the temptations of evil doers, and we trust the various authorities of the Territory will meet the exigency with their accustomed zeal and additional precautionary vigilance." The Governor, in his address to the ninth Legislative Assembly in 1877, spoke of the absence of crime in the Territory, perhaps divining the epidemic of stagecoach robberies about to commence:

> Considering our extended frontier bordering on the State of Sonora, we have been fortunate in exemption from crime and violence during the last two years. Very little trouble has been experienced from the depredations of outlaws who, in years past, hovered near the border to commit crime and then escape across the line into Mexico for security. A decided and severe policy is the only one that will keep this class of criminals in check, and this I have adopted and endeavored to carry out.
>
> The Legislature has at each session placed at my disposal two thousand dollars to be used for rewards in arresting and punishing criminals. I have never found it necessary to use the full amount so placed, but the increase of business and consequent increased transmission of money through the mails and by express companies will naturally attract the cupidity of highway robbers to this Territory from other sections, and I deem it a prudent precaution to increase the appropriation set apart for rewards. If the money is not needed it will not be used, and if needed it cannot be appropriated to a better purpose. I am desirous, if these fiends undertake to ply their nefarious vocation in Arizona, that they shall learn that those who for years braved a savage war with the Apaches will be found equal to the contest and ready with a firm unrelenting hand to put down a worse scourge to the human race.

The Apaches were wild men without education or opportunities and therefore deserving of some sympathy, but these highwaymen have had the advantages of Christian education and association and the same energy they display in obtaining the property of others, if devoted to legitimate pursuits, would enable them to lead honorable and respectable lives. While pursuing the vocation of theft and robbery they are a scourge to civilization, a disgrace to humanity, and should be swept from the face of the earth as remorselessly as the most ferocious wild beast. I would recommend that highway robbery be made a capital offense punishable with death.

By the end of 1877 Prescott's *Weekly Miner*, in stronger, simpler terms, wrote "Stage robberies in Arizona are becoming almost as frequent as Indian murders were a few years since and it is to be hoped that something may turn up that will make these low bred curs desist from going on the highway and resort to something honorable whereby they may exist."

The *San Francisco Bulletin* reported on "The Roughs in Border Lands." The editor observed, "It is the fate of border roughs to be killed sooner or later. ... The man who undertakes to make his way by a criminal life, even in a border community, does not have an uninterrupted career. He is sure to go to the wall in some tragic way. ... The fate of this element is to be killed, and the powder and ball were, probably, never put to better use. It is said that the roughs in Arizona, there living in open defiance of the law, hardly number one hundred. They have many secret confederates and a larger number of open or secret sympathizers. ... The ruffians will disappear one by one, but it ought to be in the power of the citizens of Arizona to make it so hot for these rascals that they will not stand on the order of their going."

After two decades of unchecked crime and violence related to stagecoach robberies, the editor of San Francisco's *Argonaut*, in 1896, reasoned that "Kindness to criminals is cruelty to the innocent and cruelty, too, to all who, but for the fear of punishment, would become criminals. The interests of society in the United States at this time demands an aggressive public opinion in favor of speedier trials, the withdrawal of right of appeal in criminal cases, and the rigorous enforcement of the laws against those who break them."

Proclamations and Rewards

One of the strongest tools used by law enforcement was the reward, often issued by proclamation and published in newspapers throughout the Territory. Rewards were offered to encourage Arizona's citizens, good or bad, to participate in the identification, arrest and conviction of stagecoach robbers. Rewards also provided some expectation that lawmen in the Territory would be recompensed for their expenses in pursuing stagecoach robbers.

No crime brought a greater proliferation of rewards during the pre-railroad days than stagecoach robberies. Wells, Fargo and Company, from its beginnings, implemented a policy of reimbursing customers for losses of treasure placed in their care. They also offered a percentage of the value of any treasure recovered as a reward for returning the property, and additionally a reward for the arrest and conviction of robbers molesting their treasure boxes. The standing reward, which had been set in California much earlier, was three hundred dollars for each robber.

The Legislature, each year, authorized a cash reserve for the Territorial Governor to be used for rewards. In 1878 the amount established per robbery was five hundred dollars, and twice that if two robberies were proven against the same person or persons, but the amount was not increased for multiple offenders as with the Wells, Fargo and Company policy, but rather was divided among them.

In 1878 the Postal Department offered an additional reward of two hundred fifty dollars for the arrest and conviction of any persons robbing the U. S. mail and the following year the Postmaster General doubled that amount to a five hundred dollars reward, paid for the arrest any robber of the United States mail. A decade later the Postmaster General informed Arizonians that the Federal Government would pay a reward of one thousand dollars for arrest and conviction of every person convicted in a U. S. Court of armed attack on a stagecoach or a railway car carrying government mail, whether the mails were molested or not.

In 1879 Acting Governor J. J. Gosper departed from the standard of requiring arrest or conviction and offered a reward of five hundred dollars for the killing of any stagecoach robber while in the act of committing a robbery, but only three hundred dollars for the capture and conviction of that same robber. However, with a standing reward of three hundred dollars from Wells, Fargo and Company for arrest and conviction of each robber, there was more money to be made by taking the robber alive than by killing him.

Counties where stagecoach robberies occurred also began offering rewards in aggravated circumstances. In 1882 the Board of Supervisors for Yavapai County offered six hundred dollars each for the arrest and conviction of two stagecoach robbers. The following year the Board of Supervisors of Pinal County authorized the Sheriff to offer a reward of three hundred dollars, and for the first time mentioned the offense of robbing the passengers.

Settlers of the Territory refused to be left out of the reward business. In 1878 the citizens of Tucson offered five hundred dollars for the capture of any stagecoach robber. In addition to the reward offered, they subscribed funds to pay Indian trailers to track stagecoach robbers. They made arrangements to employ Pima, Maricopa and Papago Indians and were negotiating with Yuma Indians, and simplified the arrangement by making the offer dead or alive.

Rewards were cumulative, so that a robber who stopped a stagecoach and rifled the mails could bring from two hundred fifty dollars to one thousand dollars reward, depending on the period in which he committed his crime. If that same robber molested the Wells, Fargo and Company box he was worth another three hundred dollars. The Territory might add another three hundred dollars to five hundred dollars to the reward, the city of Tucson and certain counties at various times added three hundred dollars to six hundred dollars. Thus a single robber could be worth from eleven hundred fifty dollars to twenty-four hundred dollars, and this was multiplied by the number of robbers engaged in that particular business.

Stagecoach robbers who were killed during arrest, and there were very few, died because they resisted lawful authority to a degree that justified the use of deadly force. The robbers who were captured were examined at a preliminary hearing, indicted by a grand jury, tried and, if convicted, received prison terms. If they were convicted on the

Territorial charge they were sent to the territorial prison near Yuma; but, if they were convicted on a federal charge they were sent to a prison outside the Territory. Stagecoach robbers were never lynched or legally hanged for that crime.

The Territorial Penitentiary

As the Territory matured crimes grew in frequency, boldness and gravity. Territorial prisoners were held in the county jails during the first decade, with the result that many escaped before or after conviction. There was a strong need for a Territorial prison. On January 22, 1867, by an act of Congress, the net proceeds of the Internal Revenue of the Territory for the fiscal year ending June 1866 were appropriated for the purpose of erecting a penitentiary building, but there was not enough money. The Territorial legislature of 1874 authorized the issuance of bonds to the sum of twenty-five thousand dollars for construction of a Territorial Prison.

On February 12, 1875 the Legislature, after reviewing various proposals, selected Yuma as the permanent site and designated the Yuma county jail a temporary territorial prison. The first territorial prisoner arrived at Yuma's county jail on May 20, 1875. In September the design of the new territorial prison was accepted and a ten acre plot of ground was selected on the bank of the Colorado River where it was joined by the Gila River.

The Territorial prisoners held at the temporary penitentiary – the Yuma county jail – were employed in building the prison and each new prisoner who arrived at Yuma joined a work crew constructing the cells that would restrain them. In June 1876 the first section of the prison had been completed and the inmates were removed to the new prison on July 1st. The prison could accommodate from twelve to fifteen prisoners. There were two cells with a capacity of four prisoners and the outside building of adobes contained two prison rooms with barred windows and anchors to secure prisoners, which could confine ten prisoners. The adobe building also had a warden's room, a hall for guards, a kitchen and a store room. Although the prison had not reached capacity, work on the prison continued at a slow but steady pace nevertheless.

The inmate population had reached one hundred thirty-two prisoners by the end of 1884, one hundred forty-three prisoners two years later and near one hundred ninety by the end of the century. Over crowding was a continual problem and by 1907 the prison was aging badly and housed three hundred sixty-three prisoners in a space designed for two hundred forty. A new prison was needed and the Legislature voted to build it at Florence. On September 15th, 1909 the last prisoner left the Territorial Prison at Yuma.

During its thirty-three years of operation twenty-six stagecoach robbers were sentenced to the Territorial Prison, one of which was Arizona's only recorded female stagecoach robber – Pearl Hart. Two stagecoach robbers escaped while en route to the prison, one of whom died in the attempt while the other prisoner was never heard from again. One stagecoach robber – Pearl Hart's accomplice Joe Boot – was one of few men who successfully escaped from the prison.

Men convicted on the federal charge of robbing the U. S. mail, during the early days, served out their sentences at the House of Corrections in Detroit, Michigan.

Detroit House of Corrections, Michigan

Stagecoach robbery was a Territorial offense, prosecuted in the Territorial district courts. The offense included theft of the contents of Wells, Fargo and Company's treasure boxes, robbing passengers and stage line employees, stealing bullion, payrolls and other treasure belonging to the mines. However, in the course of committing a stagecoach robbery there was often a federal offense committed – robbing the U.S. mail. Robbing the U. S. mail was an offense tried in the U. S. Circuit Courts independently of the Territorial charge, and sometimes after a trial on the Territorial charge failed to achieve a conviction.

Sentences for federal offenses were served in prisons outside the Territory. In the early years U. S. prisoners were sent to the Detroit House of Correction because the federal government did not have a prison facility during the nineteenth century so contracted with various existing facilities to house their prisoners. Five stagecoach robbers were sent to the Detroit House of Corrections from the Arizona Territory.

The Detroit House of Corrections was first conceived as a workhouse to help Detroit's city government recover the cost of jailing misdemeanants.The workhouse was funded by bonds in 1859 and the building was completed in mid-1861. The facility was much larger than the city required so the state legislature designated it as an alternative to the aging Jackson State Penitentiary for the confinement of felons.

Later, federal prisoners were sent to the penitentiary at Point San Quentin, California.

San Quentin Prison, California

During the last decade of the nineteenth century U.S. prisoners from the Arizona Territory were sentenced to San Quentin Prison, rather than to the Detroit House of Corrections. Eight of Arizona's stagecoach robbers were sentenced to serve their terms at San Quentin.

California established its prison system in 1851 to accommodate the burgeoning criminal population which had followed the sudden influx of gold seekers. The original prison was a two hundred sixty-eight ton bark docked at Waban. This ship, managed by a private company, soon proved to be inadequate in size and security. The overcrowding and frequent escapes energized the search for a permanent facility.

Point San Quentin, directly across from the prison ship, was selected as the site for building the new prison, and work began in 1852. San Quentin Prison was well established by the time Arizona's first stagecoach bandit arrived in the early 1890s, and no Arizona stagecoach robber ever escaped from behind its walls.

The Pardoning Power

The Governor held the power of pardon for crimes committed within his territory, including violations of the territorial criminal code as well as violations of U. S. laws. The Governor of the Arizona Territory exercised that power regularly, even when a prisoner had served-out his entire sentence, thus enfranchising him and restoring all his other rights of citizenship as well. By 1896 many believed that the pardoning power was being abused.

An application for a pardon usually began with a petition signed by leading citizens, including friends of the prisoner, but as often included signatures of members of the prison board, the prison superintendent or his assistant, guards, members of the jury which convicted him, and even the sentencing judge. The petition had been used often to commute sentences and Governor Murphy in 1898, set out guidelines for pardon applications:

> Notice for application for pardon should be published for at least two weeks in some newspaper in the county where the crime was committed, for which the applicant was convicted.
>
> All applications for pardon should be accompanied by a petition signed by at least twenty-five reputable citizens of the locality where the crime was committed.
>
> There should accompany the application a recommendation to clemency and the reasons therefor signed by two-thirds of the grand jury which indicted, and two-thirds of the trial jury which convicted, the district attorney who prosecuted, and the judge who sentenced the prisoner.
>
> If the required signatures of the judge, district attorney and the jury cannot be obtained because of death or the absence of any number of them from the territory, the fact in that regard should be stated.
>
> After an application for pardon in due form and in accordance with these requirements is received at the executive office, it will be forwarded to the superintendent of the territorial prison for a report as to the prisoner's conduct while in confinement and for the recommendation of the superintendent.
>
> After the latter recommendation is received by the executive, the case will be reviewed and considered by him, and such action will be taken as he may deem proper.
>
> These rules do not apply to pardons for the restoration of citizenship at the expiration of a prisoner's term when such pardon appears deserved.
>
> A strict compliance with the above regulations will expedite action in pardon cases.

Women were usually pardoned well in advance of the date their sentence was completed, partly because they were such a problem in an all male prison environment, but also because there were so few women in prison at any one time they could hardly behave in any other manner than as model prisoners.

However, not even the men who were sentenced to prison, but received no pardon or parole, ever served an entire sentence because they received credits under the Goodwin Act:

SENTENCE, IN YEARS.	CREDITS, IN MONTHS.	ACTUAL TIME, WITH CREDITS DEDUCTED.	
		YEARS.	MONTHS.
One	2		10
Two	4	1	8
Three	8	2	4
Four	12	3	
Five	17	3	7
Six	22	4	2
Seven	27	4	9
Eight	32	5	4
Nine	37	5	11
Ten	42	6	6
Eleven	47	7	1
Twelve	52	7	8
Thirteen	57	8	3
Fourteen	62	8	10
Fifteen	67	9	5

Stagecoach robbers never received sentences exceeding fifteen years.

APPENDIX

Chronology of Stagecoach Robberies

1875	October 2	Pima County
1876	December 7	Yavapai County
1877	January 5	Yavapai County
	April 12	Yavapai County
	May 12	Maricopa County
	September 27	Yavapai County
	December 12	Pima County
	December 22	Pima County
1878	January 30	Yuma County
	April 19	Maricopa County
	July 31	Pima County
	August 14	Pima County
	August 14	Pima County [2]
	August 15	Maricopa County
	September 2	Maricopa County
	October 6	Yavapai County
	November 11	Yavapai County
	November 14	Yavapai County
1879	February 13	Pinal County
	February 19	Pinal County
	May 5	Maricopa County
	June 10	Yavapai County
	June 20	Maricopa County
	July 11	Maricopa County
	August 14	Maricopa County
	September 16	Pima County
	November 19	Yavapai County
	November 27	Yavapai County
1880	May 21	Pima County
	July 12	Maricopa County
1881	February 16	Gila County
	February 25	Cochise County
	March 15	Cochise County
	May 10	Yavapai County
	June 11	Gila County
	August 17	Cochise County
	September 8	Cochise County
	September 13	Maricopa County
	October 8	Cochise County
	November 29	Gila County
	December 14	Cochise County

1882	January 6	Cochise County
	January 7	Cochise County
	May 2	Yavapai County [2]
	May 10	Maricopa County
	August 26	Yavapai County [2]
	September 19	Apache County
	December 3	Graham County
1883	February 4	Graham County
	March 2	Gila County
	March 17	Yavapai County
	April 12	Yavapai County
	April 16	Gila County
	June 27	Yavapai County
	July 1	Yavapai County
	August 10	Yavapai County
	August 10	Pinal County
	October 9	Yavapai County
	November 5	Graham County
	November 6	Graham County
	December 20	Pima County
	December 31	Pinal County
1884	January 1	Pinal County
	January 13	Yavapai County
	January 19	Maricopa County
	April 21	Yavapai County
	June 1	Yavapai County
	October 19	Yavapai County
	November 14	Pinal County
	November 17	Maricopa County
1885	February 2	Pinal County
	February 23	Pinal County
	July 23	Pima County
	August 7	Pinal County
	August 18	Maricopa County [2]
	September 1	Apache County
	November 20	Pinal County
	November 28	Pinal County
	December 13	Pinal County
1886	January 23	Pinal County
	June 4	Yavapai County
1887	October 30	Apache County [2]
	November 7	Maricopa County
1888	October 2	Pinal County
	October 17	Pima County
	November 1	Cochise County
	November 3	Maricopa County
	November 10	Maricopa County
	November 12	Yavapai County
	November 16	Maricopa County

	November 19	Yavapai County.
	November 22	Pinal County
	November 23	Pinal County
	December 24	Cochise County
1889	January 1	Pinal County
	July 31	Pinal County
	September 26	Yavapai County
	October 2	Pinal County
1890	February 6	Pinal County
	March 20	Pinal County
	May 1	Graham County
	October 17	Cochise County
	October 31	Cochise County
1891	April 1	Pinal County
	May 16	Cochise County
	June 2	Cochise County
	December 20	Pinal County
1892	January 5	Pinal County
	August 10	Pima County
1893	June 28	Yavapai County
1894	January 6	Pinal County
	March 20	Graham County
	August 24	Yavapai County
	August 26	Pinal County
	September 1	Gila County
	September 11	Yavapai County
	December 13	Pinal County
1895	September 2	Yavapai County
	October 3	Pinal County
1897	July 9	Graham County
	November 1	Yuma County
1898	April 20	Graham County
	April 26	Yavapai County
1899	May 30	Pinal County
1901	January 2	Yavapai County
1902	August 25	Santa Cruz County
	December 23	Cochise County
1903	October 27	Yuma County

LAWMEN of the ARIZONA TERRITORY

County Sheriffs

When the Territory was first organized the governor divided it into three judicial districts and four counties and appointed a sheriff for each county. The first assembly also authorized general elections in September 1865. During these elections the Sheriff of each county was elected to a term of one year. This changed in 1870 when terms were extended to two years, effective January 1, 1871 as the newly elected Sheriffs took office. Below are listed the Sheriffs of each county and their dates of service:

Armstrong, W. T.	1899-1900	Gila County
Barnett, W. A.	1899	Santa Cruz County
Barnum, Thomas	1871	Maricopa County
Beeler, Edward	1899-1900	Apache County
Behan, John H.	1871-1872	Yavapai County
Behan, John H.	1881-1882	Cochise County
Berry, William Wiley	1896 & 1898	Apache County
Birchfield, William P.	1897-1898	Graham County
Bourke, John P.	1865-1867	Yavapai County
Bowers, Edward F.	1875-1878	Yavapai County
Bradshaw, Isaac C.	1864	Yuma County
Brady, Peter R., Sr.	1877-1878	Pinal County
Brady, Peter R., Sr.	1867-1870	Pima County
Breon, Paul	1870-1871	Mohave County
Broadway, Noah M.	1885-1886	Maricopa County
Broderick, Thomas F.	1900	Santa Cruz County
Brown, J. R.	1891-1892	Pima County
Calkins, Jerome B.	1864-1865	Yavapai County
Cameron, Ralph Henry	1891 & 1895-'98	Coconino County
Campbell, W. R.	1893-1894	Apache County
Clark, Ben R.	1899-1900	Graham County
Comstock, A.	1875-1880	Mohave County
Cook, William W.	1903-1904	Maricopa County
Crawford, Ben M.	1885-1888	Graham County
Creaghe, St. George	1889-'90 & 1897-'98	Apache County

Dana, James T.	1869-1871	Yuma County
DeArmitt, Hill Barry	1864-1866	Pima County
Dobbins, Marcus D.	1866-1867	Yuma County
Donahue, Jerome J.	1893-1894	Coconino County
Doran, Andrew	1883-1884	Pinal County
Drais, L. K.	1893	Pinal County
Fairchild, Fletcher	1899	Coconino County
Flower, William T.	1866	Yuma County
Fly, Camillus Sidney	1895-1896	Cochise County
Francis, John W.	1891-1892	Coconino County
Fryer, Jere	1887-1890	Pinal County
Gabriel, John Peter	1879-'82 & 1885-'86	Pinal County
Goodwin, Francis Henri	1873-1874	Yuma County
Gray, William T. "Bud"	1889-1890	Maricopa County
Greenleaf, Mel	1893-1898	Yuma County
Halbert, Andrew J.	1887-1888	Maricopa County
Hancock, William A.	1871	Maricopa County.
Hatch, Robert S.	1885-1886	Cochise County
Hayes, Thomas C.	1873-1874	Maricopa County
Henkle, Jacob	1883-1884	Yavapai County
Herbert, Henry M.	1874	Yavapai County
Hodges, F. M.	1878-1881	Yuma County
Hodgson, E. E.	1887	Gila County
Houck, Chester I.	1903-1906	Navajo County
Hubbell, John Lorenzo	1885-1886	Apache County
Hubbs, Harvey	1899-1900	Mohave County
Johnson, James A.	1899-1904	Coconino County
Kelton, Carlton B.	1891-1892	Cochise County
King, David	1867-1869	Yuma County
Lake, William H.	1889-1892	Mohave County
Leatherwood, Robert N.	1895-1898	Pima County
Lewis, Adelbert "Del"	1901-1904	Cochise County
Little, O. B.	1891-1892	Apache County
Livingston, Gus M.	1901-1912	Yuma County
Lovin, Henry	1900-1904	Mohave County
Lowry, James R.	1891-1894	Yavapai County
Lowther, W. W. "Tip"	1881-1882	Gila County
Martin, Luther	1879-1880	Apache County
Mathews, Thomas J.	1866	Mohave County
McKey, Alexander	1865-1866	Yuma County
Montgomery, John Britt	1891-1892	Maricopa County
Moore, Andrew J.	1867-1869	Yavapai County
Moore, Milton C.	1865 & 1867-'68	Mohave County
Mowry, George	1875-1878	Maricopa County

Mulvenon, William	1885-1888	Yavapai County
Munds, John L.	1899-1902	Yavapai County
Murphy, James K.	1893-1894	Maricopa County
Murphy, William	1881	Gila County
Murphy, David L.	1899-1900	Maricopa County
Murphy, Frank E.	1901-1904	Pima County
Nugent, Michael J.	1887-1892	Yuma County
O'Neill, William	1889-1890	Yavapai County
Olney, George A.	1891-1894	Graham County
Orme, Lindley H.	1881-'84 & 1895-'98	Maricopa County
Ortega, Leandro	1901-1902	Apache County
Ott, Charles Hyler	1871-1872	Pima County
Oury, William Sanders	1873-1876	Pima County
Owens, Commodore Perry	1887-1888	Apache County
Owens, Commodore Perry	1895-1896	Navajo County
Parks, James V.	1901-1906	Graham County.
Pascoe, Benjamin F.	1883-1886	Gila County
Paul, Robert A.	1881-1886	Pima County
Peralta, Alejandro	1879	Apache County
Peralta, Sylvestre	1903-1912	Apache County
Perez, Thomas	1883-1884	Apache County
Ports, John C.	1881-'82 & 1895-'98	Mohave County
Prather, A. P.	1869-1870	Mohave County
Reynolds, Glen	1889	Gila County
Roberts, Joseph I.	1903-1904	Yavapai County
Rogers, C. R.	1903-1904	Gila County
Rogers, Michael	1875-1876	Pinal County
Rosborough, James	1893-1894	Mohave County
Rose, C. B.	1881	Graham County
Ruffner, George C.	1895-1898	Yavapai County
Ryan, Jerry	1889-1890	Gila County
Sage, Cornelius	1864-'65	Yuma County
Scott, James	1895-1896	Apache County
Scott, Joseph B.	1893-1894	Pima County
Secrist, F. P.	1901-1902	Navajo County
Shaw, Eugene O.	1886-1887	Pima County
Shaw, Matthew Fasion	1887-1890	Pima County
Shibell, Charles A.	1877-1881	Pima County
Shute, George E.	1887-1888	Gila County
Slaughter, John H.	1887-1890	Cochise County
Smith, Van Ness C.	1864	Yavapai County
Smith, Edward L.	1873-1874	Mohave County
Smith, Edward H.	1868-'69	Mohave County
Spees, John M.	1899-1900	Yuma County

Stein, Robert	1883-1888	Mohave County
Stevens, George H.	1882-1884	Graham County
Stout, Samuel S.	1901-1902	Maricopa County
Stover, Ephram S.	1881-1882	Apache County
Taylor, John Langford	1869-1870	Yavapai County
Thomas, James S.	1874	Yavapai County
Thomas, Reuben S.	1879-1880	Maricopa County
Thompson, John Henry	1891-'96 & 1901-'02	Gila County
Townsend, Oscar Frank	1871-1872	Yuma County
Truman, William C.	1891-'92 & 1894-'02	Pinal County
Turner, Thomas J.	1901-1904	Santa Cruz County
Tyner, Andrew	1881-1886	Yuma County
Tyng, George	1872-1873	Yuma County
Wakefield, Lyman W.	1899-1900	Pima County
Walker, Joseph R.	1879-1882	Yavapai County
Ward, Jerome L.	1883-1884	Cochise County
Wattron, Frank J.	1897-1900	Navajo County
Welbourn, L. C.	1872-'73	Mohave County
Werninger, William C.	1864 & 1875-'78	Yuma County
Whelan, William Baird	1889-1890	Graham County
White, Scott	1893-'94 & 1897-'00	Cochise County
Wicks, Thomas	1870-'71	Mohave County
Williamson, Dan H.	1897-1898	Gila County
Wills, Thomas N.	1903-1906	Pinal County
Worden, T. C.	1871-1872	Maricopa County
Wright, Arthur A.	1895-1896	Graham County

U.S. Marshals

A U. S. Marshal, appointed for the Arizona Territory by the President, was charged with enforcement of federal laws only. The Marshal was empowered to appoint as many deputies as he thought necessary. The Marshal's term was limited to the period he remained in favor with the President, or until he resigned or was removed, or he was unable to fulfill his duties due to illness, or he died. Thus, the position of Marshal changed regularly in the Territory. A Marshal could also hold office as the Sheriff of a County or serve as a deputy sheriff or as a Town Marshal while continuing in the office of U. S. Marshal, or might serve in other related positions such as Wells, Fargo messenger or driver. The Marshals serving the Territory of Arizona during the era of stagecoach robbery includes:

Milton B. Duffield	March 10, 1863
Edward Phelps	June 18, 1866
Isaac Q. Dickson	April 15, 1871
George Tyng	January 30, 1874
Francis H. Goodwin	December 23, 1874
W. W. Standifer	August 15, 1876
Crowley P. Dake	June 12, 1878
Zan L. Tidball	July 18, 1882
William K. Meade	July 8, 1885
Robert H. Paul	March 4, 1890
William K. Meade	May 8, 1893
William M. Griffith	June 15, 1897
Myron H. McCord	June 6, 1901

One deputy U. S. Marshal deserves special attention. Joseph Wiley Evans was the most successful stagecoach robbery detective in the Arizona Territory. Evans had come to Arizona in the early 1870s as a line superintendent for the California & Arizona Stage Co. In those days stagecoach robberies had not yet begun but, with progress, stagecoach robberies commenced with boldness and frequency. In January 1877 Evans became the first man in the Arizona Territory to capture stagecoach robbers. On May 17, 1877 he again captured two desperate road agents, this time in a harrowing shoot-out that left three men wounded, including Evans.

Crowley P. Dake received his appointment as U. S. Marshal and appointed J. W. Evans chief deputy, even though Evans was handicapped by the loss of one arm. In February 1875 Evans had a disagreement with James Carroll, a driver for the California & Arizona Stage Company, which led to a shooting affray. Carroll was killed and Evans wounded. Within a month Evans' arm, at a very definite line of demarcation below the elbow, began to decay. The arm was amputated by Dr. Lippencott in mid-March.

In 1881 Evans was assigned to Tucson, the Pima County seat, and primarily worked the southern region which was where stagecoach robberies were occurring during that period.

During his career Evans brought many stagecoach robbers to justice and in doing so collected numerous rewards, including more than eleven from the postal department alone. He retired from law enforcement in the mid-1880s, began speculating in Phoenix real estate, and established the Evans Loan and Investment Co. Evans had been "slightly ill" for several weeks when he suffered a fit of apoplexy and died on May 28, 1902.

U. S. Postal Guards & Detectives

The U. S. Postal Department did not provide detectives for the Arizona Territory, preferring to rely upon the U.S. Marshals and other law enforcement officers in the Territory who were doing an acceptable job of capturing and convicting stagecoach robbers. The public, outraged at having their mail pilfered and mutilated, in a petition circulated throughout the Territory in September 1878 called for guards to be placed on stagecoaches. The petition read as follows:

> The undersigned citizens of the Territory of Arizona beg respectfully to represent that the coaches bearing the United States mails are continually robbed in this territory and elsewhere, to the disgrace of the nation and the detriment of its citizens. We therefore beg to petition that the Postmaster General of the United States be authorized to employ a "Postal Guard" of sufficient number and with adequate armament to protect the mails of the United States wherever they are carried, with authority to kill and destroy any person or persons who may molest them. That the expense of maintaining said "postal guard' may be paid out of the revenue of the Post Office Department and that its organization may be regulated by the Postmaster General of the United States.

The Postmaster General never authorized the use of postal guards in the Territory but a postal agent named John Mantel worked undercover to find stagecoach robbers.

A postal detective from Los Angeles occasionally assisted Arizona's lawmen. J. H. Mahony assisted J. W. Evans in the capture of James F. Rhodes and later brought in Leandro Imperial, a postal rider who began rifling the mail entrusted to him.

In August 1879 a Colton, California newspaper remarked, "J. H. Mahoney, Special Agent Post Office Department, passed through town Thursday morning en route for home. He has been scouring the unknown wilds of Arizona after stage robbers and mail depredators generally and has inflicted a very healthy scare among the knights of the road. A few such men as Mahoney and robberies would become very scarce."

Wells, Fargo & Company Detectives

Early in the history of stagecoach robbery in the west Wells, Fargo & Company began employing shotgun messengers to protect shipments of treasure. The messenger rode with the driver, the green treasure box nestled between his feet. This often had very positive results, but just as often the robbers anticipated the guard's presence and would be sure to "get the drop" on him before proceeding with their business. Where messengers were involved they are named in the text or among the listing of "Knights of the Lash" but four Wells, Fargo and Company detectives worked in the Arizona Territory and deserve individual attention.

James B. Hume arrived in the Arizona Territory in November 1878 and the *Weekly Miner* reported, "J. B. Hume, chief detective officer for Wells, Fargo & Co. on this coast came in on last night's stage from Yuma. Mr. Hume has been with Wells, Fargo and Company many years and done them valuable services in capturing robbers, recovering stolen treasure, etc., and now comes to Arizona with a view of adopting some more efficient means of preventing express robberies here and of apprehending and bringing to punishment robbers who, in spite of every precaution, yet succeed in robbing the stages."

Nine months later Hume was in Phoenix "taking a look at the lay of the land, having special reference to the frequency with which robberies are occurring in that locality ... if anybody can, [he] will figure the matter out and if the successful operators of the past few months really think of building a house and going into the business regularly at that particular favored spot near the river, he will be apt to catch them at it."

Hume was assisted by Robert H. Paul. Paul had joined Wells, Fargo and Company in 1872 and was sent to the Arizona Territory in 1878. He served as sheriff of Pima County from 1881 to 1886 and then took a position as a detective for the Southern Pacific Railroad.

In 1890 he was appointed U. S. Marshal for the Arizona Territory and served until 1893.

Agent Frederick J. Dodge was sent to Tombstone in 1881 as undercover operative for Wells, Fargo and Company. He took a position as a faro dealer at Hafford's saloon, from where he was able to keep a close watch and attentive ear. He rode with the Earp posse when they arrested Spence and Stillwell for the September 1881 stagecoach robbery near Bisbee. However, he is probably remembered best for his persistent assertion that "Doc" Holliday was involved in the stagecoach robbery during which Budd Philpott was murdered.

John N. Thacker was active in the Territory from time to time, but worked mostly in California and Nevada. He became involved in pursuits several times, including the pursuit and capture of Juan Ruibal.

Knights of the Lash

Stagecoach drivers were known by the sobriquets "Knight" or "Knight of the Lash", "Whip", "sagebrush navigator", or the biblical "Jehu." Jehu was often reserved for a driver who drove at a very fast pace, seeming reckless to his passengers. But, no stage driver kept his job for long if his recklessness endangered his passengers, or if he was a regular drinker. Drivers were a hardy lot representing a cross section of the nation's citizenry. Many chewed, smoked, or cussed mercilessly, but others were kind and gentle, especially toward the ladies riding in their coaches.

The stagecoach driver was captain of his vessel. He commanded all who boarded and was always respected, usually appreciated, and often admired. Not every man could handle the ribbons of a four-up or six-up, so the stagecoach driver was quite a peculiar sort. Many times it was only his iron will and bravado which brought the coach through bad weather, across swollen rivers, over treacherous roads, with poor stock, while surviving attacks by highwaymen or Indians. Handling the ribbons often seemed an impossible task for a man with two hands, but in Arizona there was one driver who handled the reins with skill equal to any man, though he had but one arm:

... A one-armed driver is reported from Prescott. He, too, is a careful man, likewise guides teams over dangerous roads, but he only has one hand with which to do it.

His name is Pete Collack. He drives from Prescott to Jerome, 35 miles, ten of which is rough mountain road, and four "around the horseshoe" creeping close to the steep sides of mountains over precipices 500, 600 and in places 700 feet to the rocks below. Yet one armed Pete steers his coach and four as safely as though he had never seen the army and had his left hand to grasp the reins, leaving his right to swing the whip and "touch up" the leaders when they might shirk their portion of duties. ...

Pete buckles his reins to the stump of his left arm, amputated below the elbow, and cracks his whip with one hand. Occasionally he picks out one or the other reins and the coach jogs easily along.

There were many stagecoach drivers in the Arizona Territory who deserve accolades, but fifty-eight were memorialized because of their involvement with Knights of the Road, the good Knights and the bad jousting on the barren roadways. These *Knights of the Lash* included:

William C. Ayers
R. T. Bolen
Joseph Boley
Johnny Bullock
Nelson Caplett
Sam Childs
Dan Clayton
Charles Colbath
Pete Collack
Johnny Collins
George Cumins
George DeJarnett
Mr. Engle
Dick Farrel
George Gage
Mr. Goff
Andy Hall
John Hance
Jimmy Harrington
Sam Hattabaugh
John Henry
Arthur Hill
Charles Hooker
Mr. Humphrey
J. W. Jackson
Jesus Johann
Robert Joyce
Ira Kempton
Charles Kenyon
"Dutch" John Lance
Barney Lee
Al Livermore
Jesus Lujan

Charles McCool
Z. C. McCullough
Levi McDaniels
Mr. McKenny
O. Mercer
Eugene Middleton
Leroy Middleton
Charles Miller
George Miller
Amos Niccolls
Billy Osborne
F. M. Peterson
Budd Philpott
Nathan Powell
Bill Reed
E. A. Saxe
Mr. Sheldon
James Stewart
George Thompson
Richard Thompson
J. Towbride
Antonio Valdez
S. W. Waite
Eugene Whitcomb
E. H. Williams

Messengers sat beside the driver and shared the discomfort and the danger, often more so because they were the first target of a highwayman's bullets. Several messengers were recognized for their bravery during encounters with highwaymen, others should have been.

Law enforcement officers occasionally worked as messengers when not performing their regular duties but were not often involved with robbers, perhaps because of their presence on the coach. To name only a few of Arizona's stagecoach messengers the list must include Wyatt and Morgan Earp, Bob Paul, Johnny Collins [also a driver], William Blankenship, Charles A. Bartholomew, Tom Childs, Andy Hall, and Messrs. Chavis and Jilson.

BIBLIOGRAPHY

Bailey, Lynn R.; *A Tenderfoot in Tombstone, the private journal of George Whitwell Parsons* (Westernlore Press; Tucson, AZ; 1997)

Bailey, Lynn R.; *The Devil has Foreclosed: the private journal of George Whitwell Parsons, the concluding years 1882-1887* (Westernlore Press; Tucson, AZ; 1997)

Ball, Larry D.; *Desert Lawmen – The United States Marshals of New Mexico and Arizona Territories, 1846 - 1912* (University of New Mexico Press; Albuquerque, NM; 1992)

Block, Eugene B.; *Great Stagecoach Robbers of the West* (Doubleday & Company, Inc.; Garden City, NJ; 1962)

Calhoun, Frederick S.; *THE LAWMEN – United States Marshals and their deputies, 1789 - 1989* (Smithsonian Institution Press; Washington, D.C.; 1989)

Elman, Robert; *Badmen of the West* (Castle Books; Secaucus, NJ; 1974)

Frederick, J. V.; *BEN HOLLADY, the Stagecoach King* (Arthur H. Clark Co.; Glendale, CA; 1940)

Hafen, Leroy; *The Overland Mail* (Arthur H. Clark Co.; Glendale, CA;1929)

Hungerford, Edward; *Wells Fargo, Advancing the American Frontier* (Bonanza Books; New York, N.Y.; 1949)

Jeffrey, John M.; *ADOBE AND IRON, the story of the Arizona Territorial Prison at Yuma* (Arts & Crafts Press; San Diego, CA; 1979)

Loomis, Noel M.; *WELLS FARGO, an Illustrated History* (Bramhall House, New York, NY; 1968)

Lutrell, Estelle; *Newspapers and Periodicals of Arizona, 1859-1911* (University of Arizona Bulletin; Tucson, AZ; 1949)

McLoughlin, Denis; *Wild and Woolly, an Encyclopedia of the Old West* (Barnes & Noble; New York, NY; 1975)

Newspapers referenced:

Arizona Citizen: established at Tucson as a weekly, 1870; expanded to a daily in 1879

Arizona Enterprise: established at Prescott as a semi-weekly, 1877; moved to Florence as a weekly, 1881

Arizona Champion: established at Peach Springs as a weekly, 1882; moved to Flagstaff, 1883

Arizona Gazette: established Phoenix as a daily & weekly, 1880

Arizona Graphic: established at Phoenix as a weekly, 1899

Arizona Miner: established at Prescott as semi-monthly; weekly 1867; daily & weekly 1873

Arizona Republican: established at Phoenix as a daily & weekly, 1890

Arizona Sentinel: established at Yuma as a weekly, 1872

Arizona Star: established at Tucson as a daily/tri-weekly, 1877

Evening News: San Jose, California

Globe Chronicle: established at Globe; 1880

Oasis: established at Nogales as a weekly, 1893

Phoenix Herald: see Salt River Herald

Pinal County Record: established at Pinal City as a weekly; 1885

Prescott Morning Courier: established at Prescott as a daily & weekly, 1882

Salt River Herald: established at Phoenix as a weekly, 1878; name changed to *Phoenix Herald*, 1879

San Bernardino Guardian: San Bernardino, California

St. Johns Herald: established at St. Johns as a weekly, 1885

Tombstone Epitaph: established at Tombstone as a daily & weekly, 1880

Tombstone Nugget: established at Tombstone as a weekly, 1879; expanded to a daily 1880

Topeka Blade: Topeka, Kansas

Wallapai Tribune; established at Kingman as a weekly, 1885

Pinkerton, Robert E.; *The First Overland Mail* (Random House; New York, NY; 1953)

Robertson, Dale; *Wells Fargo, the Legend* (Celestial Arts; Millbrae, CA; 1975)

Theobald, John & Lillian; *WELLS FARGO in Arizona Territory* (Arizona Historical Foundation; Tempe, AZ; 1978)

Wilson, Neill C.; *Treasure Express, Epic Days of the Wells Fargo* (Macmillan Co.; New York, NY; 1936)

Wilson, R. Michael; *DRENCHED IN BLOOD, RIGID IN DEATH; the true story of the Wickenburg massacre* (RaMA PRESS; Las Vegas, NV; 2000)

Wilson, R. Michael; *TRAGIC JACK; the true story of Arizona Pioneer John William Swilling* (RaMA PRESS; Las Vegas, NV; 2000)

Winther, Oscar O.; *Via Western Express & Stagecoach* (Stanford University Press, Stanford, CA; 1945)

INDEX

C

Watch for
forthcoming works by *R. Michael Wilson!*

ENCYCLOPEDIA of Frontier Justice in Arizona

A comprehensive survey of every lynching, legal hanging, and imprisonment during Arizona's Territorial period.

also

ENCYCLOPEDIA of Stagecoach Robbery in Nevada

and

ENCYCLOPEDIA of Frontier Justice in Nevada